`A LIFE IN FOOTBALL WITH

Chris Jo

First edition printed and published in
Great Britain 2007.

Cover photograph shows the Charity Shield and
League Championship.

ISBN No. 0 9537853 9 4

Published, printed and typeset by
Sovereign Bookcare
Stoke on Trent
Staffordshire

`A LIFE IN FOOTBALL WITHOUT KICKING A BALL'.

By Christopher Jones.

Tells of the author's life in football spanning over forty years, half of which he was involved in the world of professional football - during which time, he continued to play an active role in the administration of football at grass roots level.

Born in Crewe, the book tells of his footballing experiences on the administration side (for he never kicked a ball in anger) which ran from being involved with the England set up whilst at the Football Association to Crewe Corinthians, a local football club, who are very shortly to celebrate their fiftieth year.

It takes in spells at Manchester City, Crewe Alexandra, Everton and Leeds United during the seventies and eighties, when many of these clubs were at their peak, serving under such illustrious managers as Sir Alf Ramsey, Malcolm Allison, Johnny Hart, Ron Saunders, Tony Book, Harry Gregg, Gordon Lee, Howard Kendall and Howard Wilkinson, whilst at the same time being involved with local clubs such as Traffic, Cholmondeley County, Crewe Youth Centre and Rolls Royce.

It is a journey through football on both sides of the equation - grass roots and professional, which the author has enjoyed and tells of his dealings with the one common factor in both - people who love the beautiful game.

Some of the stories are funny, some factual and others critical of the game in general.

So, just sit back, read and enjoy it.

' A LIFE IN FOOTBALL WITHOUT KICKING A BALL '

By Chris Jones.

Tribute to Gordon Anderson.

I have dedicated this book to Gordon Anderson who, in 1957, was one of the founder members of Crewe Corinthians Football Club and without whom many hours of enjoyment that I have received from the amateur game, and certainly the last two chapters of this book, would have been lost.

Gordon was born in Lincoln on the 16th July 1927, the younger of two sons, Darys being the elder, to Richard, who was a station master in the railways and Clare. Gordon did have an older sister but unfortunately she passed away early in his life.

Gordon was educated at Shrewsbury School and then went on to do his national service in the Army, being based in this country. On completing this, he joined the railways where he worked for the Inspectorate, until his early retirement in 1982. His love of the railways led him to becoming an active member of the Ffestiniog Railway Society and his own model railway set in his attic at his Chester home had to be seen to be believed, such was its splendour.

He married Joan in 1951 and they set up home in Crewe. However, they were divorced in 1979 and Gordon moved to Chester, where he met Alma, who already had two daughters from a previous marriage. They lived together until 1990, when Alma suffered a brain tumour, which was to turn fatal some years later. During his time with Alma, the Corinthians players were to come into contact with a marvellous old lady who was referred to as 'Granny' and who acted as Gordon's secretary- this was Alma's mother, who had come to live with them and stayed with him until her death, just twelve months or so after Alma had passed away.

It was at that time that Gordon renewed an acquaintance with an old friend, Margaret, whom he had known since 1951, when they had travelled to work together on the local Crewe to Stoke train. When Margaret finally retired a few years ago, Gordon came to live with her in her bungalow just outside Crewe, where together they were very happy until, on 27th May 2004, Gordon, who had been suffering from prostrate cancer, finally passed away.

During his life, Gordon, as well as being a railway enthusiast, was also chairman of the English Speaking Union, based at Stanley Palace in Chester.

He loved spending his time in the football close season on his boat in the Norfolk Broads.

His boat, the first having been destroyed by fire, not surprisingly was called "Corinthian". He had inherited his love of boats from his parents and Gordon had a plaque placed on his boat in their memory.

It was of course because of football and watching those Corinthians games from the early nineties that I first met Gordon Anderson. Gordon enjoyed the game and the friendships that it brought about. Starting as a player and later becoming secretary and chairman, his teams always played in the true corinthian spirit. The definition of corinthian being "amateur". Always a keen competitor, Gordon was humble in victory and complimentary in defeat.

The Corinthian Society, which he set up, organised tours and holidays, the profits being donated in most cases to his Corinthians football team.

He was the true corinthian and will be sorely missed by all who knew him, both friend and opponent. His life after retiring was dedicated to the Corinthians and a lasting memory to me came at his funeral, when our veteran goalkeeper, Clive Reade, turned up in his goalkeeping jersey and that said what we all felt!

Thanks Gordon, for bringing the enjoyment back to me so soon after Heysel and Hillsborough had darkened the game and my own career in football.

All that needs to be said to those who knew the man is, `Three cheers for Gordon', which was always his rallying call at the end of every Corinthians game, except of course, directed in favour of his opponents.

THANKS:

I would firstly like to place on record my appreciation of the many people who have given me support throughout my life in football and secondly, to those people who have helped me in the compiling of this book.

More especially, however, I would like to thank my family. My father, Joseph, who, during my schooldays, unfortunately, because of work commitments in his job with British Railways, spent many hours away from home but who, on his retirement, was able to follow my career by travelling down to London to watch the England matches, to Manchester to watch City, to Liverpool to watch Everton and the short walk to Gresty Road to watch the Alex and who, on every one of these moves, because he had enjoyed his visits to the club in question, felt that I should never have moved. The final one he did get right, which took me from Everton to Leeds United and so quickly out of football. As a result of my father taking my brother's stepson, Brian, as a youngster to Maine Road, Brian was encouraged to become a City supporter, which he still is some thirty years on, often making a round trip of some four hundred miles to watch City's home games. However, my father's proudest moment came as a result of my travelling with the chief executive of Everton Football Club, Jim Greenwood and our commercial manager, Ralph Williams, to Norwich City to look at their ticket computing system, after which, we joined up with the team, who only the previous season had been First Division Champions (in those days there was no posh title like Premier) for their game at Tottenham. The three of us travelled back that night on the team coach. Living in Crewe and off the beaten track, the team coach took a detour to drop me off in the early hours of the morning at my doorstep. Watching and waiting for my return was an aghast but very proud father, who ensured that everybody in the street knew that the team coach of the Football League Champions had stopped outside his door. To me, trivial at the time but to him, definitely his proudest moment.

To my mother, Christine, for her continuous love and support until her death, some six years prior to my father in 1985 and to my sister, Marilyn, who like my mother, has always supported me in my career. Finally, as far as my family are concerned, my brother, Alec, and his wife, Connie, especially for their help after my experiences in the commercial world proved disastrous.

Lastly, to my ` adopted' family. In December 1975, I visited the Mayman family at their home in Carlisle Street with a view to asking if their son, Paul, whom I knew had been watched by Manchester City, whom I had just left, would be willing to spend the Christmas holiday period training with the first team of my new club, Crewe Alexandra. Within three months and still at school taking his 'A'Levels, he was playing in the first team and attracting the interest of the top clubs. I have remained close to their family since and the last thirty years or so has seen me attend Paul's marriage to Diane in 1980, the birth of their son, Craig, in 1985 and sadly, the death of his mother, Joyce, some twelve or so years ago and more recently, unfortunately, their separation. Many a game have I attended at Nantwich, Northwich or Telford with Paul's father, Frank.

So once again to Paul, Diane and Craig many thanks for your support over the years. I will always treasure the wonderful memories of the days spent in Crickhowell, a scenic village just outside Abergavenny, where Craig was born. Two special occasions will always remain in my mind, the first being just two weeks after his birth, travelling down straight after the Everton home game with Watford to spend the weekend with them and the second occasion being his first birthday party held at his grandparent's, Ken and Nora's home on the Saturday evening after our home game with Arsenal and then travelling back to South Wales for a couple of days holiday, before travelling over to nearby Newport County for a League Cup tie.

Nice memories and the meals that I received for baby sitting duties were of the highest quality. So, I suppose that with Paul and Craig both playing for their respective Corinthians teams, which I am of course still involved in, it has just been a continuation of those early days.

FOREWORD BY HOWARD KENDALL.

When told by Chris that he was writing a book about his experiences on the administration side of football over the past forty years at both professional and grass roots level and that because he felt that I had been the most influential person in that career, he would like me to do the foreword to the book, I was only too pleased to accept.

My spell as manager of Everton Football Club between 1981 and 1987 brought the club an unprecedented spell of success, during which two League Championships and both the F.A.Cup and European Cup Winners Cup found themselves in the Goodison Road boardroom. To achieve this success, a manager has to have behind him an excellent coaching, scouting and medical staff and ofcourse, the quality of players to achieve the success on the field. Allied to this ofcourse, he needs the backing of his chairman and directors but then a vaste workload falls onto the administration staff to ensure that the most important people of all, the fans, are looked after.

I know that the team's success in those memorable days of the mid eighties brought the Goodison Road box office staff, led by Chris, very many long hours of work to ensure that our fans had the type of treatment that they deserved from our great club. To do that, you have to love the club and the game. I can honestly say that I never heard them complain once about the extra work brought about by our success on the field, they just seemed to thrive on it and wanted more.

All of us connected with Everton Football Club have many happy memories about those days and to me, it is interesting to read about some of the stories that Chris tells from the other angle of a football club than my own.

I hope that Chris never loses his enthusiasm and enjoyment of the game. He was quite unique in that, for nearly twenty years, he shared that commitment both professionally and in his own time, at grass roots level. The game of football certainly needs the likes of Chris for it to survive at any level.

Good Luck

Howard Kendall.

INTRODUCTION

My aim in this book is to show, through my experiences, a comparison between life in football at the top with that at the grass roots level. I appreciate that I have been fortunate enough to have experienced both ends of the scale and I am grateful to fate for this opportunity. Finding the time to be involved at both levels is the underlying factor present in my case. This can only be obtained by a complete love of the game of football, which allows for a willingness to give up one's time and effort for other people in order that they can enjoy the beauty and friendship that the game of football provides.

Football is a competitive sport but it is important that any rivalry on the pitch should always be quickly forgotten when the game is over in order to allow for opponents to socialise together in the player's lounges at the professional level or in the local pub at grass roots. Sure enough, the next time that the two teams play, it is just as competitive. Long may this continue, for therein lies the beauty of football. It is a sport and like all games is played by human beings. They are the lifeblood of the game. It is often remarked that 'football is more important than life and death'. To me, it is about people and life. Players, officials and supporters are real people and should be treated in the same manner as we ourselves would like to be treated. It does not matter whether they are top internationals or local lads playing for fun. They all basically play the game because they enjoy it and possible financial rewards should be the last thing on the mind of any youngster starting out to play football, or indeed any professional come to that.

I know that, at twenty years of age, when given the opportunity to work for the Football Association in London, being based then at Lancaster Gate, an area more fitting than the present area of Soho Square, I had to give one hundred per cent commitment to the job in hand. Being based in London and with the capital's great number of both Football League and non League clubs being on the doorstep and with, ofcourse, the privilege of working for the Football Association, by which I mean, often being able to receive complimentary tickets for the many games that I wanted to attend, I found myself watching football seven days a week and when coupled with working normal office hours, my only break from football was when I was asleep. Football was my life and has continued to be so. In many ways I am selfish, in that I have only ever done what has suited me and that is why remaining single has suited me best. For me, marriage is about putting other people first, especially children, and there was never any room in my football life for that. This book, or rather my life in football, would not have been possible without the time that I have given to football. The grass roots game had always run parallel to the professional game for me and if that time had not been available, my involvement in the amateur game would have to have been curtailed and so much enjoyment lost. The negatives of this are not having a family of one's own but I suppose that the clubs and the people in them have always been regarded as a family.

To compare the game at professional and grass roots level, I have drawn a comparison between my first job in football and what is, as far as this book is concerned, my last- although my enthusiasm perhaps one day may allow me to be involved, if asked, with a team with one of the sons of today's Corinthians team in it - but I am not holding my breath on that one!

My start in football could not have been higher. In November 1970, just six months after the 1970 World Cup in Mexico, I joined the Football Association, where my first boss was the legendary Sir Alf Ramsey, without doubt, the greatest England manager of all time.

Alfred Ernest Ramsey was born in 1920 in Dagenham, Essex. He turned professional in 1944 with Southampton but due to the war years, only turned professional at the age of twenty four. In 1948, he made his England debut against Switzerland at Highbury in a 6-0 win but was left out of the next game by the old Selection Committee, not returning until part way through the following season for the game against Italy, after his predecessor had played in a 9-2 win against Ireland, never to be picked again. The Selection Committee system certainly made some rather bizarre decisions in those days. Alf then had a continuous run of two years in the England team after his move to Spurs in 1949. In 1950, Spurs won the Second Division championship, followed by the First Division the following season- a feat Alf was to repeat with Ipswich in 1961 and 1962 after he had taken over as manager in 1955. He won his last international cap at the age of thirty two and in 1963, became manager of England, replacing Walter Winterbottom, but with one strict proviso- that he had full control of team selection, no doubt, being influenced by his own experiences whilst playing for England.

The Football Association's governing body were made up of officials placed on the F.A.Council by nomination from their County or Representative Football Associations and as such, the International Selection Committee was made up from these representatives and it was they that, prior to Sir Alf, selected the England team that his predecessor, Walter Winterbottom, had to play. Alf insisted on and was granted, for the first time in its ninety one year history, the right to select his own England team. The selection powers of the committee had been in existence from 1871 to 1963 but even though the committee continued to exist, its loss of power in later years was to be held against Sir Alf, creating enemies for him within the corridors of power at the Football Association. Alf, on his appointment, had made the brave statement that,` England will win the World Cup'. His comments, seriously meant and spoken with determination and resolution, were scoffed at by the national press and media but Alf was proved correct in England's greatest football moment when, on 30th July 1966, they picked up the World Cup, by beating West

Germany 4-2 after extra time. So, in 1967, Alf was rewarded by the country with a knighthood and took the team to the 1970 World Cup in Mexico with what he thought may be an even better team. However, 1970 was to see the emergence of probably the best ever football team the world had ever seen. The Brazilians were far superior to any side in the competition and really only second place was up for grabs. England, unfortunately, were knocked out by West Germany 2-3, after leading for so long, but were probably the one team to really give the Brazilians a game in a Group stage match, losing by the only goal of the game.

In the eighteen months or so that I worked for Sir Alf at the Football Association, November 1970 to July 1972, I found him to be loyal to his staff and players and a true professional.

His knowledge of the game was first class. Critics said of him that he destroyed wingers and put the game back as far as entertainment went, `Ramsey's wingless wonders' was often quoted as a slight against him. Malcolm Allison said of him, `that he was a bad manager of a good team but a good manager of a poor team'. I have never been able to associate that statement with Alf and his teams but there again, my next job after leaving the Football Association saw me join Manchester City, where big Mal was manager and I continued to be mystified by some of his antics at Maine Road. The blame placed on Sir Alf for the non existence of wingers in the England team should not, I believe, be directed against him. If he placed his hand in a fire and pulled out a five pound note, surely, he could not be blamed if somebody else following suit, had their hand burned. Alf played without wingers with success. Other people doing so who failed, should not be able to point the blame against the England manager.

Sir Alf's private life always appeared to be kept apart from his football working life. His wife, Lady Vicky, rarely featured in public, unlike certain ladies in football today. He was a very articulate person, always appearing to think very carefully about what he was to say. His cockney accent had disappeared apparently over the years due to elocution lessons. I did however experience it slipping back in on one occasion after he had been upset about an article of sensationalism in one of our leading popular newspapers which, although only lasting for twenty four hours, could have had far reaching effects on the England team spirit. Luckily, Alf managed to pacify the players concerned who had felt that they were going to be discarded by the England manager from what they had read in the newspaper concerned. That was never Sir Alf's policy. His players were his family and there would never have been a possibility of them finding out that they were out of his squad via the press. It was that policy that made him popular with his squad - or rather respected but when he needed to have an aloofness with his players he could have, if only to ensure that they could never take their place for granted. On his farewells after games, we all knew that when any of his players mentioned that they would see him next game, Sir Alf's reply was always, `perhaps', if only to keep them on their toes in order to maintain their form on the pitch.

After I left the Football Association in 1972 to join Manchester City, Sir Alf, on his visits to Maine Road, always found time to search me out and have a small chat. This made me very proud to have known the greatest manager that England have ever had and one who was so supportive towards those who had helped him.

It was a sad moment for the English game when his enemies in the press and his own F.A.Council finally had their revenge and dismissed him after England had failed to qualify for the 1974 World Cup finals by losing out to Poland in the qualifying group. In those days, only one team from the group qualified- as football aimed at finding out the true champions and not allow teams to get through the qualifying rounds via the backdoor, or second place, or as now, in the European Champions League- top four places, making a mockery of the word "Champions". How can a team be regarded as winners of the European Champions Cup when it can not even win the Championship of its own country? Money not sport rules.

After a brief spell as Birmingham City manager, Sir Alf died in 1999 and it was only then that the world of football paid their long overdue respects to him with a one minute silence observed at all grounds in England.

During all of this time, Alf continued to live in his semi-detached house in Ipswich. He was never motivated by money but by football, which was just as well really because his bosses at the Football Association were not over generous with his salary, which was a reputed seven thousand pounds a year- my own being one thousand. How I wish I could be on one seventh of the present England manager's wage now, or indeed, I am sure, would any of the present F.A. staff doing the same job as I did in the early seventies!

I was proud to have known Sir Alf, whose success today would no doubt have made him a multi-millionaire but I am sure that it would not have altered the great man's personality.

So what about the comparison with today's manager of my Crewe Corinthians Football Club?

This honour is held by Jeremy John Hulme, known affectionately by the many people who know him as "Jed".

Jed was born in Crewe on 1st November 1952, as a twin to his sister, Robina. Jed's parents, Roy and Lily, both now in their eighties, find that the figure five features prominently in their lives. They had been married for just five weeks, when Roy was sent to Burma in the fight against Japan in the Second World War. During which, he was taken prisoner and remained as such for five years, without Lily knowing about his well being until, without notice, he just returned home on the conclusion of the War and the two of them had- five children. As well as Jed and Robina, their other children are Clive, the eldest, with Greg and

Gary younger than Jed. Therefore, large families have always been part of Jed's life.

Jed married Sue, who gave him his first son, Steve, who has since emigrated to Thailand, where, for the last few years, Jed with his present family, wife, Emma and children, Josh and Jack, have spent their holidays. On splitting up with Sue, Jed met another Sue- Sue Tagg and together they had three children- Jeremy, who prefers to be known as "Jez" and is infact our centre-forward and twins Philippa and Stephanie. The relationship between Jed and Sue did not work out however and they went their separate ways.

On the 24th July 1999, Jed married his present wife, Emma Cartwright, at St.Andrew's Church in Crewe. Although Emma is considerably younger than Jed, she is also considerably taller, so much so that Emma had to admit that when Jed was told that he could kiss the bride at their wedding, he had to climb the three altar steps to do so. They are happily married and run the local Thorougoods Shop in Somerville Street in Crewe. In addition to this, Jed is also a milkman, with his own Express Dairy franchise. In fact, Jed and Emma are never short of anything to do. Having six children, albeit four of them at adult or late teenage years, a convenience store to run, the milkround to do, in which, Emma even has to help out on that by doing two evening collections each week, Jed, being a joiner by trade, also enjoys trying his hand with property and any spare time that he has, is spent doing work renovating a church which he has converted into a house in Loggerheads. So the chap, who was educated at Bedford Street Infants and Senior School and Mill Street Junior School and who puts his football experiences as playing for St Andrews Scouts, the P. Way and Audlem Royal and in seven a side with Old Villa and Oakfield Racing playing where short, but mainly in goal (despite his size, his bravery went unquestioned), has a very full timetable and that is before he finds time to be manager of Crewe Corinthians.

On interviewing Jed, two amusing stories came to light. The first occurred when Jed owned the newsagents shop across the road from the Crewe Alexandra ground in Gresty Road, which incidentally has been owned for the last twenty years or so by his brother, Greg. The shop, positioned as such, was obviously used by most of the Alex players. On this one occasion, a certain young player, David Platt, who used to drive over from Rochdale in his little red Ford Escort, had his backside window smashed and amongst the things stolen were his football boots. Rather than tell his manager, Dario Gradi, he borrowed a pair of Jed's boots that day for training. As Jed recalled, David was one of the most approachable players at Gresty Road and so Jed set him up with a deal of a free bottle of lucozade for every goal that he scored for Crewe. After he left Crewe, David went on to play for Aston Villa and England, where he scored that all important goal against Belgium in the quarter final of the World Cup. I bet that David's reward for scoring that goal was more than a bottle of lucozade!

Another interesting story tells of Jed's one television appearance- if one could call it that. Jed was working for a local milkman, when he realised that a cash book that he should have ordered several weeks ago had not been done. So, rather cheekily, he decided to use the milkman's van to do a four hundred mile round trip to Reading to the suppliers to collect the book. Unfortunately, on the way back, a major hold up on the motorway produced tailbacks so long that they made national news on television. Unfortunately for Jed, cameras zoomed in on Jed and his mate, Neil Atkinson, in the milkvan, some two hundred miles away from where the owner thought that it was parked up for the night. Fortunately the owner, who saw his van on television's `News at Ten', saw the funny side of the incident and ofcourse the free TV advertising and forgave Jed.

When entry into the Regional League for the young Crewe Corinthians team was first muted, Jed, who had previously managed a successful Wolverton, for whom several of the lads had played, was an obvious choice to be approached to become manager. The type of manager that Jed is, was soon to be shown by a gesture in his first season, when he promised that if the team achieved twenty five points he would pay everything towards the cost of an end of season party for them. A tough task but one which the lads just missed out on by one point but Jed and his wife, Emma, still gave them their free evening at a personal cost to themselves of several hundred pounds. Fortunately for the team, Jed is backed all the way by his wife, Emma, who even finds time to wash the kit and never charges, which in this day is a big financial saving.

What of the players?

Here, I was lucky in that the first captain of a team that I was involved in, was probably the greatest player that England has ever produced and certainly the most successful captain. Working for the Football Association, who ofcourse ran the England team, gave me the privilege to come into contact with Robert Frederick Chelsea Moore.

Born in Barking, just a few miles from Sir Alf, in 1941, he made his West Ham debut at seventeen and in 1965, led the Hammers to their one and only European trophy win, the Cup Winners Cup against Munich 1860. The following year saw him, as captain of England, lift the World Cup and in recognition of this he received the OBE in 1967. In 1970, he led England to Mexico to defend the trophy. However, controversy was to follow. At Bogota, he was accused of stealing a bracelet, a charge later dropped but not before it had left a scar on the great man's reputation. True to the great professional that he was, he gave an outstanding performance in the World Cup which warranted Pele, probably the greatest player ever to play the game, to describe Bobby as probably the best defender he had played against. What higher accolade is needed to judge Bobby Moore's status in the game?

In 1973, he played his one hundred and eighth and last international against Italy at Wembley. The following year he joined Fulham, playing against his beloved West Ham in the 1975 F.A.Cup Final. He retired from professional football in 1977 and after short spells as manager of Oxford City and Southend between 1984-1986 he left football, before dying of cancer in 1993.

I always found Bobby to be polite and immaculate, both in appearance and performance. In training and in games, as well as off the pitch, his presence was awesome and on the occasions that I was lucky enough to watch the England team train, Bobby was simply immaculate. Not the quickest in sprints, but he was so quick in thought on the pitch and like all great sportsmen always had time to do things. On the occasions I spoke to him, a cheeky grin always gave me the idea that he could be a live-wire character behind that immaculate exterior.

One question to me that will always remain unsatisfactory answered was why England's greatest captain and possibly footballer, Bobby Moore, never received a knighthood, when that honour has been bestowed on other members of that 1966 team and has since been bestowed upon others with not as much achievement in the world game?

Perhaps honours nowadays are easier to receive but hopefully one day that will be rectified and the just rewards made to a player who, to me, was simply the best.

What of our Corinthians team ?

Here I have chosen a young lad, David Griffin, who joined us from Nantwich Town Youth, along with Wayne Beggs and Graham Smalley, after they had all become too old for their Staffs Minor County Youth League team.

Born on the 25th April 1986 in Crewe, David has a sister, Emma, who is two years older. David's mother, Christine, is marketing manager at the South Cheshire Private Hospital and his father, Mike, is self employed. Christine and Mike split up when David was about two. Having lived the early part of his life in Shavington, David moved the short distance to his present home in Wistaston, when his mother remarried Graham Tressider, a local funeral director with Nantwich Funeral Services. His stepdad, Graham, infact having a spell as a player with Port Vale Football Club.

David went to Shavington Infants, Junior and Secondary Schools but it was at secondary school, that I first recall seeing "Griff" play in midfield with another of our players, Wayne Beggs, in a team that throughout their five years were constantly chasing for honours. The pair impressed but typically of the Crewe Schools F.A., there was no representative team, a situation that still applies today some years on, which is an absolute disgrace and should be rectified immediately.

David therefore gained his football experience, like many of his contemporaries, in the Lads and Dads League- courtesy of the likes of the Jed Hulmes of this world, but in David's case, thanks were to go to Derek

Harding and John Landstrom for running Shavington Shooters. Dave then spent two years playing for Sandbach Ramblers before joining Nantwich Town, under the managership of Francis dechoux, where he spent the next two years playing in the Staffordshire County Youth League under eighteen section, getting into the side by being willing to fill a vacancy in central defence, despite always playing in midfield prior to that.

David, after completing his studies at Shavington Secondary School, then moved on to South Cheshire College to take his`A'Levels and it was whilst he was there, that his football career could have taken off for the first time. He had been made captain of the college first team, where his performances as sweeper/central defender had earned him selection for the Cheshire team. He played in the first six county games of the 2003/4 season and following on impressive performances for his county, had been selected to play in the England under eighteen schoolboy trials to be held at Altrincham Football Club on Saturday 25th October 2003. Before that, however, David had to play in a county game against Shropshire on the Wednesday prior. It was then that fate played its cruel hand. The worst possible scenario happened, David sustained in that game a serious ankle ligament injury. Because of his mother's position at the South Cheshire Private Hospital, he was entitled to private health checks but this only confirmed his worst fears and he was advised not to play. Fearing that his chance had gone, young Dave decided that with strapping he could give it a go and play. Although he did his best, it was not good enough. The full extent of the injury being shown in the fact that it was some four months before he could play again. He has, in his possession, a letter from the E.S.F.A thanking him for attending the trial. It is a letter that he should treasure. His achievement in at least getting this trial is quite remarkable for lads in our area and makes him unique in our team and a fitting comparison at our level to the great Bobby Moore.

David's first three seasons at Nantwich Town were to see him figure firstly in the youth team on a regular basis for two seasons in the Staffs County Youth League but for all the wrong reasons in their F.A.Youth Cup team when, on his debut in that competition against Gresley Rovers, he got sent off. So his F.A.Youth Cup record was played one, sent off one!

The 2004/5 season saw David move on to captain the reserve team in the Mid Cheshire League, under the managership of former Crewe Alexandra player, Dave Pullar. Towards the end of that season, Dave earned selection for the first team, making his debut on 5th March 2005 at Formby. I was proud of what the lad had achieved. He was the first of our young Corinthians team to play in a higher League- North West Counties. Regretfully, not being able to witness his debut at Formby, matters were rectified when David played three home games for the first team against Ramsbottom, Skelmersdale and Great Harwood and I was duly impressed. I had always said that if any of our players succeeded in being selected to play at a higher level, I would endeavour to help them further

8

their career in football by getting in touch with some of the many contacts that I had made in twenty years of football at the top level. True to my word, I contacted one of the coaching staff of a Championship League team, who agreed to send a scout down to watch the lad play. His performance impressed and details of future games were given to that club by of all people, David's dad, Mike, when we were at the home game against Great Harwood on Easter Monday, so that the club in question could follow up their initial interest. I had asked Mike if he could use his mobile phone to ring a number for me, knowing that it was the interested club and that when they answered, if he could hand me the phone. Unsuspecting of what really was going on, he did this for me. When the club answered his call, I took over the phone, proceeding to give them the next few games young Dave may feature in. Mike then realised, probably for the first time, just how close his son could be to having a chance with a top Football League club. Here, for the second occasion, fate played young "Griff" a cruel hand. A week later, on Friday 8th April 2005, Dave rang me to inform me that he had been struck down by a serious throat infection, thought at first by his doctor to be tonsillitis, but which turned out to be far more serious. It was soon to force him into hospital for two spells totalling nine days in April, which prematurely finished his season. To avoid any inconvenience to the interested club, I immediately contacted them to advise them of the lad's condition and they gave me their word that they would look again when he had recovered his place in the team- so hopefully, it may be third time lucky for a talented youngster who epitomises what the bread and butter grass roots game is all about.

The talent is there, it just needs developing. Unfortunately, with the introduction of academies and the influx of foreign players over the last fifteen years or so, the chances of the late developers in football, which for one produced the greatest captain that Manchester City have ever had in Tony Book, have almost disappeared, despite the fact that in England's greatest footballing era, the sixties, regulations would not even permit lads to be associated with a Football League club until the age of fourteen and not play for any of their teams until the age of sixteen and yet we still managed to produce far more world class English players than we do now.

In September 2004, David started his first year of a three year Bsc Degree course on Sport and Exercise at the Manchester Metropolitan University (Alsager site).and supplements his week at university with a part time bar job at the Crewe Arms Hotel.

On interviewing Dave, he mentioned his stepmum, Anne, her younger sister, Clare, and a twinkle appeared in his eye when he mentioned Clare's little boy, Matthew, aged then just two and a half and who refers to Dave as "uncle". Young Matthew had been to a number of both our and Nantwich games, running about either in the stand or on the school field at Brine Leas where we play. We had agreed that if ever we were to appear in any final, young Matthew, along with Jed's own son, Jack, some four years older, would be our joint mascots for the day, with Jack looking after his younger counterpart. Unfortunately, AC Wickstead, in an early April semi-final, put paid to that. However, the offer still remains for future years and at least, it was our attempt to make our club into a family club, by bringing the younger members of our player's families into the set up.

So there are the four comparisons-each very different in what the game has given them. The greatest English manager and player of all time, Sir Alf Ramsey and Bobby Moore OBE, whose privilege it had been mine to know and of equal importance to me, Jed Hulme and David Griffin. All four have or had a love for the game and give or gave a lot back. Young lads do not start playing football because it gives them fame and riches, they play because they enjoy it. The likes of the Jed Hulmes and David Griffins are just as important to the welfare of this great game as are some of their famous counterparts. I know that they were held with respect by the likes of Sir Alf and Bobby Moore as such, because they were gentlemen of the game - humble in their fame.

It is important that people running the game continue to recognise this fact and that perhaps some of the silly money paid out by our top clubs can be given to the grass roots level to ensure its continuation. In all my years in football, and I am sure that I speak for a good number of old-timers, I have never come across a player whose performance could be enhanced by the payment of big financial bonuses- if it did, I would not hesitate to call him a cheat.

The David Griffins and Jed Hulmes epitomise our grass roots game. With Dave, it is his potential to play at a higher level, its unlucky breaks and his continued enthusiasm which allows him to play two games each weekend and train on three nights a week and continue to have a ball in the boot of his car. With Jed, it is the time that he gives up to help others to play despite having a hectic work and family life. They are the bread and butter of the game and there are thousands like them throughout the country who make the game so rich, which is loved and played or watched by millions throughout the world each week.

This book is about life on both sides of the equation- the administration of the professional and that of the amateur game which so often ran concurrently for me but with equal enjoyment.

CHAPTER ONE : HOW IT ALL BEGAN.

I was born in Crewe on 21st August 1950. My dad, Joseph, worked on the Signal and Telegraph in the railways and my mother, Christine, had been trained both as a hairdresser and a pianist but her full time job, like most women in those days, was as a wife and mother. Both my parents were born in 1914 and I was one of four children born to them. My eldest sister, Wendy, unfortunately died of leukemia in September 1953, at the age of just fourteen. My elder brother, Alec, is some eight years older than myself and my younger sister, Marilyn, was born just three months after my sister Wendy's death, in December 1953.

My parents always recalled that my sister had died in Manchester Royal Hospital and that on her deathbed she had spoken fluent German, so well in fact, that the doctors attending to her believed her to be a young German orphan girl- remember that the War had just finished some eight years previously, and they possessed until their dying day, a poem allegedly spoken by my sister in German at her death and dictated to a German speaking doctor at the hospital, basically telling my parents that she wanted to say goodbye with a smile. That incident has certainly remained in my mind and makes me believe that there is something far advanced after death to what exists in this world- after all, my sister had never received any German lessons in her life and the fluency that she spoke the language defied all reasonable logic.

My mother's family consisted of four sisters- Lil, Wyn, Marjory and Joan and one brother, Granville, who all incredibly ended up in the teaching profession. Her parents were quite wealthy, my grandfather, Si, a carpenter by trade, owning numerous properties that were later to befall to my family, including the house in Earle Street, a four bedroom, two toilet and bathroom, kitchen and three living room town terrace house, where they had brought up my mother and her brother and sisters, was far removed from where, for my first eleven years, my life had been spent in a two bedroomed terrace house in Ford Lane.

It was whilst at Ford Lane that I first recollect having a keen interest in football and my second love, cricket. We played both on a large span of green field in Badger Avenue, just off Ford Lane, or in the entries to our homes. Here, unlike today, numerous games would be going on, with just two coats down at each end to represent the goals. Now, unfortunately, one would rarely see children organising games of this nature for themselves, relying heavily instead on willing parents organising teams and games for them. If only the two situations could exist together, I am certain the standard of football would improve greatly. My generation would certainly have benefited from the organisation of games and teams by adults but similarly, I am sure today's youngsters would benefit from my generation's ability to just get a group of lads together for games that went on until darkness fell, where skills came from trial and error together with practice, rather than by coaching. Our games were based on streets-lads from Ford Lane would become Ford Rovers and would play Peel Street, becoming Peel United, both home and away, the organisation being done by ourselves and it was both great fun and good experience at an early age.

At the tender age of ten, I regarded myself as a left back or left half but unfortunately fell at the first selection hurdle for my school team, Adelaide Street Junior School. I had attended Adelaide Street Infants and Junior School, where our games were confined mainly to the school playground, until our final year when trials for the school team were held. Unfortunately, I did not make the team and there were no substitutes in those days but I doubt whether I would have got in there either. So I did what anybody keen on sport but not good enough to play would do, I did the next best thing, I got involved in the team in another way, by becoming the sports reporter to the school magazine. The school's headmaster, Gerald Durber, had decided to start a school magazine and I was asked to be the sports reporter, which I gratefully accepted. Equipped with note pad and a little camera, I would troop down to Middlewich Street playing fields, or wherever we would be playing, by walking or, if lucky, cycling to the games, another thing that seems to have disappeared from children's ways of life today. Nowadays they are ferried about in cars and I often wonder that if they had to do what we did to play our sport, whether they would have bothered - and this can certainly show in their attitude and performance.

Our school team was run by Mr Kearton and Mr Wilson and featured two friends of mine from those early days. Tony Wakefield, who lived just a few doors away from me in Ford Lane, was a brave little goalkeeper who was also an adequate outfield player and big Chris Jaycott, whose parents ran a local sewing machine shop, who, at centre half, could kick the ball farther than most, which was so important in those early days. However, every school fell below the high standard set by Mill Street Junior School, run by Mr West and their headmaster, Mr McCandless, who easily won both the League and Timperley Shield, often winning games by double figure scorelines.

In those days, children at eleven years of age had to take what was called the Eleven Plus, which were tests in English, Arithmetic and Intelligence, which would then determine whether they went on to grammar school or to the local secondary school, which in my case would have been Ludford Street. Fortunately, I passed the exams and went to grammar school in the September of 1962. The local grammar school had previously been a mixed school but the opening of a local girls grammar school in Buchan Grove increased the opportunities for children in the area to benefit from grammar school education. I was grateful for this because academically it gave me the opportunity to take GCE exams, whereas at secondary school, only exceptional pupils could be transferred at the end of their four years and they would then have to be transferred back a year in order to commence their studies for the two years of GCEs- three good schoolfriends of mine, Tony and Paul Latham and David Johnson, who all played cricket for us, having come through this procedure.

Equally as important to me was the fact that both football and cricket were far better catered for at the local grammar school. Unlike all of the local secondary schools at the time, we had our own sports field, well looked after by our own groundsman. Our fixtures were far more varied, playing against other grammar schools in the Cheshire and Staffordshire area, football games being held every Saturday morning from mid September to mid April and thereafter Saturday afternoon for cricket until the break for the summer holidays.

Academically, we were not graded in the first year, just being placed into our house names- I being placed into Dutton. At the end of that first year we were graded into A and B streams, I unfortunately being graded into the lower. However, by the end of the third year, I had progressed into the higher stream, where I stayed doing my ` O Levels', picking up eight passes in all, moving on to pass two of my three ` A Levels' in English and History.

On the sports side, we played both form and house games during the week after school and although I managed to get into both and indeed the school team at cricket, football was a different matter. However, because of my love for the game and the fact that many of my schoolmates had known me as the sports reporter of my junior school, I ended up playing an active role in the running of the school football teams from an early age. It was therefore a natural progression for the sports masters, Randel Jones and Phil Howell, to make me secretary of both football and cricket when I was in the fourth year, a position that I was to hold for a record term of office of four years. In fact, very rarely had anybody been secretary of football and cricket at the same time but it gave me great enjoyment and experience. There were under 12, 13, 14 and 15 matches to arrange for the first four years and first and second team fixtures for those pupils in the 5th and two years of 6th form education. Unlike secondary schools then and now, where fixtures are local and shoved in after school and few in numbers, our fixtures and travel were quite extensive and took some organising. Therefore, PE lessons for me were spent in the PE Masters room, often on the phone to the various schools in Cheshire and Staffordshire or to the local coach company, possibly spending more money on phone calls than the school registrar. Cheshire Schoolboy trials had be arranged for the most promising of our players and with it the appropriate time off lessons and arranging their travel. Through this, I quickly became known on the schools football and cricket circuit.

The majority of the schools that we played against were grammar schools, such as Nantwich, Helsby, Winsford Verdin, Macclesfield, Chester City and Kings and Sandbach, with games played on a Saturday. Teachers gave of their time on a Saturday, allowing games to be played in their entirety, unlike today, where few of our local schools have any sport on a Saturday, just a shortened midweek version. We also had our own groundsman and were only too willing to help him, which is certainly not the case today. Many school grounds are contracted out to an often indifferent standard. School pitches in the Crewe area have continued to deteriorate in the last thirty years or so, since many of the new comprehensive schools were built. Many have never seen a roller and the grass is so high that it makes playing to a good standard difficult. Schools must continue to press for improved facilities for their pupils by strengthening their links with the governing bodies of sports who, in return, should do all they can to assist with much needed finance. I am glad that I went to school during the golden era of grammar schools, when teachers gave of their time more freely and pitches were cared for by professional groundsmen. Our fixtures were interesting and varied and good players could always reach a representative level - a lot of this regretfully does not exist in the Crewe area now and I am sure that this is the same throughout the country.

Going back to my schooldays, several of our school games were incident packed. I remember vividly the time when our school first team were due to play Stockport School at football. In their six years together, I believe, Stockport had been unbeaten. They were held together by a wonderful player, who was very shortly to play in the First Division for Manchester United and have a long and illustrious career in football, culminating in him becoming chairman of the Professional Footballers Association. That player was Alan Gowling. We had talked about and trained the lads for the game all week and had motivated a boy called Tony Latham to mark Alan Gowling. Tony was the nephew of Frank Blunstone, a local lad who had moved to Chelsea as a young player from Crewe Alexandra, going on to gain international honours with England, before injury had finished his playing days forcing him onto the coaching side where he was at that time youth team coach. Tony played like a man inspired. Not just did he mark Alan Gowling out of the game but he scored both of our goals in a fine 2-1 win and earned himself selection for the County schoolboy squad going to Bognor for its annual football competition. Tony later tragically died of a heart condition, which he sustained whilst driving, which sadly involved another motorist, just one week after I had had the pleasure of showing him around Goodison Park during my spell there as box office manager.

We also had needle confrontations with Hanley High School over the years, which was mainly due to the ill feeling that existed between the two respective PE masters, Randel Jones and Selwyn Whalley from Hanley High School, who for many years had played right back for Port

Vale. The previous year, Hanley had become Staffordshire under nineteen champions and with many of that side still remaining, were regarded as a very formidable team. The week before the game had been very cold and with overnight frosts forecasted from Wednesday onwards, it was necessary for us to spend time rolling the pitches in order for them to be playable at the weekend. With the football pitch being rolled, the surface, although hard due to a few days of frost, was playable. The game therefore went ahead with Randel refereeing. Selwyn had been upset by Randel's decision to play and it was both embarrassing and amusing to see the two teachers at each other's throats. The game ended with us winning 2-1 to beat the current Staffordshire champions. However, that was not to be the end of the matter. We had arranged a cricket fixture with them to be played at Hanley later in the year. Randel had decided, much to our alarm, to umpire the game. Selwyn, fortunately, was not involved but on arriving at Hanley, we found the wicket so poorly prepared, with grass several inches high. Mr Jones took some pieces as evidence, which he would later send to Hanley with a letter of complaint. Luckily, we won the toss and elected to bowl. The wicket was so dangerous, that within half an hour and with half of their side out and with most of their batsmen being hit around the body with deliveries flying dangerously off a length, the game was abandoned. That incident ended fixtures between Crewe Grammar School and Hanley High School, two schools with an excellent sporting reputation. It had been caused really by teachers who should have known better but whose personal feud was so evident for all to see.

The other incident involved myself and resulted in the only time that I have ever had to be disciplined in sport. Our first eleven cricket team, with myself included as a medium pace bowler, had been thwarted by time wasting tactics by a visiting Crewe Vagrants team, led by Jeff Minshull, a local councillor, who in later years was to be instrumental in getting today's Corinthians team into the Regional Sunday Football League. In a game scheduled to play for set hours (2-7pm), we had batted first and were forcing the pace when the Vagrants started to time waste. In the end, we declared with a total short of what we would have made if they had bowled their overs at a rate of which they were capable. When they started their innings, they also found runs easy to come by on the excellent wicket that I had helped to produce. Therefore, in retaliation, we started to waste time and I am afraid that being a bowler, I was the worst culprit and, as secretary, the chief instigator. Words were said at the end of the game and accusations and threats followed. As a result of this, a complaint was sent to Randel about our and my behaviour in particular. At assembly, the headmaster, Mr Lucas, a giant of a man, being well over six foot tall, asked for the cricket committee to meet Mr Jones in the PE masters office at lunch time. At that meeting, I am afraid that I was'hung, drawn and quartered'. In a meeting, where I took the minutes, I was suspended for two games and even had to write and inform myself of the decision- talk about rubbing salt into the wound!

The day that I returned from suspension though was to see my best sporting performance. We were due to play our local rivals, Nantwich and Acton Grammar School, at home and I had helped the groundsman to produce a wicket that would help the bowler - one end of the wicket being constantly watered and with more grass left on it than the other end. Our regular opening bowler, Chris Hunt, was out injured and so I opened as second string bowler to a lad called Charlie Musker. We had struggled on the wicket batting first and totalled just over the fifty mark. Nantwich, with Ian Cowap in their line-up, who went on to play at full level for the County and have an illustrious career in local cricket, where he played as a professional for several leading amateur clubs, just never came to terms with the indifferent bounce of the wicket and I obviously chosing the correct end to bowl from, recorded the best ever bowling figures for the school by taking seven wickets for just seven runs, as we bowled out Nantwich to win by twenty runs or so. That Saturday evening just happened to also be our sixth form leaving do and I celebrated by spending a fortune on getting drunk along with most of my team mates, for in true cricket spirit, a player getting five wickets or more ends up buying a round-or two for his team mates.

One of the masters that we had looking after our cricket team was my old Maths teacher, Ed Lewis, who lived in North Wales but stayed over in Crewe for the week. Ed was an Evertonian and it gave me great pleasure when, as box office manager of Everton, I was asked to get him an Everton season ticket as his retirement present from teaching some fifteen years later in the eighties.

Our other teacher who helped us with our cricket was David Cleland, my history teacher, who, in his first year at Crewe, had succeeded in becoming a Cheshire selector and was to get me involved in the Cheshire set up on occasions as scorer, the highlight of which featured a game between Cheshire and Yorkshire at the beautiful school of St Peters at York in which I witnessed one of the very few ties that I have ever seen. Yorkshire, chasing something like 180, were level with four wickets intact when, if my memory serves me right, they failed to succeed in getting that elusive run in one of the most dramatic finishes that I have ever witnessed. Included in the Yorkshire team that day was David Bairstow, who later played for England and included in the Cheshire team were two lads from my school- Paul Latham, younger brother to Tony and Norman Hughes, who was later to represent England and Great Britain at hockey, having taken up the sport and being encouraged by one of our PE masters, Phil Howell- to give up football in the process, in which he was no mean player. Also included in that Cheshire team was an opening batsman from Sale, Steve Smith, who later was to make his mark as a rugby union international with England.

In the mid sixties, there was no organised football for lads of our age except ofcourse school football, so we therefore decided to organise our own League. We felt that we would struggle to get many teams of eleven a side and therefore opted for a seven a side League but played on the same basis as the eleven a side game, with offsides, normal goals on full sized pitches etc. We decided to make the League open to teams within a fifteen miles radius of Crewe, which allowed teams from Stoke on Trent to enter. As it was my idea, I was designated at the inaugural meeting, held at my home and attended by ten clubs- three from the Potteries, the remainder from Crewe, Nantwich, Alsager and Sandbach, to become secretary. The local evening paper, the Sentinel, gave good coverage for us, reporting in detail any information that I sent to them. The League got underway in late September 1966 but as teams started to drop out of the title race and with the difficulty faced with travel to and from the Potteries, we began to see fixtures being unfulfilled. It was therefore apparent, early in 1967, that the League fixtures would not be completed.

Parental help in those days was virtually non existent and teams had to rely on public transport to get them to the Potteries or vice-versa, as very few families had cars. The quality of players playing in the League however had started to attract the scouts of Football League clubs and Stoke City's chief scout, Cliff Birks, twice invited us down to the Stoke City training ground at Lilleshall Road to play their under seventeen team. We lost the games 1-3 and 0-2 but gave a very creditable performance, which resulted in two of our players, Paul Latham and Steven Bache, being invited back on occasions to play for the Stoke City youth team. I was later to find out, through getting to know Tony Waddington, the Stoke City manager, that it was he who, by living in Crewe, had heard and read about the League and had arranged for his scouting staff to keep a watchful eye.

Another club to take an interest was to be a club and gentleman who I was to get to know well in the mid seventies and eighties, some ten years later, namely Everton and their chief scout, Harry Cooke. Everton invited two players from our League, Colin Neale and Francis Robinson, over to their training ground at Bellefield to take part in a trial game. With the invitation in my pocket as League secretary and with all expenses to be re-imbursed, we set out by train from Crewe to Liverpool. Everything was running smoothly, until the ticket collector asked the two lads for their tickets. Colin passed him his ticket and he asked him to show him his privilege card - which was given to all railway employees to enable them to obtain reduced or free rail travel, which he did. On turning to Francis, he asked him the same. I immediately knew that something was amiss, as I knew that Francis was still at school. As a result, the two lads, on completing the journey, were escorted to the police station on Lime Street Station. What a start. I told the Police of the reason why we were going to Liverpool and the explanation must have fallen on the kind heart of an Evertonian railway transport police official, and because I had that letter

17

from Everton with me I was able to verify my address and guarantee them full assistance with any future enquiries, the lads were released and we hastily ran to get a taxi to take us to the Everton training ground for the trial game. It later came to light that the lads had purchased their tickets the previous night and Francis, with Colin's help, had tried to make a few pence in the process. In the trial game, both did relatively well but were not invited back.

In later years, Franny was to have a short spell playing in the youth team at Blackpool, before returning locally to play in the Sunday League. Colin or "Ted" as he was popularly known, went on to play for Winsford United and Nantwich Town, where he was a member of their championship winning side in the early eighties and was also to become a legend in the local Sunday Regional League, where his epic battles with Roy Harding, once led to both men standing in a bucket of ice to find out who was the harder, after Ted had been challenged by Roy to meet him outside, for what Ted considered to be a case of fisticuffs. Ted, sadly, was to die of cancer just a few years ago.

With the seven-a-side fixtures failing to be fulfilled, the League had to be disbanded in its first season. We had made a brave attempt to provide youths in the area with football without any real adult assistance. The standard of play was excellent - thus the interest from two of the country's leading clubs but transport difficulties perhaps were too difficult to overcome without that adult interest. The experience that I gained from running the League at such a young age, only sixteen, was tremendous. The trophies, which had been donated by my brother, Alec, were played off for at the local grammar school, as so many of the League's players attended that school - but I did retain one plaque, which I still have today, some forty years on.

During all of this time, I continued to follow my local club, Crewe Alexandra, right from the time of being introduced to them by my next door neighbour, Ted Tunstall, who was in his early teenage years and therefore a few years older than me, watching my first game on 30th August 1958 in the newly formed Fourth Division against Chester at Gresty Road, which the Alex lost 2-4 in front of a crowd of 8657 - not bad considering that for the previous three seasons in the old Third Division North, the club had finished bottom. Other games that stick out in that first season were the two games against Port Vale played in front of 15350 at Gresty Road and 20524 at Vale Park. I was also present at the famous 2-2 draw against the great Tottenham team, when twenty thousand were at Gresty Road, qualifying for our tickets by attending a previous match against Chester, when over twelve thousand had attended, an increase of five thousand on the previous home game against Barrow.

The visit to Chelsea as a youngster for the famous 2-1 win will always remain in my memory, as will the days spent as a member of the Junior Supporters Club, started by Harold Finch, which, when I became secretary, some ten years later in 1975, I resurrected, because I knew how much enjoyment I had received as a youngster from attending their meetings and the fun that we had on going on organised trips to away games. I even spent part of my school summer holiday one year, along with David Johnson, who was later to join the church, working on the ground, by cleaning all the seats in the old wooden stand. Our boss for that venture was Syd Barratt, the groundsman, who I was to get to know well when I became secretary of the club in 1975.

Cleaning the seats of the stand to becoming secretary of the club ten years later. Life in football for me was certainly to be in the fast lane over the next few years.

CHAPTER TWO: TO THE FOOTBALL ASSOCIATION AND ENGLAND

I had started on a three year HND Business Studies course in September 1969, of which six months of the year were to be spent in college at the Mid Cheshire College of Further Education at Hartford and the other six months gaining practical experience in a firm. Unfortunately for me, the firm that the college allocated, English Calico, in Congleton, gave me so much mundane work to do, that the most testing thing that I had to do was to remember which staff had tea and who had coffee at their breaks.

It was the summer of 1970 and probably the best World Cup of all was taking place in Mexico. England were the reigning champions but in Brazil, they were to come across a team basically regarded by many as the best team ever. The nation was gripped with excitement and not unnaturally I began to miss the active role that I had played in football administration over the last few years at school. I therefore decided to try to get an administration job within a football club.

To try to achieve this, I decided to write to all ninety two Football League clubs in the hope that one of them may have a suitable vacancy. After all, what was I to lose, a few pounds in postage and stationery. This was in late June and replies soon began to filter back, all polite but unsuccessful, until a ray of hope came through a reply from Arsenal Football Club and their secretary, Ken Friar, who stated that if I wanted to make an appointment, he would be willing to talk to me. I knew that there was no offer of a job on the table but the opportunity of talking to somebody in football was too good to turn down. Therefore, I rang and made an appointment to meet him.

So, in mid October, 1970, I boarded a train to London to meet Mr Friar. I arrived at Highbury Stadium an hour early and just walked around the famous stadium to kill time, soaking up the atmosphere, before bracing myself to walk up the steps leading to the entrance of Arsenal Football Club. I approached the reception area and told the receptionist of the nature of my visit. I was nervous, even though I knew that it was not an interview for a job, but I still so much wanted to make a favourable impression. Mr Friar soon made me feel at ease in our conversation.

At the end of our meeting, he stated that although no vacancies existed at Arsenal Football Club, I should contact the Football Association at their headquarters in Lancaster Gate, as they may be recruiting. On leaving the meeting, I could not wait to return home in order to put pen to paper with an application to the Football Association, just in case a vacancy existed.

Sure enough, within a week, a reply came back stating that a vacancy existed which may be suitable and inviting me to ring and make an appointment to attend an interview. Within five minutes of opening that letter, I had fixed a date and time for an interview, that was to be the most daunting one that I could have ever imagined.

The interview was fixed for a Monday afternoon in early November. Ensuring that I would be on time and being a student, not having the finances for an overnight stay, I caught the early morning train from Crewe. It arrived late morning at Euston, a two hours journey and fortunately on time, which then gave me three hours to eat some lunch and to get the short distance from Euston to Lancaster Gate by tube. It was the longest lunch I have ever had and after finding out where the Football Association offices were, in order that I could arrive back in time for the interview, I went and spent an hour or so in the nearby Hyde Park, before entering the doors of Lancaster Gate to report for my interview. Those few hours waiting to attend the interview for the job I wanted so much were amongst the most nerve racking of my life.

Typically, as with all interviews, they are always running late, as if deliberately to make the applicant even more nervous. Sure enough, mine was running fifteen minutes late, before I was finally summoned into the room for my first ever job interview.

Facing me were three men, one of whom every football fan in the world would recognise. Sitting on my first ever interview panel was the manager of the England 1966 World Cup winners, Sir Alf Ramsey. A rather large gentleman sat in the middle of the three, he just happened to be the secretary of the Football Association, Sir Denis Follows - the top administrator of the game in this country, although his counterpart at the Football League, Alan Hardaker, may have contested this fact and on the other side to Sir Denis was Ken Young, the chief accountant of the Football Association. In appearance, Mr Young was very similar to Fulton Mackay out of the comedy programme, `Porridge' and just as regimental in the way that I found he ran the F.A.Accounts Department.

After the nerves had settled, which was sooner than I could realistically have hoped for in view of facing such an illustrious interview panel, I gave what I can honestly say was an excellent interview, so that, when I left the room half an hour later, I at least knew that I had done myself justice.

The next few days waiting for the outcome of that interview were amongst the longest of my life. Finally, on the Saturday morning, the fateful letter from the Football Association, bearing the three lions crest mark, finally arrived. The memory of opening and reading that letter will remain with me for ever and the joy of being successful in getting the job was to rank amongst one of my proudest moments. I know that to offer the job to me, knowing that I would have to leave a home two hundred or so miles away, must have meant that I made a real impression at that interview. My starting date was fixed for a week later and arrangements for my accommodation would have to be made hastily in order for me to commence work on the agreed date.

Fortunately for me, two of my old school pals, Merfyn John and Michael Dodd, had twelve months previously moved down from Crewe to Chelsea College and had rented a terraced house in Battersea, where they had been joined a few months later by Paul Latham, another school mate, who had figured prominently in the football and cricket teams at the old school. I therefore approached Merfyn and Michael to see if they could accommodate me. The twenty pounds a week rent that they had taken on, would therefore be halved from its original with the extra two of us. They readily agreed and I handed in my notice at Hartford College and packed my bags for the capital and a job that I had always dreamt of.

To have impressed the secretary of the Football Association and the England team manager, both Knights of the Realm, was something I am proud of, especially at the age of twenty, but I can not help but think that Ken Friar at Arsenal, who was to serve the Gunners as chief executive for the next thirty years, may have been instrumental in my appointment. His suggestion to contact the Football Association led me to believe that he knew something. It is, however, something that I will never know, as I never had reason to find out and no doubt, he would struggle to remember a young man who came down from Crewe to meet him one midweek Autumn day in 1970.

Settling into the house at Battersea with three mates was a godsend, which I was to later appreciate when, in 1989, I was to move from Everton to Leeds United and have to endure various lonely accommodations. To Merfyn, Michael and Paul, I am eternally grateful for putting up with me and thus allowing me to settle at the Football Association so very quickly. Michael and Paul had, like I say, played for the school and in the 7-a-side league with Brookfield United whom, even though I was secretary of the League, I was also secretary to that club as well, and both lads had played for the representative team that our 7-a-side League had sent to play against the Stoke City youth eleven on two occasions. Michael had, at school, however, fallen foul of the PE master, Mr Jones, for showing dissent to a sportsmaster of an opposing school, who refereed one of our games. His crime? When asked for his name, he gave it rather sarcastically as, "Harold Wilson", who just happened to be Prime Minister at the time. The teacher concerned took this to be true, which all the players found to be hilarious, not least of all our opponents, until one of Michael's team mates shouted his real name. Whereupon, the teacher, realising that he had been made to look foolish, sent Michael off, reporting the matter to our PE master, who decided that he should be suspended. Unfortunately, that suspension was never lifted. Mike also had a footballing background in that his father, Walter Dodd, was a former director of Crewe Alexandra Football Club in the sixties.

Merfyn John, a fanatical Welsh lad, was a bubbly character who, unfortunately for me, had a quick temper, especially when one criticised the Welsh, as I did one evening after watching Wales play football on the TV highlights. I had seen enough of the game and decided to go to bed. Holding onto the door to say my farewells, I muttered something detrimental in fun at the poor Welsh performance and Merfyn, just like the fiery little Welsh patriot he was, just kicked out so hard at the door, that my hand slipped and my little finger was caught in the door as it closed. In agony, but with howls of laughter about, I went to bed. I did not get much sleep with the pain though and so the next morning, I had no alternative but to visit the hospital, where the finger was declared broken. I don't think that I will upset the Welsh again so quickly!

Our weekend lifestyle was great. Paul was working for Kodak and had managed to become a member of the Playboy Club and so many of our weekends were spent visiting what was then the `club of all clubs', where we just soaked up the atmosphere and on occasions were joined by mates from back home, tasting that exclusive London nightlife. Unfortunately, all good things come to an end when Paul's job moved him from London to Hemel Hempstead and the four became three.

On the football side, the first international that I saw at the Football Association came within a few weeks of joining. However, for the first six months or so, I was delegated to work on the accounts side, as only that one international against East Germany was scheduled to be held until the two European Championship games against Malta in early February and Greece in the middle of April.

Work in the accounts department was very varied. It involved the actual accounting of running the F.A. premises in Lancaster Gate from the wages of the staff to the overheads of the building. After which came the accounting of various functions that the Football Association controlled, such as representative and international matches, which I was more directly involved in. To the average football fan, the number of teams run by the Football Association would surprise them. In those days, we had not just the full England team, `B'internationals, under 23, 21 and 18 and Amateur teams but then we had the representative team playing against teams such as the Armed Services and Oxford and Cambridge University. Each had running cost involved, such as the expenses of players and fees for playing in these fixtures and then ofcourse, the final accounting of those matches, showing whether the game made a profit or loss. Then there was the F.A.Cup, the big money spinner for the Football Association, together with the affiliation fees received from all the teams registered with the Football Association which came in from the various counties which, in those days, was all profit, as nearly every County was administered by honorary secretaries and treasurers, unlike today, when many County Football Association's have their own full time staff and offices to pay for.

My boss in the Accounts Department was Ken Young, a real regimental type who accounted for every single penny, a policy which led

24

to many minor conflicts with leading players over their expense claim - although, there was only ever one winner and that was not the player!

I wonder how different that is to today's football ?

F.A.regulations only permitted international players to claim the equivalent to second class rail fares and only hotel accommodation if their journey was over a certain time. Footballers, and more especially international players, were never ones to itemise their travel, hotel and meal expenses to the nearest penny but Mr Young would never permit this and I, on many occasions, had to ring up to find exact fares and adjust their expense sheet accordingly. This obviously caused a certain amount of animosity and was very embarrassing for yours truly, but I do admit, many years on, that I did explain to some angry players, that it was my boss, Mr Young, who was such a stickler- after all, why should I make myself unpopular when I had to come into contact with them on travel etc? Just imagine having to find out the second class rail fare between Barking in Essex to Wembley and finding it less than the England skipper, Bobby Moore, had claimed and then reducing his expenses accordingly- but that was what we had to do.

Penny pinching - that was the F.A, until it came to their own after match functions, then I saw for myself just how much money was lavishly spent on after the match banquets for the F.A and all of their guests, the profits of which all ended up in the coffers of Wembley Stadium Limited, a private concern, who, because of the short sightedness of the Football Association, creamed off much of the profit generated from the game and regretfully, because of infighting between the clubs, have continued to do so, when football should have been looking, like rugby has done, to build its own stadium to hold its prestigious events.

The failure to build our own national football stadium at that time was one of the most detrimental allegations I could make against the Football Association. If this had been done by the clubs who, after all, formed the Football Association's greatest source of income, they would have had a vested interest in its financial success. That in turn would have meant more internationals, instead of the meagre fifteen matches held during my spell at the F.A. between November 1970 and August 1972. Those fifteen games comprised of eight European Championship games (Greece, Malta, Switzerland and West Germany twice), six home internationals (Wales, Northern Ireland and Scotland twice) and just one other international, a friendly against the German Democratic Republic on the 25th November 1970, before the next friendly nearly two years later on 10th October 1972.

If, as England had done in 1966 and won the World Cup and in 1970 just failed to retain it, with what many experts felt was probably a stronger squad, I am sure that our present day marketing men at the Football Association would have certainly arranged more games and generated far more revenue. The Football Association should shoulder the blame for not seizing this golden opportunity. The England shirt had always been sacred - replica shirts were not allowed. Just imagine how short sighted this was and how much lost revenue had been incurred by this stubborn stance against change.

On a footballing side, Sir Alf, undoubtedly the best and most successful manager of all time, was given just fifteen games in two years against just eight opponents to try to produce a team to become World Champions. Imagine the outcry from today's England management if the same restrictions had been placed on them. We had the quality of players and management required for success. Unfortunately, the decision men of both the governing bodies of football, The Football League and the Football Association, never gave them the necessary backing and football missed out on the golden opportunity to build on its popularity after that '66 World Cup triumph. It really was amateurs running the game, where as today, it is greed. If only a happy medium could be arrived at between the high ideals of football in the past and today's ability to generate revenue, but with the benefit going to all playing the beautiful game.

The ruling bodies in football had always had a rather stormy relationship with the television authorities, with revenue often only being negligible. The only international that I can remember being shown live during my two year stay at the Football Association was the home leg of the European Championships against West Germany and the receipts from that were hardly gigantic. I think that the players received the princely sum of ten pounds each for a TV appearance, compared to their international match fee of one hundred pounds. This came from a one hundred thousand sell out crowd, with just as much being spent on after the match entertainment for the F.A. and their guests.

The first international that I was involved in occurred shortly after joining the Football Association, when goals from Francis Lee, Allan Clarke and Martin Peters gave England a 3-1 win against the German Democratic Republic at Wembley, but the most important fact about this game was that it was England's only friendly that season, which involved important European Championship games. This was due entirely, I believe, to the constant in fighting between the game's two controlling bodies for ultimate power, namely the Football Association and the Football League, with the loser being the England team.

The Football Association ran the game and had under its jurisdiction all clubs, both professional and amateur and, as such, were regarded by the world's governing bodies, FIFA for World football and UEFA for European football, as the controlling authority for football in this country. However, the Football League clubs, although only ninety two in number out of the many thousands of clubs in England, provided nearly all of the Football Association's revenue and therefore wanted a far greater say on how the game was to be run. The Football League only had a few voices in the corridors of power at the Football Association and so could easily be outvoted. The Football Association was run by a Council, with the great majority of the members being the representatives of their County Football Associations or other select bodies or organisations, such as the Armed Services and the two leading Universities - Oxford and Cambridge. It was therefore only fair to say that the running of the Football Association really antagonised the chairman of the great majority of affluent Football League clubs. The detrimental side to this was that the Football League chairman therefore showed very little interest in the welfare of an England team that was being run by the Football Association. Managers needed very little excuse to withdraw their players from international squads in order to save them for their own League games and in doing so were backed by their own club chairmen.

As a result of this, in the fifteen internationals in two years between 1970 and 1972 during which I worked for the Football Association, when Sir Alf should have been allowed to attempt to bring together a settled squad, thirty players actually played for England- Gordon Banks, Alan Ball, Tony Brown, Colin Bell, Martin Chivers, Terry Cooper, Allan Clarke, Tony Currie, Ralph Coates, Emelyn Hughes, Norman Hunter, Colin Harvey, Geoff Hurst, Francis Lee, Chris Lawler, Larry Lloyd, Alan Mullery, Roy McFarland, Bobby Moore, Paul Madeley, Malcolm MacDonald, Rodney Marsh, Martin Peters, Paul Reaney, Joe Royle, Peter Storey, Peter Shilton, Tommy Smith, Mike Summerbee and Colin Todd.

England training sessions were virtually forgotten as players were withdrawn by their clubs on pretence of injury, an injury that always seemed to respond to treatment that made them available for their club's next fixture. It was this constant withdrawal of players that saw the number of England matches reduced to an insufficient figure to prepare a team for success in a major competition.

In order to try to remedy the problem, the Football Association brought in a payment system, whereby clubs were to be compensated financially if their players were selected in the squad to represent England. A club would receive a fee based on the player's basic wage, with a minimum payment made of one hundred pounds if he was selected for the squad. The figure of the fee payable to the club being fixed initially at fifty per cent of the player's basic wage. This, in effect, therefore meant that both the club and the player were receiving a one hundred pound fee if, as was the case, the player's basic wage was two hundred pounds a week, which nearly all were on at that time. These fees paid out to the clubs, however, did not have the desired effect and the clubs continued to withdraw players from selected squads, as the battle between the two governing bodies continued to grow. If England were to succeed, one felt that it would be in spite of the leading clubs rather than because of them. Sir Alf always had an excellent relationship with his experienced players with regard to loyalty and that always gave him and his team a chance. However, with such a high number of players having to be called upon, the loyalty relationship that he had had with his World Cup winning squad could never develop to the same extent.

After the German Democratic Republic friendly, the first European Championship fixture saw England visit Malta in February 1971. A Martin Peters goal saw England secure a scrappy 1-0 win, the team having to show seven changes from the one that had played so well in the previous friendly game. Comfortable home victories followed against Greece (3-0) and Malta (5-0) in a three week spell between mid-April and mid-May. The Championship had started well with three wins and not having conceded a goal but already nineteen players had been used. The Home Internationals, with games against Northern Ireland, Wales and Scotland, fell just three days after the Malta home game and saw a further five players play in wins against Northern Ireland in Belfast by the solitary goal and a 3-1 win against the old enemy, Scotland, at Wembley, which was enough to give England the Championship, despite a lack lustre goalless draw against the Welsh.

Confidence was high going into the1971/72 season when the great test would come against our old rivals, the West Germans. First though, there were still three tricky games to play, both home and away against the Swiss and away in Greece. The game in Switzerland, played in the October, saw England win by the odd goal in five, but it was to all go pear-shaped some four weeks later at Wembley when, with only five players in the team that had done so well in winning in Switzerland, England could only manage a 1-1 draw . A two goals to nil win in Athens was recorded but the disastrous draw at home to the Swiss had given the West Germans the advantage. In those days, only the champions of each group qualified for the next stage of the competition. There was no entry through the backdoor, as there is now, no doubt done for financial rather than sporting reasons. The two games against the West Germans had been arranged to be the last two played in the Group, with the game at Wembley Stadium scheduled for Saturday 29th April 1972 and the return in Germany two weeks later.

Once a sell out was guaranteed for the Wembley game, television was allowed to show the game live- a rarity in those days but, with the strict proviso, that the game kicked off on the Saturday evening so as not to clash with any other fixtures being played that day. Along with a colleague of mine, Dave Barber, we had followed the progress of the West German party since their arrival in Britain. Their manager, Helmut Schoen, was a wily old fox and he possessed in his squad three world class players, Franz Beckenbauer, Gunter Netzer and Gerd Muller. It was these three that saw the Germans record a 3-1 win, which gave them qualification for the final stages of the European Nations Cup and saw England eliminated. On the Friday evening prior to the game, Dave and myself had marvelled at how Netzer could strike a dead ball, as we watched the Germans train on the Wembley pitch. The next day, he was to give a world class performance, which was to be so instrumental in the German victory.

Numerous people had travelled down from Crewe for the game and I travelled back with them on the same midnight train from Euston, having to stand all the way with my father. Their disappointment was nothing compared to my own, or so I thought. I had planned to go to Germany for the second leg but gave this a miss as the Home Internationals followed a week later and felt that the time would be better spent preparing for them. It was the only England international that I missed in the two years. A goalless draw in Germany gave us some pride back, but elimination at the expense of the Germans was something England fans would have to face again, and ofcourse, 1970 had still not been avenged.

The last three games of the 1971-72 season fell into insignificance after the West German defeat. Two wins were recorded, one against the Welsh by three goals to nil and then in a most hostile atmosphere at Hampden Park against the Scots, where we won by a single goal. Despite having several thousand tickets available for the game, which we had allocated mainly to our clubs and County Associations, being English that day at Hampden Park was indeed a rarity. Where did all our allocation of tickets go ? It seemed that every ticket sent across the border to England ended up in the hands of an exiled Scot making his bi-annual pilgrimage home and this certainly left any England supporter intimidated and very isolated that day.

One lasting story that will remain in my memory was told to me by Alan O'Dell, Sir Alf's personal assistant for many years at the Football Association, of how Sir Alf had been sitting in a first class compartment with a group of elderly F.A.councillors returning by train from Glasgow after the game, when a group of Scots, much younger in age and much the worse for wear because of drink, mistakenly opened the door to where Sir Alf and his bosses were sat. On seeing Sir Alf, they told him in no uncertain terms how lucky they felt England had been that afternoon. Sir Alf quickly retorted by telling them, in equally rude terms, where they should go, much to the consternation of Alan and his bosses. Aghast, they accepted the England manager's rebuke and departed quietly, much to the relief of the others in the compartment. That was the man, courageous with his actions and also with his words.

The season, though, was soon to fall flat again with a single goal defeat against Northern Ireland at Wembley. Little did I realise it but that was to be the end of my association with the England team at the Football Asssociation, for within three months, I was to move back nearer to home with a move to a top Football League club.

Ofcourse, working for the Football Association had its advantages, such as complimentary tickets for matches. London, in those days, had a large number of big clubs and amongst the games I was fortunate enough to see was the one in which Arsenal, by winning at Spurs of all places, obtained their first double to equal their North London rivals and for which, I was sat just three seats away from the great Portuguese footballer, Eusebio, obtaining his autograph in the only thing that I had on me at the time, a cricket league handbook.

I was also present on three other big match occasions. Firstly, when Chelsea, for whom I had always had a soft spot, being the nearest club to my digs in Battersea when I first moved down to London, pulled back a two goal deficit by beating Bruges in the European Cup Winners Cup and then going on to win that trophy, their first triumph in Europe.

The other two games of note were both finals, but firsts for me. The European Cup Final was staged at Wembley between Ajax, featuring the great Johann Cruyff and Panathinakos from Greece, with the Dutch team triumphing in an era of Dutch dominance, both nationally and at club level. The other final was our very own F.A.Cup Final, which was extra special, not because of the standard of football but because of the occasion. It was none other than the Centenary F.A.Cup Final and it was to mark a lot of milestones in the great game that I was fortunate enough to be in a position to attend in later years at Manchester City for the Golden Jubilee of the Maine Road ground and at both Crewe Alexandra and Everton, where I was on the staff during their centenary year. All these centenary celebrations made me realise just how quickly the game and its clubs had developed, the fact that so many centenary celebrations had occurred for me in such a short period of time. The Football Association had quite rightly placed great emphasis on its Centenary F.A.Cup Final and numerous souvenirs were presented to all and sundry. Unfortunately, the match itself never lived up to the occasion as Leeds United beat Arsenal by the single goal in that 1972 Final.

Working in London had been a tremendous experience and the huge number of clubs, both professional and amateur, in the big city allowed me to attend a high number of games but all that was to change in the summer of 1972.

CHAPTER THREE : TO A FOOTBALL LEAGUE CLUB- AND THEY DON'T COME MUCH BIGGER THAN MALCOLM ALLISON'S MANCHESTER CITY.

Although I had enjoyed my two years at the Football Association, it had always been my ambition to work for a Football League club. Therefore, just as I had done two years previously, I decided to put pen to paper and write to all the clubs but with one big difference, this time I would be able to say that I had experience in football administration with the highest body in the English game.

Letters went out in early 1972 and a few days later a reply came back from Derby County, who at the time were one of the four leading clubs in the First Division (in those days there was no glorified title such as "Premier" League, it was just a simple First, Second, Third and Fourth division and that is how it would remain in all my time in football). This letter invited me to attend an interview at the old Derby County Baseball Ground.

It was a Friday afternoon and I had travelled up from London to attend the interview. It was a cold, wet March day and the walk from Derby Railway Station to the Baseball Ground, about a mile, ensured that I was wet and cold by the time that I had arrived for the interview, which was conducted by the Derby County secretary, Stuart Webb, who firmly controlled the commercial as well as the administration side at Derby.

The interview went well and at the end of which, I was introduced to the Derby County manager, the one and only, Brian Clough, who had been informed that I was from the Football Association, a body that he had had his fair degree of confrontations with in the past. I believed that our meeting went well and I left under the impression that I was to be offered the job of assistant secretary, or some similar role in the very near future. I left Derby that day excited by the prospect of joining them and started to follow their results with added interest. This culminated in myself and my father, who was equally as excited at the possibility of me joining Derby County, travelling to Maine Road, Manchester, to watch Derby in a crucial match that looked like having a big say on where the League Championship ended up.

Disappointingly, Derby were beaten two goals to nil by a Rodney Marsh inspired Manchester City who, surprisingly, had themselves slipped up in the title race since the signing of Rodney from Queens Park Rangers but who, on the day, had dented Derby's hopes.

However, the following week, Derby, whilst on holiday, were crowned Champions, as their rivals' results went in their favour.

So, during the Summer of 1972, I expected to receive a letter from

Derby County informing me of the date to commence my employment with them. I am still awaiting that letter some thirty plus years on!

The summer was passing by and then, in late July, a letter appeared - but from Manchester City, asking if I could attend an interview. They had kept my application on file as promised in March and some five months later a vacancy had arisen. Only too willingly, I accepted their invitation. In my mind, I had decided that if I was fortunate enough to be offered a job at Manchester City, it would now take preference over any offer from Derby County whom, on a matter of principle, I had not contacted since my original interview, believing that they knew my address if they wanted to contact me regarding my services.

I attended the interview at Manchester City on a Saturday morning in early August. It was conducted in the Maine Road boardroom by the City secretary, Walter Griffiths. In that boardroom, I could not help but notice the many fine souvenirs that City had acquired over the years but Derby, with no where near as fine a boardroom as City, did have that League Championship trophy. I left the interview at Maine Road knowing that I had the job in the administration office and agreed a starting date of a fortnight on the Monday, which was the week leading up to the start of the 1972-73 season. I will always remember the pride that I had when landing the job at the Football Association and this same pride was present again on getting this position at Maine Road. I could now look forward to returning to the Football Association on the Monday to hand in my notice and to inform my many friends and colleagues of my impending move to Maine Road. Most of the people I worked with at the Football Association knew of my desire to want to join a club. My work at the Football Association, enjoyable that it was, did not have that end product that football is all about - the game at the end of the week. There was no greater buzz for me than working at a football club on matchdays. The atmosphere created by the crowd, the expectation of the game, the result, disappointment or elation, all so important in the great game of football, were missing ingredients of my work at the Football Association and it was that I wished to savour so much.

On the Monday morning, after being successful in my interview that weekend at Manchester City, I returned to the Football Association and arranged to see the secretary of the F.A, Sir Denis Follows, to inform him of my forthcoming move. His personal secretary, Patricia Smith, a loyal and faithful servant of the Football Association, called me into his office, whereupon, I entered and told him of my appointment. His congratulations and later those of Sir Alf and my many colleagues, together with the farewell card that they all signed and the many gifts that I received, will always make that part of my life so special to me. The next step of the ladder had been reached, one which would hopefully see me eventually landing a club secretary position but firstly, I had to gain the necessary experience of a League club and no better than one near to my home town.

The administration staff at Manchester City consisted of Walter Griffiths, the secretary, who had been a long time servant of the club, joining them from Wolverhampton Wanderers, where he had been assistant secretary in the days of the legendary managership of Major Buckley. Keith, his son, was responsible for the wages and the match day programme. Bill Adamson and Walter Rowlands, both retired bank managers, were responsible for the Football Club and Social Club accounts respectively. My job was to incorporate all match day organising plus help with the accounts and wages. Our typist and personal secretary to Walter Griffiths was Dorothy McLeavy. I was immediately made to feel welcome and knew almost immediately that I had made the right decision to move from the F.A.to further my career, the only disappointment being that the first few weeks of the season had not seen City play to their previous season's high performance on the pitch.

My first game at Maine Road, although only a reserve game, was certainly incident packed, resulting in a rather humiliating seven goals to nil thrashing by Sheffield Wednesday, for whom a striker called Roger Wylde scored six. This was then followed by our first team losing by the only goal to Everton, in which the problems on the pitch were also present off it. The North Stand, which had previously been a standing area behind the goal, had been converted to seating in the close season. Unfortunately, neither the architects or our staff had checked the first few rows of the stand and as a result, those supporters sat there were unable to see over the barrier wall, which had not been lowered. With a near capacity crowd in that area, it was virtually impossible to relocate those supporters together, just in seats scattered throughout the stand. Thus many supporters that night left the ground at the end of the game rather irate, not just by the team's inept performance and a successive defeat to follow that opening day defeat at Liverpool in front of a gate of over fifty five thousand, but also by the inconvenience they had been subjected to with having to move to alternative seating, in a first League home gate of over thirty eight thousand.

The poor run continued on the field in those first few weeks, as a team that had run Derby County close to the Championship the previous season, lost five out of the first six games as well as going out to Bury in the League Cup, a major shock, as Bury were two divisions lower than City. A further setback came when Valencia knocked us out of the UEFA Cup in the first round, after we could only draw two each at Maine Road, in front of only twenty one and a half thousand.

So, even as early as October, as far as honours were concerned, only the F.A.Cup remained to be played for. The Mercer-Allison combination that had served City so well over the last few years seemed light years away, as an aging team were only a shadow of their previous adventurous best. The irony became such that it haunted me about how I had gone to Maine Road a few months previously thinking that I would be joining the Rams and had instead joined City who were now showing signs of requiring major surgery on the pitch, whilst Derby, under Clough and Taylor, had started so well in their quest to retain the title.

Off the field, there were also problems in the boardroom which started to affect everybody in the offices. The old Board of Directors, which featured Albert and Eric Alexander, who was chairman of the club, Sydney Rose, the club surgeon and John Humphreys, managing director of Umbro Sports, had been opposed by a takeover group featuring Joe Smith, the owner of a window conversion firm, Ian Niven, a local publican, Chris Muir, a newsagent and local councillor, Robert Harris, chairman of Great Universal Stores and Simon Cousins of Cousins Imperial Soaps Ltd. To keep the peace between the two sides, Peter Swales was appointed to the Board of Directors. Mr Swales had been chairman of Altrincham Football Club and also served on the Council of the Football Association. A very experienced and demanding chairman, he was very soon to be able to control the club and the two opposing factions. The new members to the Board had firmly backed the claims of Malcolm Allison, who had made demands to be given full charge of team affairs which, in turn, had forced the amiable Joe Mercer out of the club, breaking up the most successful management team that Manchester City had seen, in which the club had won both the First and Second Division Championships along with the F.A.Cup, League Cup and European Cup Winners Cup.

1973 opened therefore with that one remaining competition still available for City to win- the F.A.Cup. A third round draw had seen us drawn at home against Stoke City, a fellow First Division side, well respected under the astute management of Tony Waddington, who I was to get to know quite well over the years, as we found ourselves commuting together back from matches at Maine Road by rail after one of his scouting missions.

A convincing win unfortunately was only rewarded by a difficult away draw at Liverpool in the next round. The club realised that this was to be the most important game of the season and arranged for coaches to take all the staff to the game. Big Mal was full of himself that day. With the adrenalin running high, he appeared on the pitch before the game arms aloft, a show of defiance to the awesome Kop and to confident acclaim from the thousands of City supporters who helped to make Anfield a sell out that day. The City team played to their full potential and thoroughly deserved the goalless draw to bring Liverpool, who were to become Champions that season, back to Maine Road for the replay. An all ticket replay four days later, with fifty two and a half thousand tickets to sell, resulted in my first experience of late night working. The end product, a sell out and a deserved two goals to nil win, saw Malcolm and City at their highest spot together in his short managerial career.

The fifth round saw the club draw Second Division Sunderland at home. The one certain thing however about sport is its uncertainty and this was certainly to be the case as far as the Sunderland tie was concerned. On a nightmare Saturday, City were always chasing the game. The feeling inside the club after the Liverpool victory was of confidence that we could go on to win the Cup. Behind twice in the game to glaring errors, the team managed to get a draw two each and prepared to go to Sunderland for the replay, where Malcolm stated emphatically that matters would be put right and was confident of progressing to the next round. A staff coach was again arranged for the game but in a nightmare for City, Sunderland ran out worthy winners by three goals to one. In the Sunderland team that day were three players who were to later sign for City, two of whom, Dave Watson, a central defender and Denis Tueart, a winger, were to figure regularly in some of City's better days in future years, the third, Micky Horswill, a midfield player, never quite made the same impression. That Sunderland team, however, under the management of Bob Stokoe, were to later return to Maine Road to play their Semi-final against Wolverhampton Wanderers and in winning, go on to play the formidable Leeds United in a Final, which saw probably the biggest F.A.Cup Final shock of all time, when they beat their more illustrious opponents, to become one of the few Second Division sides ever to win the coveted F.A.Cup.

Travelling to Sunderland for the replay had, because of the timings involved, meant that I was unable to travel back home by train that night and having never driven a car, the only alternative was an overnight stop. This resulted in me sleeping in the players lounge. No problem with that you may think, except rumour had it that the Main Stand, where the office block and more importantly the players lounge were situated, was allegedly haunted. On the journey back, we had talked and joked about my forthcoming ordeal as much as we could laugh and joke after witnessing our dismal exit from the F.A.Cup and a premature end to our season with regards the possibility of winning a trophy. Being the last one left on the coach on its arrival at Maine Road, I alighted, walked up the steps, opened the gates to the official entrance and switched off the alarms and made my way to the lounge where I was to stay the night. Luckily, the only haunting that I experienced that night came from the nightmares of the match. I awoke the next morning to do a days work, not having been bothered by John Worsley, for that, according to our head cleaner, Mary May, was his name. Mary, infact, had such special powers that allowed her apparently to be able to contact people that had passed away, so much so, that the Police even allegedly made use of those powers in solving crimes.

After the cup exit at Sunderland, things were to go worse in the league campaign. Coventry City, under the managership of Joe Mercer, who received a fantastic reception from the fans on his return to Maine

Road, returned with an odd goal in five win, to send the club too near for comfort to the relegation zone. Reports in the press began to link Malcolm Allison with a move away from the club and this was finally brought about, I believe, by the Board of Directors, under the chairmanship of Peter Swales, who had taken over midway through that season from Eric Alexander, enforcing the sale of Ian Mellor, a winger, to Norwich City, against Malcolm's wishes. Malcolm then went missing from the club for a few days, before it was announced that he was to become manager of Crystal Palace.

The club turned to one of its loyal servants, Johnny Hart, to finish off the season and to try to get the few points that were still required to ensure their survival in the First Division. John was just the opposite in personality to Malcolm. Quiet and unassuming, John had been a one club man, serving as an inside forward in his playing days, before moving on to the coaching side, where he had become well respected as youth team manager, bringing through to first team status such illustrious names as Joe Corrigan, Glyn Pardoe, Willie Donachie, Mike Doyle, Tony Towers, Tommy Booth, Alan Oakes, Frank Carrodus, Derek Jeffries and Ian Mellor to name just a few. The players responded well to John and the club moved clear of any relegation worries.

On the administration side, just as on the playing side, the club had undergone changes at the top. Walter Griffiths, our secretary, during the boardroom battle for power had antagonised the takeover group and with their ultimate success, had left himself short of support in the boardroom and was sacked. In the office, we had began to feel the tension that existed between Mr Griffiths and some of his new directors, which had also spilled over into a hatred between Walter and Malcolm Allison. The respective characters of the secretary and manager could not have been more contrasting. Walter was of the old school type, trained to account for every penny, straight faced and reliable. Malcolm, meanwhile, was flamboyant in every sense of the word. Malcolm would often call into the office to take some money as expenses, often amounting to twenty pounds or so. This would therefore run up a sizeable amount of cash not accounted for in the club's petty cash, which Walter every week insisted on checking. When coming across these IOU slips, Walter would vent off his anger and the more irate he became with Malcolm's extravagance, the more Malcom appeared to enjoy the confrontation. The only trouble was that Walter would hardly ever speak to Malcolm unless he had to, and therefore it was left to yours truly to try to obtain a detailed expense sheet from Malcolm to show how he had spent the money he had taken from petty cash. Malcolm's idea of an expense sheet to validate his claim was usually just four or five words, which would infuriate Walter even more. Fortunately, I soon discovered a method of appeasing both parties without the other one knowing. I would approach Malcolm's secretary, Julia Cannon, and together we would ensure that the expense sheet showed full details of how the money had been spent by Malcolm and then getting him to sign it, which in turn would satisfy Walter. For several weeks however, before we had worked out this solution, I had worn away the carpet between the secretary's office and that of the manager.

Walter had also upset a close friend to the new chairman, Peter Swales, namely Paul Doherty, a leading football reporter then with the Sunday People, who was very shortly to become head of Granada's television programme, 'Kick Off', which featured weekly all the North West clubs and was the lead up to its recorded highlights shown each Sunday afternoon featuring leading games in the North West. Therefore, it had only ever been a matter of time before Walter would be forced out of Manchester City.

At my interview with Walter at the start of the season, he had indicated that shortly I would be made assistant secretary or some such similar role because he felt that his own son, Keith, would never be accepted as such because of the animosity shown by certain members of the Board of Directors towards himself. The atmosphere in the office was beginning to get to everybody and it was a relief, I am sure for all concerned, when the Board and Walter parted company. In Walter's position came a young secretary from Oldham Athletic called Bernard Halford who, over the next thirty years, was to become a key figure at Maine Road. Walter Griffiths ironically was to move in the reverse direction, joining Oldham Athletic as their Secretary/Commercial Manager, where he stayed for a few seasons.

The move to bring in Bernard was a godsend. He was a lot younger than Walter and although Mr Griffiths had always been all right with me and had been instrumental in bringing me to Maine Road, the atmosphere that had been present between certain members of the Board and Walter had gone. Bernard was more approachable, an excellent club secretary, whom I learnt a lot from, whose enthusiasm and willingness to put his hand to any task, which he always said came from his days at Oldham, were soon to rub off on the staff. The clouds over the office had been lifted like a breath of fresh air. Keith, Walter's son, naturally left with the departure of his father and Bill Adamson decided to call it a day.

Bernard immediately brought with him Maurice Watkins from Oldham. Maurice, in his late fifties, was to do the wages and his previous experience of being secretary of Crewe Alexandra and his home town club, Stockport County, were to be both very useful for City and myself, as I was so eager to learn from him. I was quickly to set up a good friendship with Maurice and his wife, Ethel, and on his retirement from Maine Road, some seven or so years later, when they moved to their favourite spot in Llandudno, I found myself spending several summer days in their pleasant company, often on their local bowling green. A wonderful couple, I was shocked and saddened when, without warning, Ethel, who was a retired nurse, suddenly passed away. Maurice, a very nervous person, never recovered from this shock, falling ill himself and was taken to Walton Hospital in Liverpool. Being at Everton at the time, I was fortunate enough to visit him on several occasions before his death in the 1980s. Maurice had been a good friend, who had given me good advice and help over the years.

The office was also to see the introduction of Ian Niven, whose father of the same name, was a director of the club and who, on Bernard's appointment, had been moved up from the ticket office. Along with Walter Rowlands, who still did the City Social Club books, the club offices became a happier place to work, as Ian's jovial approach to life and his love of City certainly added to the new and improved atmosphere. Although my hopes of now being officially appointed as assistant secretary were very much on hold, this did not matter in the slightest, as the newly found atmosphere more than compensated and I was to get excellent experience working for and with people which I was to enjoy so much. I was also aware that people in high places knew that I could do the job, which I was to later prove- but not at Maine Road.

Therefore, with these alterations to both on and off the field made, we looked forward to the 1973/74 season, which was to have far reaching consequences on our local rivals at Old Trafford. Johnny Hart had signed on a free transfer the legendary Denis Law from Manchester United in the summer. Unfortunately for John, he was never to witness as manager the full extent of his signing, as very early in the season his health broke down and he was unable to cope with the stress of management placed on him by a City Board of Directors determined to overtake their rivals across the city, who were starting to age and showing rapid signs of decline. We, in the office at Maine Road, had witnessed at first hand the stress that John was under when, on the day that we were due to play at Walsall in the League Cup, John took a turn for the worse and it came as no surprise to any of us that John was to take no further part in the running of the City team. I suppose that everybody at City had always been envious of the attendances that the Old Trafford club were able to get, despite in the late sixties and early seventies being inferior to City on the pitch. This desire to overtake United, by a Board of Directors with blue blood in its veins, would always lean heavily on the shoulders of any manager that City had and its first real casualty was unfortunately, John.

Tony Book, affectionately referred to as "Skip", due to the fact that he had captained City in the golden era of the Mercer-Allison years, was appointed caretaker manager for the Walsall tie. The game finished goalless, as did the replay at Maine Road, before City saw off the underdogs in a second replay at Old Trafford to the tune of four goals to nil. Tony, who was now virtually to call a halt to his playing days, appointed Dave Ewing, the reserve team coach, as his assistant. Dave had been a no-nonsense centre half with City in the fifties before moving to my home town club, Crewe Alexandra, in the twilight of his career where, after initial barracking by the home fans, he won over his critics, to play a captain's role in the club's first ever promotion season in 1962, before returning in the mid sixties to join the City coaching staff.

City's League form was erratic but the League Cup offered us a chance of honours as the next round saw us record a single goal win at Carlisle United and then dispose of York City 4-1 after a goalless draw at Boothen Crescent. The club therefore found itself in the last eight of the competition. It was at this point that the club made, what many of us at the time felt, a rather hasty decision. Tony, who had been put in as caretaker manager and had taken us into the last eight of the League Cup, was replaced by the Norwich City manager, Ron Saunders, who brought with him Terry Alcock who, just like Ron, was a no nonsense sergeant major type, who had made Norwich into a fit unit, although lacking in star quality players, the likes of which City had, with such household names as Summerbee, Bell, Lee, Law and Marsh- a forward line of internationals and flamboyant in their character. Rumours of discontent in the dressing room were soon circulating around the club. All nearer to their thirties than their twenties, the last thing they wanted and needed were the regimental training methods that allegedly were being imposed by the new manager. Many of us felt that players such as Mike Summerbee, Francis Lee, Rodney Marsh and Denis Law were too extrovert for the new management team and were about to be forced out of the club. With the influence these lads held in the dressing room, it obviously led to an atmosphere being created within the club.

However, a quarter final win against Coventry City and victory over lowly Plymouth Argyle in a two legged semi-final led us to a League Cup Final against Wolverhampton Wanderers. City's League form, however, continued to be erratic and there was still this growing feeling within the club and supporters that the team were not behind the new manager.

For the League Cup Final, City had organised two overnight stops at the Royal Garden Hotel in Kensington. The club booked the hotel for both the Friday and Saturday evenings, when the official banquet would be held, before travelling back on the Sunday lunch time for a Civic Reception in the Town Hall, courtesy of the Lord Mayor and Corporation of Manchester. It was then back to the City Social Club for an evening to commemorate our appearance at Wembley, in which Bernard Manning was top of the bill.

That weekend turned out to be the best organised one that I have ever been fortunate enough to attend, far surpassing those organised later for us at Everton in the mid eighties for their three consecutive F.A.Cup Final and Charity Shield appearances and the European Cup Winners Cup final in Rotterdam, the only downside was to be the result. The style that City put on that weekend, from the 1st to 3rd March 1972, was of the highest quality, with no expense spared and a true reward for the efforts made by all of the staff, from the laundry ladies to team manager. It was a pity though that the Final turned out to be a bitter disappointment on the field for a City team, who had started the game as clear favourites with all the pundits. A forward line of Summerbee, Bell, Lee, Law and Marsh, although nearing the end of their careers in some cases, should have been far too good for a Wolves side, whose main strike force was the charasmatic Derek Dougan and John Richards and whose skipper, Mike Bailey, was a driving force in midfield.

Losing that final by the odd goal in three, meant that the after match banquet started in a very subdued mood. However, during the course of the evening, as the wine began to flow, the dejection of defeat started to disappear, as we all started to come to terms with the fact that there were ninety other Football League clubs who would willingly have changed places with us that evening. At the end of an evening, which had been enjoyed by the directors, players, staff and their guests, one was left with the thought that if it had been as enjoyable as this when losing, what would winning have been like? The party went on long into the early hours of Sunday morning before people gradually started to drift away to their rooms for just a few hours sleep to try to get over any hangover before facing the two hundred mile coach trip back to Manchester for the Civic Reception. A few of the more sober staff managed a Sunday lunch but the great majority of us could hardly bare to look at food never mind eat anything. Luckily, by the time we arrived back in Manchester, we had all recovered sufficiently to enjoy the buffet and drinks that had been put on for us by the Lord Mayor and his Corporation.

We had followed the team's open top bus on its scheduled tour of Manchester, where many thousands of City supporters had turned out to welcome them back. If anybody had ever needed any proof of the wonderful support that City possessed, that turnout was it.

At the Civic Reception, several thousand more City supporters were outside on a cold Sunday afternoon in very early March when the players went on to the balcony to be greeted by those fans. The reception they received made everybody, including those of us stood behind them, so proud to be associated with this great club. City fans have been very loyal and regretfully have not, over the last thirty years, had the success that they deserve, the only major honour being the League Cup win in 1976.

The tremendous warmth that the City fans have for their team was also to be shown that evening at the function arranged for us all at the Social Club. The Club was managed by Roy Clarke, a left winger, who played for City and Wales in the fifties and by his wife, Kath, both lovely people, who were very popular with the punters. Those fans in the packed Social Club that evening made everybody feel like heroes and the atmosphere generated and enjoyed by supporters, players, directors and staff and their guests was definitely the best club spirit that it has ever been my pleasure to have witnessed in the many years that I was fortunate enough to spend within the professional game. It is always easy to be supportive in victory but these fans had shown their support in defeat and that made the weekend extra special and placed the City fans at the top of the ladder as far as I was concerned.

Rather tired and fairly drunk after the most hectic weekend of my life, a taxi journey to Piccadilly Station, saw me catch the last train that evening back to Crewe. I remember closing my eyes on the train journey home and then opening them again, to see the train had stopped. Realising that I had fallen asleep, I looked frantically at my watch, which showed that it was after the time that the train was due in at Crewe and began to contemplate spending a cold early Monday morning on some far away platform. The thought of this soon sobered me up. The train then started to move slowly and within seconds, although at the time it seemed like hours, I realised that I was in luck. The train had been delayed a few minutes and was just arriving into Crewe. A grateful one mile walk home, which could have been so much worse, like a bench on a cold platform many miles away, saw me get the first real sleep of the weekend but it was still early to rise next morning to catch the 7.35 am train back to Manchester to start another week's work - but what a weekend!

Unfortunately, after the League Cup defeat, a decline in performances and results on the pitch saw the club facing the real threat of relegation. Not many points were realistically required but the way the team were playing, one struggled to see where these points would come from. Team spirit, according to the press and rumours floating around the club, was at an all time low and suddenly, after another defeat, this time at Queens Park Rangers, Ron Saunders was dismissed by the Board of Directors. Ron was not a bad manager because, prior to coming to Maine Road, he had made Norwich City into a respectable First Division outfit and then, just four years later, in 1978, he guided Aston Villa to the First Division title, a feat that has not been achieved by his countless successors at Maine Road. It was just, I believe, as did the majority of City fans, that he was the wrong type of manager for City at that particular time. Ron had tried to rebuild City overnight, upsetting many of the established players in the dressing room in the process and this had backfired on him, just as it did with the legendary Brian Clough when he took over from Don Revie at Leeds United. If only he had tried to make the changes more gradually, things may have been different for both him and City, for, just like Brian Clough, he was to later prove himself to be an excellent manager.

The job of rebuilding City and initially earning those few points that ensured their First Division status fell once again to Tony Book, who had temporarily taken over the reigns when Johnny Hart had fallen ill earler in the season but who then had stepped down with the appointment of Ron Saunders, after steering the club into a mid-table position and the last eight of the League Cup. Tony had the full backing of all the players but most importantly, the influential senior ones, whom Ron had reportedly upset. The club, under `Skip', not surprisingly gained those few remaining points that ensured First Division survival. Tony had been a loyal servant and as a right back had captained the City team in the late sixties and early seventies, becoming the most successful captain that the club had ever had in the picking up of major trophies, despite only turning professional in his late twenties and not moving to City until around the thirty mark, proving the old adage that, `if you are good enough you are young enough'- perhaps a timely reminder to all aspirant footballers and club scouts, although I do admit that perhaps there are not too many like Tony around, but there could be some!

The 1973/74 season still had one final twist in the tail for City. Our big rivals, Manchester United, under the managership of Tommy Docherty, had struggled that season and needed a large victory against us in their last home match to stand any chance of avoiding relegation. Ironically, it was Denis Law, who had been signed on a free transfer from United at the start of the season and whose form had seen him picked again by Scotland, who was to score the only goal of the game on his return to Old Trafford, the scene of so many of his great scoring feats, that was to send Manchester United into the Second Division.

The game ofcourse has been well documented many times since, especially Denis's goal, but for myself and the many City staff and supporters present at the game that afternoon, the atmosphere was frightening to say the least - more hostile even than that faced by being English at Hampden Park for the Scotland versus England fixture. We, as a group, were sat behind the Scoreboard end goal where Denis was to score that goal, immediately standing up to acclaim the goal, only to realise the folly of our actions and hastily sat down, as one had the thought of thousands of eyes with hatred in them staring in our direction. The game still had several minutes to go, when the crowd came onto the pitch. The referee, quite correctly, took the players off the pitch for their own safety and despite appeals to clear the pitch, which were unsuccessful, the match was never finished. The Football Authorities decided, quite sensibly, that as the game only had minutes left, the result should stand. The possibility of them ordering the game to be replayed, as indeed they could have done, did not bear contemplating about in view of the hostile atmosphere that had prevailed on the terraces at Old Trafford that afternoon. Very quietly, we made our way out of Old Trafford that afternoon. It was the first and perhaps only time that I can recall never seeing a City fan with a scarf on - that would have been suicidal on that day of hatred. For United to have been relegated was hard enough for their fans to take but for it to be City and a goal by their old hero, Denis Law, that had eventually brought about this outcome was just too much to accept for many of them. The atmosphere in Manchester that evening, travelling away from the ground, continued to be so hostile as I witnessed numerous acts of vandalism which the Police just could not control. To start the following season, United had their ground closed as a disciplinary action for what had occurred but, within a season, were to bounce back a young and rejuvenated team under Tommy Docherty.

1974 had also seen the Jubilee Year of Manchester City playing at Maine Road. With this in mind, the Supporters Association had organised an evening to celebrate the occasion and I was very honoured to be invited, along with many of the old great players from City teams of the past and present, to listen to some of the marvellous stories told by them that evening of the old ground, now sadly no more, but with so many happy memories for players and fans alike.

Maine Road will always be linked for me to Stan Gibson, our chief groundsman at the time, who was to spend many years in the service of the club and became, without doubt, one of the best groundsmen in the League, nurturing the pitch from an indifferent standard to become one of the best. Stan was City through and through, living in a club house situated between the Main Stand and the Social Club, where he spent many a happy hour making many friends with the City fans who used the Club after the match or in the evenings during the week and where, at one time, his daughter, Janice, worked.

The 1974/75 season was to be my last full season at Maine Road. Tony Book had appointed Ian MacFarlane as his assistant manager. Ian had had a host of clubs but his main role had been at Carlisle United, where he had a spell as manager, during which he had taken the notorious Stan Bowles, a very gifted player from Crewe, after Crewe had taken him on after he had been sacked at Maine Road. Ian quickly reformed Stan sufficiently to sell him on to Queens Park Rangers for a handsome profit, a move which also resulted in the player showing his true class to gain international recognition with England. Ian loved to refer to himself as "the big man". Just the opposite to Tony in personality but both had charm in abundance but in different ways. Ian was loud and infectious with his bubbly character, whereas Tony was more resolute, a deep and genuine figure and very determined but together they complimented each other by their opposite personalities. They set about the job of rebuilding City that Ron Saunders had tried probably too drastically to do. Asa Hartford, a midfield player, from West Bromwich Albion and Joe Royle, a striker, from Everton, were brought into the club, Joe Corrigan was restored to the goalkeeping position and a gifted young left winger, Peter Barnes, son of Ken, who at the time was on our coaching staff but was later to become chief scout, was drafted into the first team with such effect that he was soon to become a regular in the England team and receive the PFA Young Player of the Year award. Peter was one of the most exciting players I have ever watched. He would attack full backs with pace and real dribbling ability and be able to cross the ball. We were to finish in a respectable eighth position in the League that season but without making any impression in the Cup competitions.

The 1975/76 season saw Dave Watson join Manchester City from Sunderland, whilst Francis Lee had departed to Derby County where, for one incredible season, he was to finish with a League Championship medal.

Once again, away form continued to be City's undoing in their quest for a League placing high enough to qualify them for a place in Europe and it was therefore left again to the League Cup to give City their best chance of any silverware.

The League Cup started with a game against Norwich City. Coincidence saw the tie go to three games, just as it had done two years previously when City had ended up by reaching the Final. Just as in that Walsall tie, Norwich were emphatically defeated on a neutral ground, this time, Stamford Bridge, to the tune of six goals to one but in front of only 6238. In those days, a third game nearly always went to a neutral ground which, although fairer on a sporting context, rarely broke even financially, something that would certainly not be tolerated today. There are however merits behind the decision to play any third game at one of the opponents ground - at least only one of the two competing club's supporters are inconvenienced in having to travel.

Other changes in the modern day game I find difficult to come to terms with, for example, how our football authorities have revamped the old European Cup, a competition that was designed to find the champions of Europe. To me, the sporting context of finding the champions of Europe in no way allows for any team that can not even win its own domestic championship to be entitled to be acclaimed 'Champions of Europe'. After all, to win one's domestic competition is no fluke, it is only acquired after a season's graft and is the only true measure of finding the best team in the country. That team, if we are looking to find the top team in Europe, should then only compete against other countries' champions to find the ultimate 'Champion of Champions'. Unfortunately, today's game is all about finance and allows even teams who can finish as low as fourth to enter a competition that is aimed at finding the champions of Europe. How can they be classified as European Champions? Money certainly rules and when one sees such high wages being paid out, in most cases, to very ordinary players, whose names will not stand the test of time in supporter's memories, you can understand why this is such.

In fact, most City supporters who can recall the era of Summerbee, Bell and Lee (all Englishmen, I must add) are more likely to remember a whole team from that era of thirty years ago than a side from just five years ago! However, until our major clubs are brave enough to see their youth academies produce the majority of their first team and stop relying on agents hawking around foreign players, our system will continue to erode and with it, I am sure, England's chances of becoming World Champions. We have the best domestic league structure in the world which should benefit our players to become World Champions but not enough English born players are playing in it to take advantage.

Manchester City, in the sixties and seventies, had one of the best youth systems in the country. Scouting ran at first by a wonderful, jovial Harry Godwin, who signed so many talented lads that went on to form the basis of City's Championship winning teams of the late sixties, always claiming that the only incentive he offered them to sign were sweets - and I do mean of the toffee type. Knowing Harry, who was affectionately known as, "Uncle Harry", I can vouch that the first thing that Harry did on meeting any of us, was to offer us a sweet out of the bag that he always carried on him. Harry, a chief scout, who never drove a car, travelled miles by public transport and was so meticulous with his expenses, even accounting to the nearest penny for a cup of tea or a sandwich and always the exact rail or bus fare- how different from his manager, Malcolm Allison- but it would be boring if we were all the same! The basis of the Mercer-Allison team were produced by Harry and his scouting staff, all coming through the youth systems or being bargain signings.

The scouting system was successfully continued after Harry had retired by another true City man when Ken Barnes, who had played for City in the fifties before moving to Wrexham as player-manager, returned to City as part of the coaching staff in the days of Joe Mercer and Malcolm Allison, became chief scout. With the exception of a League Cup triumph in 1976, major honours however eluded Ken's signings but City were always amongst the leading teams in the League in those late seventies and just like Harry, his signings at junior level formed the basis of City teams that would hold up as amongst the best that the club had ever produced.

Reverting back to the League Cup - after disposing of Norwich, the next round saw us drawn against Nottingham Forest, which we won to set up a mouth watering home tie against Manchester United. A full house of over fifty thousand were present at the game to see City triumph emphatically 4-0, but the downside to that win was to be a serious injury to Colin Bell who, over the years, had proved to be one of the best, if not the best, midfield player City have ever had. Tremendous stamina, with an eye for a goal, Colin would be so difficult to replace. The reward for beating United was a relatively easy home draw against Mansfield, in which the team made no mistake in order to clinch a two legged semi-final against Middlesbrough in the New Year.

However, all was about to change for me very quickly, as a vacancy for the position of secretary of my home town club, Crewe Alexandra, would entice me away from Maine Road before the semi finals against Middlesbrough would take place. My final game at Manchester City was a home game against Queens Park Rangers on Saturday 6th December 1975, on that day being presented with a wonderful farewell card signed by all the staff, players and directors and a briefcase to "look the part" in my new job.

City had been a wonderful experience and the lasting memory to me of the club had been the formation of the Junior Blues Club, an idea that I was determined to copy at Crewe, as it creates supporters at an early age which hopefully the club can hold on to. City have certainly benefited over the years from this and I honestly believe that the Junior Blues Club and the growing bond between the numerous Supporters Clubs that had been set up throughout the country and backed so much by the management of the club, was the greatest legacy that Peter Swales, the chairman at Maine Road during my time, left the club.

Another feature that the club had introduced into football was the use of its stadium for concerts. Very few clubs had any other functions in those days except ofcourse on matchdays. Few had social clubs and even fewer had restaurants, so grounds were in general only used on some forty or so days in the year and yet rates and/or rents had to be met. It therefore started to become obvious that grounds had to be used for other functions other than on matchdays.

Manchester City, during my spell at Maine Road, became the first club in the League to use their ground for a concert, when the legendary pop star, David Cassidy, was booked to appear. With tickets initially selling well, the concert was on schedule to be a huge financial success. However, a few days before Cassidy was due to appear at Maine Road, a tragic accident occurred at a concert in which he was appearing, in which a young girl lost her life, being suffocated in the crowd. This had a complete transformation on the ticket selling, with more refunds issued than tickets sold in those last few days, as anxious parents brought back tickets. The occasion had still been a financial success however and was to lead to City continuing to stage concerts in future years, with a few other clubs following suit.

The spirit that existed at City in 1975 was amongst the best I was to ever experience. Just about everybody in the club, from chairman down to the youngest player, seemed intent on selling the club to the fans. Players were so willing to attend functions in their own time, a fact that I was to benefit from on two occasions when I was actually at Everton Football Club. My bank, in those days the TSB, had arranged a five a side football competition, featuring all of the branches in the area and had asked me, because of my connections in football, to attempt to arrange for a guest from the world of football to present the prizes at the end of the evening. Being at Everton at the time, I asked all of the first team squad and management but one excuse after another appeared, which I suppose one could understand, as it meant an eighty mile round trip and the giving up of an evening. Just about to despair and admit failure, I gave Ken Barnes at Manchester City a phone call, on the off chance that his young son, Peter, whom I had known from the day that he had started at the club, would be available. Peter had not just broken into the City team but also the England squad and had just been voted Young PFA Player of the Year. Readily, he agreed, came down to the event, did not charge a penny in expenses and was a perfect ambassador for the game.

The following season, the Bank repeated their competition and I was again asked to provide a personality to present the awards. Getting in touch with Peter again, he arranged for a mutual friend of ours to make the presentations and Gary Owen, the midfield England under 21 captain who, like Peter, was with City, came down from his St. Helens home to Crewe to present the awards, charging nothing and just like Peter, was a perfect ambassador for the City club and footballers in general. The action of those two players were just two instances of the tremendous amount of public relations work carried out by the City players, work that very few other clubs attempted to do.

I was enjoying every minute at City and with that League Cup Final pending, it really was one of the hardest decisions I have ever had to make - whether to leave in order to achieve my lifetime ambition of becoming the secretary of a Football League club- and the youngest in the League at that, or to stay at City, where I had been so happy and enjoy that Final. In the end, I chose Crewe and left behind a wonderful set of people from directors, management, players, staff and fans who, to me, there never will be any better. Naturally, I followed City's progress in the League Cup and cheered them on to a win against Middlesbrough and was pleased to be able to go down to Wembley Stadium to watch them beat Newcastle United in the Final in 1976, which unfortunately for a club, whose supporters deserve so much more, was to be, at the time of writing, their last major honour.

CHAPTER FOUR: TRAFFIC - AN INTRODUCTION TO SUNDAY FOOTBALL LEADING TO CHOLMONDELEY COUNTY AND AFC BWANAS KNOCKERS.

It was only natural, after leaving the local grammar school in the summer of 1969, that I would want to get actively involved in football, having enjoyed my time as secretary of both football and cricket for the past four years at school. So, when two friends of mine, Tony and Paul Latham, started playing in the Sunday Regional League for a newly formed team called Traffic, I began to go along to support. The team comprised of a number of former grammar school pupils and was managed by Graham Swallow, who at the time also played with Nantwich Town in the old Cheshire League, with the administration being looked after by Geoff Steele. Traffic quickly dominated the local Sunday scene, winning the Second Division in their first season and had in Roy Broughton, who averaged over two goals a game, one of the most prolific goalscorers and later to become one of the most successful coaches in local football.

That first season, Traffic lost just one game and that was shrouded in controversy when Tony Latham, a larger than life, highly competitive player, fell foul of referee, Harry Vickers, who had an equally extrovert personality and as well as being an ex Football League referee, was also chairman of the Sunday League. Harry had been a Football League referee until, I believe, a complaint was made against him by Everton Football Club, that he had targeted Dave Hickson, their volatile centre-forward, for an early bath if he stepped out of line. These remarks had been reported to the Everton club by a member of the public. Rumour had it that Harry was withdrawn from the League list of referees for this remark but was later to become one of the very few officials ever to be re-instated, albeit, as a Football League linesman. The clash of personalities was obvious throughout the game and it came as no surprise when Tony received his marching orders, which proved to all and sundry that there was only one boss out there and that was the referee - especially when it was Harry.

Traffic went on that first season to win both their Division Cup and the League Cup, beating Unicorns in the final at Gresty Road, in the days the local Football League club allowed each local League to stage its Final on the pitch, along with both the Crewe F.A. Saturday and Sunday Cup Finals, provided that all these matches could be staged after the last home Football League game. This was always regarded as a good public relations exercise for the club in order to help it bond with local football in times when the club needed all the support locally it could get in order simply to survive. Unfortunately, those days of allowing the use of the Gresty Road pitch for local Finals have since disappeared and local football is poorer as a result.

Following on Traffic's success, several of the team started to play for Whitchurch Alport on a Saturday in the Mid Cheshire League and so I started to follow their fortunes.

The Mid Cheshire League was then a feeder league to the Cheshire League, which in turn was a feeder league for the Football League - although promotion also depended upon facilities being up to standard and on teams being elected in preference to those having to apply for re-election, who were nearly always re-elected as "the closed shop" policy certainly existed in those days. The Mid Cheshire League was therefore of a relatively high standard.

Whitchurch Alport were managed by Eddie Morris, who had previously played for Crewe Alexandra as a half back and was a more than useful cricketer with Crewe L.M.R, a leading club in the old North Staffordshire League, one of the top cricket leagues in the country, where such world class cricketers as Gary Sobers, Jim Laker and Frank Tyson had played as professionals.

Under Eddie's management, Whitchurch Alport were to win the League Championship, Shropshire Amateur and Welsh Amateur Cup, before Eddie moved up the ladder to manage Winsford United in the Cheshire League, before finishing his managerial career as youth team manager at Crewe Alexandra in the days of Dennis Viollet, the ex Manchester United player, who was manager at Gresty Road at the time.

My connections with Eddie however were more to do with my second love- cricket, where, along with fellow cricket fans such as Graham Dutton, Mary Walker, Rob Proudlove and the late Jimmy Wright, Dick Brereton and Les Linnell, we followed Eddie's young son, John's progress as a fifteen year old in the Crewe first team with admiration. John had already played for the League eleven as well as representing both Cheshire and England at schoolboy level and it was quite apparent that he could have a promising future in the game. Having connections at Lancashire County Cricket Club, in that I knew their secretary, Chris Hassall, from his days as secretary of Crystal Palace, Everton and Preston North End, before acquiring his position at Lancashire County Cricket Club, I decided to inform Chris of John's potential. Chris, to his credit, duly contacted the coaching staff who, unfortunately, were not sufficiently impressed and therefore, Chris replied to inform me of their decision. That letter of rejection, pleasantly worded by Chris, I immediately gave to Eddie. Over the next few years, John, who had ended up signing for Derbyshire County Cricket Club, was to make the Lancashire coaching staff eat humble pie as he scored several big hundreds against the Red Rose, one of which, his first, I was present to witness at Aigburth, Liverpool, which earned John his County cap. Every time that John got a big score against Lancashire, that letter appeared out of Eddie's wallet, John going on to become one of Derbyshire's highest runscorers of all time, a feat which earned him recognition with England, where ironically one of the test matches that he played and I was able to witness, was against India at of all places ......Old Trafford. Nice to be proved right against the experts!

Returning to the Traffic days, their second season, one in which, because of joining the Football Associaion, I was only really involved in until November 1970, saw them pick up two knockout trophies- the Divisional Cup and the Crewe Cup.

The following two seasons (1971-72 and 1972-3) no trophies were forthcoming but this was made up for between 1974 and 1977, when six more trophies befell the club before its folding up.

However, at the start of the 1972-73 season, one of Traffic's young midfield players, John Cottrell, who played for the cricket club I supported, Crewe L.M.R, decided, along with some of his mates, to try to form a side themselves.

John, whose father, Frank, had been chairman of Crewe Alex in the early fifties, therefore approached me with the view to assisting them, provided that they could gain admission to a League. As a result of moving from the Football Association to Manchester City that summer, and thus returning to Crewe to live and commuting daily by train to Manchester, I agreed to help.

At the Annual General Meeting of the Cheshire and Border Counties Sunday Football League, we were accepted as members of their Second Division and approached Cholmondeley Football Club, whom I knew from my days in the Regional League, to play on their ground every alternate week. All the local pitches were fully booked and therefore we had no alternative but to make the thirty mile or so round trip to play our home games if we wished to join the League.

It was because of this difficulty with travel that I actually bought my first and only car. Several of our players had qualified to drive but did not possess a car and as I could easily afford a car at the time, I realised that this may be an ideal opportunity to learn to drive. The car, a Morris Minor, was bought from Jim Lockett, the father of one of our players, Barry, whose older brother, Michael, had played for Traffic. That car, however, was ill fated and on its maiden journey to Cholmondeley went off the road and into the grass verge, where it remained until the scrap metal merchants took it away. Although the car only cost a minimal sum, other costs made travelling to Cholmondeley that day quite expensive!

The team that we put together was relatively young, with an average age of around the twenty mark. In the team were two sets of brothers- the Hortons and the Turners. Andy was the younger of the two Hortons, being a full back, whilst brother, Steve, a forward. Malcolm, the younger of the two Turners, was one of our best players, a midfield player like his elder brother, Mick, Malcolm had featured in both the Stoke City and Crewe Alexandra youth teams as an amateur and associate schoolboy and was still only twenty, Mick, meanwhile, was to serve in the Army. As well as these lads, there were other trustworthy lads, such as Mick Brownell, Malcolm Madeley and ofcourse, John Cottrell, who had all played for Crewe Alex Youth, as striker, defender and midfield player respectively, along with George Mills, who, even at fifteen, must have been well over six foot and quite naturally played centre half. Our goalkeeper, Dave Harper, was also a reliable sound keeper and then we had Barry Lockett, reliable in turning up but we were never quite sure in what condition. Barry really was the character of the team. He certainly had skill but I can always remember one particular game where I just could not see him anywhere on the pitch, only to find out that he had left it the worse for drink from the previous night, been sick off the pitch on the far side where it dropped away slightly, came back on and played inspired, to be Man of the Match.

I, through my links at Manchester City with Mr Humphreys, the City director who was also managing director of Umbro at the time, had managed to get the team clad in sky blue shirts and as a second kit, red and black stripes, which obviously were City's colours. Although not popular with the great majority of the team at the time because they were United fans (how being at City, could I be involved with a team comprised mainly of United supporters. What chance did I have?) but the kits were so cheap and being a newly formed team, we could not afford to look a gift horse in the mouth.

In a poor Second Division, we gained promotion but on going up to the First Division, lack of dedication in certain positions in the team, saw us struggle to put out a team in the more demanding First Division and we were soon struggling even to field eleven players. Heavy defeats became the norm and we were not learning from the errors of our ways. It was therefore very evident that the team would fall by the wayside, which I believe it did a year after I finished at the end of that one season in the First Division, in which we were relegated, but not before we had entered a team in the Commander Bayley Cup.

This competition had been played for annually on Willaston White Star's ground for many years. It was contested by sides comprising of only a small number of league players, the rest of the team having to be made up of players who had not played any or very few league games that season. For this competition, I knew that I could call upon a couple of my colleagues on the Manchester City staff who were really enthusiastic about playing. Ian Niven and Tom McCrindle had trained hard each lunchtime for a couple of weeks in the gym at Maine Road and it seemed that just about the whole of Manchester City Football Club knew about the Commander Bayley game that was going to take place between Cholmondeley County and one of the Post Office teams. Support on the day for the two lads from Maine Road was tremendous but I am afraid the expectations of the City staff went unfounded, as the two lads failed to inspire a rather inept Cholmondeley County side, who went out of the competition that night in the first round. The two lads, on their return to their desks at Maine Road, were aching with their exertions from the previous evening and unfortunately, took some friendly ribbing from their older colleagues, especially Maurice, who was extra critical in a very humorous way.

With the demise of Cholmondeley County in the April, those lads who were still keen to play decided to form a five-a-side team that summer and enter all the local fete five-a -side competitions.

To this team, we added two very special local fifteen year old schoolboys - Ian Cooke, a midfield player, who had played that season for England Schoolboys and had agreed to sign as an apprentice professional with Manchester United on his leaving school and Colin Chesters, a striker, who had represented Cheshire Schoolboys, who was lined up to join Derby County as an apprentice professional.

The team name of AFC Bwanas Knockers had been given to us rather jokingly by Anita Dobson, our telephonist at Maine Road, when I was desperately trying to think of a catchy name to epitomise the fun that I wanted the lads to have from entering these fetes.

The lads did not win any of the competitions that we entered that summer but thoroughly enjoyed the occasions.

Of the two lads, Ian was released after his apprenticeship and went on to play local football with Nantwich Town for a few seasons. Colin, meanwhile, played several games in the Derby County first team, one of which at the very start of his career against Arsenal I witnessed, before moving on to Crewe Alexandra, before finishing at Northwich Victoria.

Before finishing with the chapter on Cholmondeley County however, it would not be complete without recalling an incident which caused me some little pain. It was coming to the end of that first season in April 1973. We used to hold regular weekly meetings at the Red Lion in Wybunbury. To get there, I had to catch the local bus and on this one occasion, getting off at my destination, I stepped out infront of the bus that had stopped to let its passengers off, in order to cross the road to the pub, only to be hit by a Robin Reliant, which was overtaking the bus and had cut in sharply. The next thing that I can remember was the bus driver coming to join a crowd of people to attend to me and eventually being taken to hospital. The next day, however, despite medical advice, I had discharged myself because the following day we had the F.A.Cup semi final being staged at Maine Road between Sunderland, who had knocked us out of the competition that year, and Wolverhampton Wanderers. That one day in "dock" was to be the only one that I had off sick in all of the time that I was in football.

The 1975/76 season was therefore to commence with me not being involved with any local club, a situation that was to remain the same for two seasons, as from December 1975, I was to become club secretary of

Crewe Alexandra and felt that a connection with a local club would have shown bias, which I was determined to avoid at all costs. I continued however to follow the local scene but from a neutral viewpoint.

CHAPTER FIVE: APPOINTED AS SECRETARY OF MY HOME TOWN CLUB - CREWE ALEXANDRA.

After five years experience on the administration side of football, firstly at the Football Association in London between November 1970 and July 1972 and following straight on from that at Manchester City until December 1975, I was now confident that I would be able to meet the demands of being "top dog" at a Football League club and occupy the role of club secretary. The experience that I had received at the F.A. and at City was varied and the advice and training was of the highest quality from the best possible bosses that one could have hoped for and whose man management skills were something that I greatly admired.

There were, however, drawbacks that I would have to accept by leaving City. Only eighteen months previously, we had been involved in a League Cup Final with Wolverhampton Wanderers in a weekend that, despite the result, had been so special and here we were again, just one tie away, a two legged semi-final against Middlesbrough, from a further trip to Wembley. This, together with the arrival of Bernard Halford, had seen the spirit lifted in the office, as the new secretary and Board of Directors were now seemingly working in harmony. The whole club, from chairman down to the tea ladies, appeared to have the club at heart and were willing to make sacrifices in order to foster the club's relationship with its fans, which in turn had made it such an enjoyable place to work.

The first time that it came to my notice that Crewe may be looking for a new secretary came in the summer of 1975, when a good old friend, Tommy Doig, approached me regarding my role at City and my future ambitions. Tom, in his late seventies, was affectionately known as "Mr Crewe Alexandra" and I think that I am right in saying that he was the first person ever to be given life membership of the club. He had served Crewe Alexandra in one capacity or another for over fifty years and in all of that time, with roles ranging from secretary to scout, had never received a wage, his only re-imbursement being his bus fares from his Willaston home to the ground, a journey of some two miles, or his rail fares, and being a British Rail employee had entitled him, even on his retirement, to reduced fares on doing any scouting for the club. A marvellous servant, he spent many hours working voluntary for the club he loved.

Tom had been to watch a couple of evening reserve team games at Maine Road at the start of the 1975/76 season and we had travelled back to Crewe together on the train after the games. It was on the second of these occasions that he informed me that they were now looking to appoint a new club secretary and asked if I would be interested in the position. Sure enough, within a few weeks, in November 1975, an advertisement appeared in the national press. I told Tom that being ambitious and as the step up to secretary was a promotion, I had to be interested, it was just a case of waiting for the right club to come along. So, when the advert appeared in the national press, I formally sent in my written application to the chairman. Almost immediately, a reply came back inviting me to attend an interview at the chairman's office at his timber and DIY Centre in Coppice Road in Willaston, just across the road from where old Tom lived.

The interview took place the morning after City had beaten Manchester United in the League Cup to enter into the last eight of the competition. At the end of the interview, the chairman, Norman Rowlinson, offered me the job and asked me to let him know my decision within the next forty eight hours, in order that he could inform his fellow directors accordingly. After the interview was over, I went across the road to Tom's house to inform him of how the interview had gone, since I felt a debt of gratitude to him for his involvement in giving me this opportunity to fulfil my ambition of becoming a secretary of a Football League club probably far earlier than I could have envisaged.

The next morning, I returned to Maine Road to inform Bernard Halford, the City secretary, of the outcome of my interview and to have a chat with Maurice Watkins who had, some ten years previously, been secretary at Gresty Road as well as having had spells at Stockport County and Oldham Athletic and whose experiences with lower League clubs would be well worth listening to. Both Bernard and Maurice advised me to accept the offer but with the proviso that I should have a contract.

Contracts, in those days, were not as common and legally insisted upon as they are today. This contract would safeguard my immediate future, for in those days, Crewe's position of having to apply for re-election to the Football League for the last three seasons had made their position in the Football League perilous to say the least. The following morning, I rang Mr Rowlinson to inform him that I would only be too pleased to accept his offer to become secretary of Crewe Alexandra but with that one condition, that I should be given a two year contract.

At first, Mr Rowlinson seemed somewhat surprised by my request but on talking it over, agreed on its merits and arranged for his vice chairman, John McHugh, who was also the club's legal expert, to draw up the appropriate document. This contract, I was later told by Mr McHugh, was, he believed, the first written contract that the club had ever given to a secretary. Whilst it was common practice for clubs to give their manager a written contract, in the past the agreement between the club secretary and the Football Club had been by word of mouth. The ironic thing was that the contract was never signed and I still have it at home as such, as I soon became confident of the future, both for the Football Club and myself.

One of the first persons I was to inform, although I suppose the club already had informed him of my decision to join the Alex, was Tom, who promptly arranged for me to have one of his two shares in the Football

Club, a fact that I have never allowed to go unnoticed, as that share (in those days there were only two and a half thousand shares as opposed to one hundred thousand now) was given to me by a very special servant of Crewe Alexandra.

A date of Monday 8th December 1975, was fixed for me to commence my duties as secretary of my home town club, Crewe Alexandra and, in doing so, I had achieved my immediate ambition, by also becoming the youngest secretary in the Football League at the age of twenty five years and three months.

In contrast to City, who were in a comfortable top half position in the First Division and had a semi-final place in the League Cup, Crewe had had to apply for re-election in three of the last four years and only twelve months previously, had a home gate of just over the thousand mark for the visit of Workington. There was therefore a doubtful future surrounding the club, thus my request for a two year contract. However, performances on the pitch had started to improve since the appointment of a new manager, Harry Gregg, who had joined the club a few months previously from Swansea City and had been instrumental in Crewe avoiding having to apply for re-election the previous season, the first time for four seasons.

Starting his career with Coleraine in Northern Ireland before moving to England to join Doncaster Rovers, Harry soon became the costliest keeper in Britain when Manchester United paid thirty thousand pounds for his services. Whilst at Old Trafford, he was involved in the Munich Air crash of 1958, in which so many of his team mates were to lose their lives. His heroism on that fateful day, as he crawled back into the wreckage to pull out survivors, being well documented. The day of the Munich aircrash and the fact that he was also to lose his first wife following a serious illness and leave him with his daughters to have to look after, made Harry very philosophical and good to listen to about life. So much tragedy had happened to one so young, at that time still in his early twenties, but the great mental strength that the man had was to see him through those times. A tremendous character who, on many an occasion, had me transfixed as he spoke about Munich, Manchester United and life in general. Not the easiest to work with at times but a great person to know and to listen to, Harry's sheer personality, his demand for total commitment from his players and the respect they had for him, were to turn a very ordinary team struggling at the bottom of the Fourth Division into a mid table unit. He was, without doubt, the strongest personality that I have ever come across in the football world, gaining every last ounce of effort from his players and it was that, rather than his tactical or coaching ability, which was to keep the club out of the relegation places in the years that he and I were at Crewe. Admittedly, not pretty to watch but effective in the Fourth Division in those days.

Sure, we had a lot of bookings compared to other teams in those days. Harry was hard but demanded discipline from his players. Dissent, that resulted in a player receiving a caution, was always dealt with internally by the player having a sizeable portion of his wage deducted as a result of that booking. I know that some of our opponents considered us to be a dirty team but Harry always boasted of the fact that he had never told a player of his to kick an opponent. I certainly never heard him make this demand and I never came across any player who stated that the manager had told him to take such an action. How many managers can make this boast with hand on heart?

On joining Crewe in December 1975, the club already had a hefty suspended fine of one thousand pounds hanging over it, following one of the poorest disciplinary records in the Football League from the previous season, in which they received close to forty bookings with eight sending offs. The significance of the size of this fine was that it was virtually the equivalent to the net receipts from two home games. Within a week of my joining the club, and with the season less than half way through, Warwick Rimmer, one of our most experienced players, who for a good number of years had featured in the Bolton Wanderers team in the First Division, became our fifth dismissal of the season at Newport for, of all things, dissent. Warwick, of all people, should have known better. It was that incident that Harry drew upon in order to virtually eliminate all bookings for dissent in the season, which was to somehow see us improve sufficiently our disciplinary record in order to avoid that hefty fine, which the club really would have struggled to find, without the financial assistance of its directors.

Harry, as a goalkeeper, had laid claim to fame with awesome performances for Northern Ireland in the 1958 World Cup held in Sweden and it was these that probably made him one of Northern Ireland's best goalkeepers, second only in my opinion to the legendary Pat Jennings. In the sixties, Harry left Manchester United for Stoke City, before moving on to the coaching and managerial side with Shrewsbury Town and Swansea City, before joining Crewe, where, because of the large size of his family, as well as himself and Caroline, whom he had married after he had lost his first wife, there were six daughters and a baby son, John Henry, to find accommodation for, eventually settling in Rope Lane, two miles or so away from the Ground.

Monday 8th December 1975 was, without doubt, the proudest day in my career, as I became the youngest secretary in the League at the age of twenty five and of my home town club, who I had supported as a boy and where I had spent part of my school summer holiday, some ten years previously, cleaning every seat in the stand in time for the first home League game of that season. The simple title "Secretary" seems, like "first" to have disappeared in today's football dictionary and been replaced by superlatives such as "Chief Executive"and "Premier", call the titles what you like to make them sound more important or higher but to many old timers, they are still the same and so were the responsibilities of the role.

On the previous Saturday evening, I had spent a memorable farewell evening with everybody at Maine Road after the home game against Queens Park Rangers, which had resulted in me catching the late train back home rather the worse for drink, having visited many of the city centre pubs. A nice gesture occurred on the Monday morning, when I received a phone call wishing me good luck from the staff at City, which brought a lump to my throat and set the day off on an emotional touch.

It was then time for me to meet the two local newspapers and their respective reporters and photographers for an interview and the customary photograph. Both the local newspapers, the Crewe Chronicle and the Evening Sentinel, were to give me full support throughout my time at Gresty Road. In my opinion, clubs need the press more than the press need the clubs. To see the way that some of the clubs treated their press always astounded me, having seen how, at Maine Road, City had always gone out of their way to assist their local reporter on the Manchester Evening News, Peter Gardner. It therefore became a priority for me to assist both newspapers wherever possible and in return, their respective sports editors or reporters, Roy Greer, from the Chronicle and Chris Proudlove, from the Evening Sentinel, returned the favour, by giving us such excellent coverage.

Over lunch on that first day, it was soon brought home to me what the real world of the small club was all about by our manager, Harry Gregg, who informed me that during his first weeks at Crewe, the club had faced financial difficulties and that he realised that he would have to sell a player in order to keep the Bank Manager happy. He had assessed his playing staff and saw that the best chance of selling a player was to sell one of his two professional goalkeepers, Geoff Crudgington or Brian Parker, as one of the two apprentice professionals he had at the time, Paul Antrobus, a local lad, was infact a goalkeeper and could make the step up, if required, to be cover goalkeeper for the first choice keeper. With this in mind, Harry decided that he would allow his first choice keeper, Geoff Crudgington, to move on and replace him with Brian, the younger and by far more inexperienced keeper, whom Harry felt was good enough to do a job in the first team.

In those days, Harry had been renowned for his goalkeeping coaching and had been responsible for resurrecting the career of Jimmy Rimmer. Jimmy, who had slipped to being third choice at Manchester United, had, by moving to Arsenal and working with Harry, not just become number one choice with the Gunners but had also been selected on a regular basis for the England squad, alongside the likes of Peter Shilton and Ray Clemence, who were without doubt two of the best ever English keepers.

With Harry's reputation at stake, he recommended his goalkeeper to Arsenal's chief scout, Gordon Clarke. Unfortunately, Geoff performed badly when Gordon had turned up to a game unannounced to watch him play. When the Arsenal chief scout rang Harry to tell him that they would not be following up their interest in Geoff, Harry quickly responded by informing Gordon that he had watched the wrong keeper and that the keeper that he was recommending to Arsenal was the younger of the two goalkeepers, Brian Parker, who he felt had a future in the game at a higher level. Harry talked Arsenal into agreeing to watch the next game when Brian, who Harry had already decided to give him his chance in the first team following Geoff's disappointing performance, would be playing. Harry then went on to tell about how, when he told Brian he would be playing that day, Brian had been so surprised, that at first, he told him that he could not play as he had arranged to go out for a meal never expecting to be considered for selection. The rest is history. Brian played well and duly impressed the Arsenal contingent and was sold for a club record fee of thirty thousand pounds and in addition, Arsenal also agreed to send their full first team to Gresty Road for a friendly at the start of the next season, with Crewe being allowed to keep all of the gate receipts.

Problem solved, or so Harry thought. The cheque had been banked but then the bank, the National Westminster, pulled the carpet from under the club's feet, by telling them that this cheque had cleared the overdraft and that they were now closing the account. So, the club found itself with no bank, a position that was only rectified by the chairman, Norman Rowlinson, getting his bank, Williams and Glyn's in Nantwich, to take over the club's account and they only did that because of the high standing that the chairman had with them and ofcourse, the fact that he was able to support the club if, as expected, the club ran into financial trouble. On hearing this story from Harry that first lunch time, I thought to myself, welcome to the real world of the Football League club at the lower level.

This story was nothing, however, compared to the nightmare that was to occur in my first week at the club. Pay day at Gresty Road was on a Friday and so, during a quiet spell on a Wednesday morning, I set about the task of doing my first weeks' wages. To do this, I had to work from the players' contracts, which gave their basic, appearance and bonus entitlement. Imagine my horror when I found out that very few of the players' contracts agreed with the wages that they were being paid. I immediately rang the manager, who was at home relaxing after finishing the morning's training session, and told him of the problem. Harry immediately returned to the ground and I showed him a list of the discrepancies which I had found.

We decided that we had no alternative but to ask the Football League and the Football Association for copies of all the contracts that the club had registered with them. These were quickly received but just confirmed our worst fears. The players had been overpaid over the last twelve months or so from what their contracts said that they were entitled to. If there had been pay increases agreed, no amended contracts existed to support this.

The gravity of the situation lay in the fact that both the Football League and the Football Association had very extensive powers regarding incorrect or illegal payments, which these would be regarded as such. Relegation had been a penalty imposed on our local rivals, Port Vale, simply for payment to schoolboys for signing. For us, relegation was a non starter as we were already in the Fourth Division. We both believed that expulsion from the League would be the most likely outcome if either of the two governing bodies had chosen to do a spot check of the club's books, which was a practice that was carried out on a regular basis of chosen clubs and was the reason for Port Vale's punishment.

We agreed that we should immediately phone the chairman to tell him of the problem and to recommend that we should inform the League of the mess that we were in with regards to our contracts and request their help in sorting out the problem. To his credit, the chairman agreed, knowing only too well that he would be the one that would have to shoulder any blame attributed at a commission for allowing the situation to occur. We also believed that by having been in touch with the football authorities for copies of the contracts, that they would now be suspicious and would choose to come down to the club to investigate. If that happened and they found the illegal payments that I had come across, which they could hardly have missed, the club would be facing expulsion from the League and almost certainly, the extinction of Crewe Alexandra.

I therefore rang the Football League at their Lytham headquarters and asked to speak to their secretary, Alan Hardaker. At this point, I must admit to being upset with the attitude of the Football League. A matter that I considered serious enough for the top man within the League to be involved in, was instead delegated to the deputy secretary, George Readle and the assistant secretary of the League, Graham Kelly, who was later to become chief executive of the Football Association. Both men were very capable and superb ambassadors for the League in the handling of the case but I always felt that if we had been a bigger club, Hardaker would have been involved. The annoying thing was that in all of the time that this case was being investigated and at our commission were Bob Lord, chairman of Burnley and Sir Matt Busby of Manchester United, two of the League's highest ranking officials, Hardaker remained so aloof that nobody at Crewe Alexandra even managed to speak to him.

George Readle and Graham Kelly came down to Crewe to investigate the problems that I had come across and fortunately gave us special dispensation to continue to pay the players the rates that they were receiving, rather than what their contracts stated. I would, however, have to get the players to sign new contracts with the revised wages. The two men continued their investigation into the club's affairs for the spell up to Christmas, compiling a report, in which we gave them full assistance, as it was now in our best interests to do. This report would then form the basis of a full commission on the affairs of the Football Club, which we were told would be held early in the New Year.

All through the Christmas and New Year period , my first month at the club, we were under the threat of an enquiry and the uncertainty that it held. We were convinced, however, that we had acted wisely by informing the League rather than, "brushing it under the carpet and hoping that it never came to light," for if it did, it would have been curtains for Crewe Alexandra - as it was, we had a realistic chance of avoiding that fate.

Sure enough, in the New Year, we were summoned to a Commission, to be held at the Crewe Arms Hotel. The manager, chairman, all the players and myself, as secretary, were all summoned to be there. The commission committee comprised of Bob Lord, an austere, abrupt down to earth Lancastrian, who was chairman of Burnley, Sir Matt Busby, who, at the time, was a director of Manchester United and had been Harry's manager at Old Trafford and finally, George Readle and Graham Kelly of the Football League, who had conducted the enquiry. I felt, and so no doubt did Harry, that the person that we had to impress was Bob Lord, the chairman of the Commission committee.

The meeting lasted from early morning until late afternoon, some six hours without a break, except for cups of coffee, tea and biscuits being brought in every two hours or so. When our chairman, Mr Rowlinson, did suggest a break in proceedings, he was abruptly shot down by Mr Lord, who informed everybody that he, "was from Burnley and the sooner he got back there, the better," and that quickly put an end to any thought of food.

Every player was brought in individually to be asked about the money they had received. The club had paid full wages to the player when off injured, with the sickness benefit money just disappearing. The players, to their credit, admitted receiving this money, when it should have been paid back into the club.

It also came to light that the increases in wages had been agreed with the previous secretary and manager but no agreements were ever signed.

A third matter was also raised at the commission. It had come to light that directors were signing blank cheques. This apparently had been done because it had been said to them by the previous administration that it was needed to assist in the running of the club because of the difficulty in obtaining two directors to call into the ground to sign cheques. Unfortunately, this had resulted in payments being made which were against Football League regulations.

At the end of the meeting, the chairman, Harry and myself were asked to leave the room, whilst the committee, under the chairmanship of Bob Lord, decided our fate. Some thirty minutes later, we were summoned back into the room. That thirty minutes was the longest thirty minutes I have ever had to endure in football. The horrible thought ran through my mind as to whether I would be remembered as, ` the local lad whose revelations had resulted in his club being kicked out of football'.

Self doubts about my actions began to appear. Whether Harry and the chairman felt the same, I don't know, because waiting, we just could not bring ourselves to talk about the possible outcome.

Luckily, all our worries were to be ill founded. Mr Lord praised Harry and myself for our actions in bringing the matter to the attention of the League, rather that trying to hide the discrepancies and then getting found out, in which case, we would have most definitely received a far harsher penalty than what we were to get. A severe reprimand was handed out to the club which, unfortunately, the chairman had to take the brunt of from the tongue of Mr Lord, who told him that the Board of Directors neglect could have cost the club dear and the old habit of signing blank cheques must stop. We were told that the club would receive a further inspection to ensure that things were running smoothly. I would always remember the closing remarks that Mr Lord made to me, which basically went along the lines of, "young man, we will be closely monitoring the affairs of your club over the next twelve months and I am sure that when we return, we will find them to be in order". Needless to say that when the League visited us, as they said that they would do, everything was found to be in order!

Now, perhaps, we could get on with the job of running a football club and I could put into operation some of the plans I had for improving the club off the field. Ideas that were so strong that I could forsake the enjoyment and relative security of Manchester City for, in order to experience the more troubled times that existed for the likes of Crewe Alexandra.

I had supported the Alex as a youngster, during which time I had been a member of the Alex Junior Supporters Club, which had been introduced in the early sixties by a true Alex supporter, Harold Finch, who for many years had produced the club programme, putting many hours of his time in for the good of Crewe Alexandra. I was therefore determined to target the young supporters and try to improve that base. At Manchester City, I had seen the birth of the Junior Blues and set about bringing a similar organisation to Gresty Road. This, with the excellent co-operation of the local press, was set up within a few weeks. I had decided that they should have their own committee, who could decide upon the way that they were to go in the future, with myself, because of my commitments to other areas of the club, acting in an advisory capacity, which would ensure that, wherever possible, all their plans could be introduced. I managed to recruit adult help in Ian Merrill, who was to later serve as secretary of Northwich Victoria and from the membership itself, Paul McCann, Andy Harrington, Malcolm Hughes, Brian Ward and Andy Norbury to name a few. A small membership fee was charged to cover the cost of printing the membership cards but my agreement with the Football Club was that the Junior Club would be self financing and the committee would have to find ways of funding their programme.

Monthly meetings were held at the club's Social Club, the room hire being free provided that no other function had been planned. We therefore tended to go along the lines of Sunday morning meetings, where we arranged for the youngsters to meet the players and staff of the club and other guests from football, such as referees. Every aspect of football was covered in my spell at the Football Club, from the role of player, manager, commercial manager, groundsman, physiotherapist, director, referee and press reporter. We even included the local bobby, PC Jack Sinclair, to do a little talk for the youngsters. In those days, the club had to pay for those police officers inside the ground and with finances being very tight, policing had to be kept to the bare minimum. For this, we were eternally grateful to Jack and his fellow officers for their assistance, which ensured that Gresty Road was always a safe place to go, with those police bills not being too much of a burden. I know that a lot of our young fans learnt a lot about the great game of ours from those meetings.

In the days of the football hooligan, which were soon to follow, I always felt that the formation of Junior Clubs, such as ours and the Junior Blues at City, were positive moves to combat the problems that the game was beginning to develop. If only more football clubs had taken the trouble to follow suit - but very few did.

Our Junior Supporters Club membership soon reached the five hundred figure and when compared to an average gate of just over two thousand, I believed this was a creditable performance and vindicated its introduction.

The Junior Club ran their own coaches to away games, held their own five-a-side competitions, coaching sessions and had their own Player of the Year presentation, which was presented to locally born and indeed the youngest member of the squad, Paul Mayman, at the last home game of that season, by the chairman of the football club, Mr Rowlinson, along with the runners up award to Kevin Tully and a commemorative plate to represent ten years as a player at the club to Tommy Lowry, who incidentally still holds the record for the most appearances for the club, that plate being ofcourse from the football club itself. However, all of this, including a wonderful Christmas party, would not have been possible without the full backing of everybody at the club, from chairman downwards.

By the time that I was to leave the club in October 1977, after just less than two years, the Junior Club committee, under the watchful eyes of Paul McCann and Malcolm Hughes, had started to organise their own eleven a side teams in different age groups. Unfortunately, the meetings were to finish and emphasis began to be placed on the playing of football. As a natural progression from that standpoint, ability became the keyword, as these two, under future managers at Gresty Road, were to commence work in a younger youth development programme than had ever been tried at Gresty Road. This, I suppose, could be described as the forerunner to today's wonderful youth set up at Gresty Road though, ofcourse, not as professional or efficient but one has to remember that in those days, schoolboys were not even allowed to go to a Football League club until the age of fourteen and only then for coaching and could only play for them at fifteen, with the permission of their headmaster, which on many an occasion had been refused and even if it was given, preference at all time had to be given to school games. It was not until a lad became sixteen and left school that he could play for a Football League Club and if he stayed on at school after that age, permission still had to be obtained from the school. The Junior Club, although it was never my idea to take it along those lines, became a way in which the football club would be able to benefit by playing youngsters at an earlier age than that permitted by Football League rules.

The Junior Club, to a large extent, was also the original attempt at a system that is now so successful throughout the country namely, `Football in the Community', based locally at the Alex Soccer Centre at Shavington. A lot of credit for this must go to the likes of Paul McCann and Malcolm Hughes for taking my idea of the Junior Club when being on its committee and on my leaving the club in October 1977 and taking it that stage further so successfully. Other praise should go to the Professional Footballers Association, who gave full backing to the idea during its infancy and ofcourse to Roger Reade, who along with Jessie Ward, was so instrumental in the formation of the Junior Blues Club at Maine Road.

The Junior Club was, without doubt, my best legacy to Crewe Alexandra Football Club. It was only fitting, therefore, that on my last day at Gresty Road, Sunday 2nd October 1977, before my move to Everton Football Club, a meeting of the Junior Club that afternoon had as its guests, Roger Reade, who brought with him from Manchester City, the England under twenty one captain, midfielder, Gary Owen, which made my last day at Crewe so very special.

Going back to my early days at Gresty Road, an additional target and a natural progression from the formation of a Junior Club, was to strengthen our liaison with the local schools. I was convinced that if we waited on the schools coming to us, we would have waited for ever and with attendances just hovering around the two thousand mark, time was not on our side. Therefore, using contacts in some of the schools that I knew from being a local lad, I started to try to get the schools interested in Crewe Alexandra. We offered the schools the opportunity whereby the manager, myself, chairman, players or other members of staff, such as the groundsman, would go down to the school to speak to classes about life in a Football League club. I obtained the Board of Directors permission to allocate up to forty complimentary tickets to the schools for each home game, provided that adequate adult supervision was present. This new found policy, through excellent co-operation from the sports editors of our two local newspapers, Chris Proudlove of the Sentinel and Roy Greer of the Crewe Chronicle, who gave us such excellent coverage, soon resulted in schools starting to queue up for our offer.

Suddenly, local interest had been aroused, with home gates up by twenty five per cent, not a lot, just five hundred people but if we could grow on this, we would be on the road to recovery. Added to this, Harry and the players had taken us into a mid table position and after Crewe's abject performances in the previous years, when they had been regularly rooted at the bottom of the table, things were looking up and the next season, which was to be my first full season at the club, was to be the Centenary season of the club. I knew from what people were saying that we were beginning to win the respect of the Crewe public for our efforts.

By getting the interest of the children, through such things as the formation of the Junior Club and by going out to the schools and offering them the opportunity to come down and meet us at our work on match days, we knew that it could have a spin off, in that it would revive the interest of the parents in the Football Club, many of whom had lost interest over the years, as the team had performed dismally on the pitch, even by its standards .

Two school visits really stand out as special to me, both of which, I attended with our manager Harry Gregg but the second one, that to Bedford Street Senior School, saw Ray Lugg, our captain, accompany us.

The first was a visit to Wistaston Berkeley School, where Harry's own children just happened to attend and had been organised with their headmaster, John White, an avid Crewe Alexandra supporter, who had also been the secretary of the local Junior Schools Football League for a good number of years. John had got together the members of his school football team and I will always remember this young ten year old standing up and telling Harry that he was the school goalkeeper and that in a game he was all right until he made a mistake and let a goal in, asking Harry's help on how best he could handle that situation. Nothing wrong in that but then came Harry's reply! `Just retrieve the ball out of the net, kick it up the field and blame some other f....' and at this point, he was half way through swearing and remembered who he was addressing and somehow in mid stream he changed the word to "person". The children knew what he was about to say and just started laughing.

Another lovely point to that meeting was that I had given Harry the forty complimentary tickets for the home game that we were going to play the following day against top of the table, Northampton Town. Harry had been so wrapped up in the occasion, that he proceeded to tell those children and their teacher, John White, that the following day he would be giving a debut to a local schoolboy, Paul Mayman. Nobody and certainly not Paul, knew the team that was to play the following day until he told those children as he gave the tickets out. John, the headmaster, in at that meeting ofcourse, just happened, through being a member of the Wistaston Tennis Club, to be very good friends of Paul's girlfriend, Diane's parents, Ken and Nora Smith and some years previously, had had Paul in his town Junior team, when he was secretary of the local Association. So, that team selection must have gone down as one of our worst kept secrets!

The other school that I can readily remember visiting was Bedford Street School to meet pupils nearing the end of their schooldays, who were looking to find jobs in the world. At this school, I was interviewed about the running of a Football League club by a young lad who wanted to become a sports reporter. I was not to meet that lad, Lance Vickers, again for some thirty years, when our Corinthians team played his Nantwich Town team in a top of the table clash and Lance reminded me of that day. Incidentally, Lance never did become a sports reporter but the interview I gave him hopefully helped him with his exam!

My third target to try to get behind the club were the local football leagues. I had, from my schooldays and throughout my time at both the Football Association and Manchester City, followed the local football scene and fully realised just how many football orientated people play or were involved in the local football scene and realised the importance of getting these people behind the club- especially with the lack of support we had. I accepted that when playing on a Saturday, they would be unable to attend our games but there were always evening games and just a support of the club can bring much welcome income from such things as selling lottery tickets, if they were made to feel important by the football club. After all, they were football orientated people.

In the past, the football club had allowed the Crewe F.A.to hold its Saturday and Sunday Cup Finals on the Gresty Road pitch and, depending on availability, each of our local Leagues could stage one of its finals. Therefore, as a public relations exercise, with the permission of the Board and the backing of the groundsman, Syd Barratt, whom I offered the fees that we would receive for the use of the ground in lieu of overtime, all the finals were to be played after our last home League game. By allocating one final to each League, which included for the first time the local Youth League, for which, I was made a honorary vice president, it gave us a full week festival of local football. The scheme worked and local football and the club came closer together. The respect that we gained as a club from the local players and governing body officials was so beneficial.

We had started in my first year to become a community football club and that, being a local lad, had always been my aim since joining from Manchester City. I knew that our only chance of survival was to try to get the public of the town behind us and thankfully, in that first year, everybody at the club, whether they were directors, manager or players gave me their support. They had all been there some time before me, it just needed somebody to come in and get things moving. Being young and enthusiastic and with the superb examples that I had seen at City fresh in my mind and a knowledge of the Crewe people, I just happened to be that person.

On the football field, results at first team level had started to improve under Harry Gregg and the team were no longer firmly entrenched at the bottom but were looking an average team in the Fourth Division, which to Crewe, in those days, was success. However, in my first week at the club, Harry stated that he felt that the reserve team should be abolished. He had been embarrassed watching them field a team one short and getting a thrashing at the hands of his old club, Manchester United, in the old Lancashire League, where our reserve team played against the "A" teams, being third or youth teams, of the big Lancashire Football League clubs. He felt that so little talent existed and being starved of cash, we could only look locally for players to form our reserve team.

By following the local football scene, I knew that the Crewe F.A. had won the Cheshire F.A.Youth Cup, a feat, to the best of my knowledge, that has not been repeated in the last thirty years and that the local Crewe F.A. Schools under fifteen team had performed admirably in the English Schools Cup, which regretfully, for several years now, they can not even find the time to put a team out to represent the area. I therefore managed to persuade Harry to give me a few weeks grace in order to arrange a match between the Crewe and District F.A.Youth team and the Crewe and District Schools team, which we would strengthen with some of our more promising seventeen year olds, in order to bring the ages of the two teams more into line.

I contacted Bernard Travis, chairman of the Crewe Schools F.A., who, at the time, just also happened to be chairman of the English Schools F.A. (how he must be turning in his grave at the sad demise of our local schools football) along with Peter Latronico, the Crewe Schools secretary and John Davies, the secretary of the Crewe Football Association, who was also assistant honorary secretary of the Cheshire Football Association and these gentlemen helped me to stage a game in front of Harry Gregg, which was to ensure the continuation of the reserve team at Gresty Road for the immediate future and also see the introduction of a youth policy, in which the football club would employ five apprentice professionals within twelve months, compared to the maximum that they had ever had in the past of two.

The game took place under floodlights at Gresty Road in late January 1976. Harry sat like a judge in the directors box surveying the potential on the pitch and it was not long before he asked me to join him, in order that I could inform him of the names of some of the lads who had started so quickly to impress him. The first lad to impress him came within fifteen minutes of the game starting, when he summoned me over to ask who the big blond haired centre forward was for the youth team. I told him that it was a lad called Colin Chesters, who was registered with Derby County as an associate schoolboy and who had been promised an apprenticeship with them on finishing school in the next six months. Within five minutes, he had summoned me over again, to enquire into the name of a strong midfield player, also for the youth team, whereupon I told him that it was Ian Cooke, who, the previous season had played for England Schoolboys and, like Colin Chesters, had been promised an apprenticeship- but with Manchester United!

He just shrugged his shoulders and exclaimed his disgust at how such local talent had been allowed to escape the net without him, as manager, even knowing that they existed. It was at this point that he asked me to join him in order that he would not get his expectations up too high, only to find that he player he had chosen was already with a League club. I did not have the heart to tell him that no other player on the pitch that evening was affiliated to another club, instead, I let him believe so many more had escaped the net.

Harry soon realised that there was a lot of potential on the pitch and made up his mind to concentrate on the younger of the two teams, the town's schoolboy team, instructing me to sign no fewer than seven of them. They were Kevin Rafferty, a goalkeeper from Sandbach, who was later to play in the first team after graduating to the professional ranks. David Cole, a full back, from Sandbach, who was to be signed as an apprentice professional. Richie Wainwright, a central defender, from Haslington, who was also to sign apprentice professional forms. Shaun Hollinshead, a striker, from Alsager, who went on to sign as a professional and play in the first team and whose father, Graham, drove the coach belonging to the family business that transported our reserve team to all their away fixtures. John Ralphs, a left winger, from Crewe, who was to later turn down apprentice professional terms but who, at just sixteen years and a couple of weeks, was named in the first team squad for the home game against Doncaster and the away game at Brentford. John did not appear on the pitch however, but if he had, we believed that he would have become the youngest player to have represented Crewe Alexandra in the Football League.

To complement these lads were the town skipper, Gary Baskerville, a midfield player, from Alsager and Phil Grocott, a midfield player, from Shavington, who, although they were signed on associate schoolboy forms, were never to be offered apprentice professional contracts.

These lads had been signed with still one full year left at school and were fifteen years old. The start of the 1976/77 season was to see their final year at school and a season in which they were to be given their opportunity in our reserve team. So, with just a few weeks coaching at the end of the 1975/76 season and the pre-season training for the 1976/77 season, the youngest reserve team that Crewe Alexandra had ever selected took the field in a game against Macclesfield Town reserves in the First Division of the Lancashire League, with seven of the eleven players being under the age of sixteen and all only being able to play because we had obtained the permission of their respective headmasters.

To their credit that day, they secured a two each draw against their far more experienced opponents.

They continued to compete admirably under the managership of John Tomlinson, a Lancastrian, who had been brought to the club by our new coach, Walter Joyce. Competing against the "A" teams of the likes of Manchester City and United, Liverpool and Everton, our opponent's teams were made up of apprentice professionals, at least one and in many cases two years older than our lads. They suffered some heavy beatings but certainly not as embarrassing as the one that Harry had witnessed against his old club, Manchester United, that had seen him threaten to abolish the reserve team. During that season, by training in the school holidays with the professionals, one could see the remarkable difference in these players, so much so, that by the end of the season, they were able to compete and secured enough wins to ensure not finishing bottom, which was indeed very creditable. At the end of the 1976/77 season, after just fifteen months with the club and all of them sixteen years of age, five were offered apprentice professional forms on leaving school.

Of the five that were offered terms, it was the one who refused to sign that had shown the most promise and looked destined for a first team opportunity well before his seventeenth birthday. John Ralphs had been with the first team without actually playing but Harry regarded him so highly that he played him in the testimonial game that the club had arranged for its long serving full back, Tommy Lowry. John had lined up in an All Star team that comprised of such famous household names as Gordon Banks, Tommy Wright, Brian Kidd, Jimmy Greenhoff, Nobby Stiles and Ian Callaghan, who had all graced the First Division and, in some cases, the national team for some considerable time. After turning down the offer of an apprentice professional contract, John was to never play for Crewe Alexandra again and thus missed out on what I am sure would have been many appearances under his mentor, Harry Gregg, and ofcourse, who knows what this may have resulted in..

Harry, whilst he had been manager of Shrewsbury Town, had come across a young Scottish junior team called Glasgow Rangers Boys Club (no connection however with the Glasgow Rangers Football Club) from whom he had signed a young full back, Ian Roberts.

Ian had since been transferred to Crewe and Harry, buoyant by the success of starting a youth policy, invited the Glasgow Rangers Boys Club over to Crewe in the Easter period of 1976 to play our youngsters, in order to assess the ability of the Scottish lads. In this game, a young gangly striker, Colin Spence, impressed sufficiently to be offered the opportunity to become our first apprentice for that 1976/77 season, later to be joined by the four local lads, who had agreed to join in time for the 1977/78 season. Colin made sufficient progress to later become the third apprentice that we had signed to have gone on to play in the first team, before moving back to Scotland to play for Falkirk.

The fourth player to make his mark in the first team and in fairness to the other three, by far the most impressive, was Paul Mayman. From my days at Manchester City, I knew that City were following his progress and had had him watched on occasions and were ready to approach the player with a view to spending a few days on trial at City. Therefore, it was only natural, on leaving Manchester City, that I should ask the manager's approval to see if we could invite the lad down to train with the team. So, on the Friday night of my first eventful week at Gresty Road, having found out where Paul lived, I left the ground and took a small detour home, calling at his parent's home in Carlisle Street. I spoke to his mother and father, Joyce and Frank, and with their backing, persuaded Paul into accepting our offer for him to spend the Christmas school holiday period training with our first team. Paul was to make an immediate impression with the players and the manager with his tireless running and not little skill and sharpness and, within three months, was to be selected for the first team against Northampton, playing a further three games that season, whilst still at the local Grammar School. Signed on associate schoolboy forms, I can honestly say that he did not receive a penny from playing those four first team games that season. His method of travel to play in those games was to cycle his way to the ground, just a mile away from his home, leaving his bike in the boot room - I can't imagine many players doing that today! Although seventeen at the time of making his debut, I believe that he was the first and only local schoolboy to ever play in the Crewe Alexandra first team. The following season, 1976/77, he made a further thirty nine appearances as a professional and his performances won him the Supporters Club Player of the Year award. His performances were being closely monitored by a number of top teams, such as Tottenham Hotspur, who were ready to act to take the lad away from Gresty Road for a transfer fee far exceeding anything the club had received in the past, when he turned his back on the professional game and quit the club.

Some lads ofcourse are salt of the earth players, never quite good enough to make the first team, but reliable and honest. One such lad that we had at Crewe was a young midfield player, Kevin Johnson, whose grandad, Jack Robinson, was a tremendous help both to me personally and to the club. Kevin was a one hundred per cent trier and if ever there was a lad who I would have liked to have been given an opportunity, it was Kevin, as his grandad would have been so proud. Alas, it was not to be and Kevin went on just to play local football.

Jack, his grandad, was a real character, the sort that one can find at every small club, giving up his time to do any little job freely and without fuss. He would use his car to convey lads to and from the training ground, run the baths and then clean them and the dressing rooms after the evening training sessions had been held in order that next morning, when the professionals came in for training, the changing rooms were clean and tidy. In those days, clubs, such as ours, depended on the Jack Robinsons of this world. They never let us down and without them clubs would have been a poorer place- unsung heroes every one of them.

On the whole though by the time that the 1976/77 season had finished, my first and only full season at Gresty Road, things were looking up, however, an undercurrent of uncertainty was very quickly to change things.

A youth policy had been set up at the club, which would see a record number of apprentice professionals for the forthcoming season being signed. Already four of the first team were under the age of twenty, namely, Paul Mayman, Hughie Cheetham, a midfield player, who had become my first player at Crewe to sign a professional contract, Paul Bowles, another Manchester lad, who had featured regularly in the team at centre-half and had come through the clubs junior ranks and finally, Dai Davies, a winger, whom Harry had brought with him from Swansea, all of whose performances were being closely monitored by the bigger clubs, which was so important as Crewe Alexandra's existence had always been dependent upon them selling a player to balance the books. In football, there had always been this equation which had been drummed into me on the financial side stating that gate receipts should equal what was paid out in wages, with any fund raising paying for the other overheads which the football club had, such as rates, travel, match expenditure etc. With Crewe, and indeed many clubs, this had always resulted in a shortfall, which meant either selling a player or the Board of Directors putting their hands into their pockets and paying out. So, the policy of Crewe had always been that of a selling club, whose main objective was simply to survive, making a youth policy an essential ingredient in that battle and just hoping every so often to be able to sell a player to the bigger, buying clubs in order to continue in business.

Crewe had been perennial strugglers, having to apply for re-election on three of the last four seasons prior to my arrival at the club in December 1975. Today, that would have meant losing their League status but in those days, the bottom four in the Fourth Division just had to apply for re-election and because of Crewe's easy accessibility with regards to travel and the chairman, Mr Rowlinson's, excellent relationship with a number of First and Second Division chairmen, who between them held forty four (one for each club) of the forty eight votes that could be cast, the other four belonging to the Third and Fourth Division clubs automatically going to the retiring clubs, Crewe had always been comfortably re-elected. However, the national press were beginning to call for the inclusion of ambitious clubs, such as Wimbledon, Wigan Athletic and Altrincham and it was becoming apparent that the "old pals act" would not go on indefinitely and there was therefore a feeling in the club that urgent improvement on the pitch was required.

In my two year spell at Crewe, what were the memorable games that were played?- well, my first home game at Gresty Road had been against Harry Gregg's previous club, Swansea. It could not have been a higher profile game for Harry and three of the players he had brought with him from the Vetch Field, Dai Davies, Micky Evans and Paul Bevan. A fairly volatile game ended in us acquiring an excellent 2-1 win against the high flying Swans, who included in their ranks two young future Welsh internationals, Robbie James and Alan Curtis, who Harry had introduced into the team during his spell as manager. If any evidence was to be required of the potential that Swansea had, it was to come fairly shortly after that when, under the management of John Toshack and with a good number of the players that played that day whom Harry had introduced into the first team, Swansea were to climb from the Fourth Division to the First in rapid seasons. One of the goals that secured our win that day was scored by Dai Davies, who incidentally moved to the Crewe area when only eighteen from Swansea and still remains in the area, working as a Postman, some thirty years on.

The tension however did not end there. One of the Swansea directors, who just happened to be a Justice of the Peace, had had a fair number of drinks in the boardroom after the game and Harry spotted him getting into his car to drive home. Immediately, he came to see me and we returned to the office to telephone the local police. I believe that he was intercepted and that the police drove him home and to our surprise and disgust, no action was taken against him. I wonder if the ratepayers paid the bill for the officer driving him home?

My second game at Crewe was also eventful, but for a different reason. We had been scheduled to play against Newport County on Boxing Day, with an afternoon kick off. Newport had contacted us, however, to state that they would re-imburse our travel and pay for overnight hotel accommodation, if we would agree to a morning kick off on Boxing Day. This would, ofcourse, mean travelling down to South Wales on Christmas Day, something the club had not done for over twenty years, when Christmas Day fixtures had been scrapped by the League. This made good financial sense for the two clubs and so we agreed to the idea. Newport had their biggest gate of the season and we actually cleared more money from that game than we would have done for a home fixture, having our share of the gate money plus, ofcourse, all of our expenditure met. The League should, however, when clubs at the lower level are struggling financially, ensure more local games are arranged for the Bank Holidays. An away game at Newport, with so many more teams within easy travelling distance of both, defied logic. The game finished as a two all draw but the fixture was more memorable for that Christmas evening spent away from home, the first and only time that I had done this in the twenty years or so in football, although ofcourse for players nowadays and in the past at top level, overnight stop overs are a common feature of their preparation for a game but for the likes of Crewe, it was nearly always there and back on the day of the match.

One exception to that being our away game at Torquay United at the end of the 1975/76 season and how we wish we had travelled there and back on the day for that game!

Torquay, just like Newport County earlier that season, had offered us a financial incentive to transfer the kick off from its scheduled afternoon slot to an evening kick off on the Saturday. Being towards the end of the season, which for Harry and his team had been the second consecutive season in which the club had avoided having to apply for re-election, we decided, that as a reward for the player's efforts, we would agree to Torquay's offer to pay for our hotel accommodation for the Saturday night after the game. So, the team were booked into a hotel. Allowing players to stay the night after a game had been played is certainly taking a chance. The night before a game, most players are disciplined in their preparation for the game, knowing that their fitness levels are to be put to the test the following day. However, after the game, they look to relax and enjoy themselves, letting off steam and when in a large group, as they were that night, far more likely, just like all young men, to get into mischief of some kind. That is just what happened. The lads went out for the evening after the game with a few bob thrown in the kitty, courtesy of Torquay United paying us for agreeing to the switch. Unfortunately, the drink began to flow and on approaching a pedestrian crossing, the lads decided that they were going to take the light out and after it had cooled , use the lamp as a rugby ball. Unfortunately, the noise they made soon drew people's attention to their rather foolish acts and it was not long before the lamp was dropped and the police arrived in great numbers to arrest this group of revellers, who were taken down to the local police station. The manager then had to be contacted and being woken in the early hours of Sunday morning, was non too pleased, having to travel down to the local police station to try to arrange for the release of those players who had been caught, for I am led to believe that some did manage to run away from the incident and escape capture by the local constabulary. So, it was not a very happy party that travelled back to Crewe that Sunday lunchtime. So much for rewarding the players with an overnight stop- never again! It had been our intention to do the Torquay trip there and back on the day, which is something that we did the following season. The press however, both nationally and locally, carried big articles, far bigger than the actual match reports, which incidentally we lost and needless to say, the players caught by the police were duly fined both by the courts and by the club.

Luckily, I had not travelled down to Torquay for the game. Firstly, for the obvious reason that I would no doubt have had this incident to deal with, but also, because I would have missed one of the best matches ever to have been staged at Gresty Road, and certainly the most entertaining game that I was to witness during my spell at the club. On the same day as the Torquay fixture, we had staged the Cheshire Senior Cup final between our neighbours, Nantwich Town, from the Cheshire League against their more illustrious opponents, Runcorn, from the Northern Premier League. A crowd of two and a half thousand, which compared very favourably with any of our first team home attendances that season, saw Nantwich Town pull off a major surprise by winning a pulsating game 5-4.

Despite relative success on the field, financial problems were still never very far away and it had became necessary for the manager to try to sell a player once more to appease the Bank Manager. This had to be done before the transfer deadline, set then for the last Thursday in March. Harry, through his days at Shrewsbury Town, had known Maurice Evans, who was now in charge of promotion chasing, Reading. He persuaded Maurice to look at Dennis Nelson, a brave, hard working striker, whom Crewe had obtained on a free transfer from Dunfermiline. Dennis impressed and Reading made an offer of ten thousand pounds, which Harry accepted and we concluded the deal just before the transfer deadline. With the cheque banked, this kept the club afloat for the remainder of the 1975/76 season and would go a long way towards meeting the summer wage bill, without having to go cap in hand again to the directors. Dennis went on to help Reading achieve promotion, which ironically was achieved in the last game of the season against ourselves, in front of a gate of over fourteen thousand, beating us 3-1. The move to Reading, however, did not really work out for Dennis and he was to return to us on a free transfer, playing out the rest of his League days at Crewe and just like team mate, Dai Davies, remaining in the area some thirty years on, working as a Postman.

Summer months wage bills at a small club, such as Crewe Alexandra, had always been a problem. Luckily, the Football League had in its rules a stipulation that four per cent of all gate receipts from all its matches would be paid into a pool, along with a percentage of any transfer fees or signing on fees (in those days clubs had to pay a minimum of five hundred pounds to register a player in the League) to be divided equally amongst all ninety two Football League clubs, with the money distributed in the close season. It was a way in which the big clubs could help the smaller clubs to exist - money paid in by the likes of Manchester United obviously being far greater than our payments but when put all together and redistributed equally, it became a real lifeline for all of the smaller clubs. This comradeship, the willingness of the big clubs to assist the smaller ones, along with the absolute total loyalty to the League, were instrumental in keeping football going in those days and ensuring that clubs could employ full time professional players. Unfortunately, this type of spirit appears to be missing in today's game and to me professional football is poorer as a result.

What of the characters of the club?

The 1975/76 season was to see the signing of one of the funniest characters I have ever come across. Kevin Tully, a winger, was a Manchester lad, who started his career with Blackpool and actually got sent off on his debut. Kevin then moved to Cambridge United, where his extrovert character soon led to him having several clashes with the then manager of Cambridge, Ron Atkinson. Kevin had ability but Ron, no doubt to save his sanity, decided to release him and Kevin signed for us on New Years Day 1976 (not April Fools day- though, that may have been more appropriate).

Kevin quickly made an impression with an outstanding debut at Huddersfield, which saw the bubbly Kevin have everybody on the coach returning that evening in stitches of laughter.

A crowd favourite, Kevin always believed in his ability to play at a higher level and was always desperate to find out from me which clubs had scouts at our games. He was often so determined to find out that on a few occasions I had actually caught him looking through the envelopes containing tickets for visiting scouts. I therefore decided, with the manager's approval, to lead him along by making up false envelopes of top clubs and leading scouts in the world of football and just happen to leave them where I knew that Kevin could not miss them. This seemed to inspire him. He was a confidence player, who just wanted to feel wanted and although Kevin may have become aware of our `set up', he never let on. Kevin's home form was inspired but, unfortunately, not his form in away games, perhaps due to those envelopes!

It was this away form that was soon to lead to him having several clashes with Harry. Kevin had been relegated to the reserve team for a midweek game at Port Vale. During the game, Harry had noticed that Kevin had actually stepped off the pitch and was talking to a supporter whilst the game was going on around him. Harry summoned Jack Robinson, who was assisting with the team that night, to go across to tell Kevin to pull his finger out. Now, anybody who knew the "Tull", was aware that Kevin could often be seen sucking his thumb. When Jack got across there, all we saw from Kevin was a gesture with his fingers (he certainly did not pull his finger out) in the general direction of the area where Harry was sat. The outcome of which, I never did find out, unlike the second occasion, which had, with the exception of Harry, the whole staff and players in uproar.

The team were holding a training session at St Joseph's, which was then a remand school in Nantwich, some three miles or so from the Gresty Road ground. The players had changed at the ground and had ran to St Joseph's to begin training that morning. The session had been underway for some time when Kevin appeared. When Kevin was questioned as to the reasons for his lateness, he openly admitted to having called off for some breakfast. Harry just exploded in rage and apparently chased after "Tull", who ran all the way back to the ground, hastily retrieved his clothes and made for a sharp exit. Ofcourse, being in the office at the time, I had no knowledge of what had happened, until the players started to arrive back laughing and smirking. I knew something had gone on and started to question everybody but nobody would say what had happened. Eventually, I managed to collar hold of our coach, Walter Joyce, who told me what I wanted to hear. When Harry appeared, he was in a foul mood and immediately started to bark out orders about writing to Kevin, fining him the maximum two weeks wages. When I questioned him as to the reasons why he wanted me to send this letter, he refused to tell me. Ofcourse, I knew and could no longer hold back my smile, whereupon, he quickly picked up on my expression and realised that I already knew about the incident and gave me a rather amusing verbal blast using a lot of words that should not have been used over the dinner table where we were sat at the time..

No doubt, every club that the "Tull" played for, had stories like this about him. Kevin could just embarrass his team mates with his actions but he always made you smile because nobody should have ever taken him too seriously, although, I bet there are a fair number of managers who pulled their hair out at his actions. What a character!

Talking of characters and one of the greatest players of all time was approached by our manager, Harry Gregg, with a view to coming to Gresty Road.

It was early in 1976, when Harry told me to pick up the phone from the club's switchboard and listen in on a phone call that he was going to make to a player he hoped that he could persuade to come to Crewe.

His opening remarks went along the lines of, `Hey, Besty, are you so short of cash that you need to go over to Ireland to play?' and then came the line that had me shaking with excitement, `Why don't you come down and play a few games for your old pal at Crewe?'.

I was listening in on an approach to a player who had been one of the world's greatest players and who, if he could be signed, would nearly fill Gresty Road to it's twenty thousand capacity, from an average gate of two thousand. Such was still the drawing power of the Irish genius, especially in a town where so many Manchester United fans existed. Harry was asking George Best, as a favour to him, to come and play a few games at Crewe.

My thoughts immediately went along the lines of whether the Board of Directors would agree to meet any financial demands which the player may have. Just for a few seconds, I hoped that we were going to make the greatest signing that Crewe Alexandra had ever made, or ever likely to. Regretfully, for everybody at the club, nothing materialised but one could instantly tell from that phone call, the respect that the Irish genius, George Best, had for his fellow Irishman, Harry Gregg and I was only left to ponder...what if?

We finished the 1975/76 season in sixteenth position and for the first time in the seventies, the club could look forward to the following season, which just happened to be the club's Centenary season, with optimism.

The chairman agreed to the club appointing a commercial manager for the first time in its history, in order to make the most out of the forthcoming Centenary season and to increase the rapidly declining amounts of money that the club, through the voluntary efforts of its Supporters Association, were receiving.

It was imperative to appoint a professional in order to realise that potential and following adverts in the national newspapers and much to my surprise and delight, a telephone call was received from an old colleague from my Maine Road days, Ken Dove.

Ken had been commercial manager at Manchester City but had left to join the David Exall Group, who were basically a group of commercial managers who ran club's commercial departments in both the football and rugby world in the north of England. Ken was now, however, keen to return back to the North West from Yorkshire, where he was, at that time, employed with one of the Rugby League clubs.

I willingly gave Ken as much information as I could and ensured that his application would not go amiss. I rang the chairman immediately and told him that he had got his man for the job of taking Crewe Alexandra forward in the commercial field and immediately set the ball rolling, by arranging a meeting between Ken, Mr Rowlinson and Harry.

Within the fortnight, Ken had joined Crewe and was certainly to become my "best ever signing", although I suppose that newspaper advert did help!

Ken's first problem was to try to get the Supporters Club working alongside his own commercial activities. In the absence of the football club not doing any fund raising of its own, the Supporters Association had taken over the role and had their own offices, some half mile away from the ground, in Edleston Road.

Friction had often existed between the Board of Directors and the committee of the Supporters Association, resulting in fund raising not been exploited for one reason or another to its full potential. Whatever had gone on in the past, for the good of the football club, had to be forgotten and a fresh start made, in order to allow Ken a chance to succeed, which I was very confident he could do, provided this very first hurdle could be cleared.

A meeting was therefore arranged between the Supporters Club, Ken, the chairman, with both Harry and myself sitting in on that meeting. The meeting went like a dream, as Ken won them over by offering them a higher commission, which covered the cost of their office overheads and allowed them to keep their identity.

The appointment of Ken Dove in the decade of the seventies was as important as that in the eighties of Dario Gradi, for it was to be Ken's expertise on the commercial field which was to keep the football club afloat in the years after I had left in 1977, before his own move to Chester in a similar capacity.

On the field, the chairman agreed that the way forward was through a youth policy, which would enhance our chances of selling a player every season or so in order to balance the books and survive. With this in mind, he agreed to Harry being allowed to advertise for a coach/assistant manager in the national press. The advert brought forward one of the best youth coaches in the North West. Walter Joyce had just finished as manager of Rochdale, having previously been youth coach at Burnley, where he had also played regularly in their First Division side as a player. Walter had also been youth team coach at Oldham Athletic and I could remember my old boss at Manchester City, Bernard Halford, speaking so highly of him, having been so impressed by him during his spell as secretary of Oldham. We could not have struck better, an excellent youth coach, who also had experience of managing a Fourth Division club.

Even the pitch was given an uplift with the first ever purchase of a decent sprinkler system, which was introduced to the Board of Directors at their pre-season meeting in July of 1976 .

The summer had been one of the driest on record and the lack of water would have caused problems for the groundsman, Syd Barratt, if not for the new system. It was rather cumbersome, in so much as pipes had to be laid lengthwise along the pitch, with the water reaching about a third of the pitch at a time. They would then have to be relaid again on two further occasions in order to complete the whole playing area but, at least, it was a real step in the right direction and Syd was pleased as punch with it, as it was our junior playing staff who did all the mauling involved with the movement of the pipes.

For the first time in the seventies, the local press were portraying a healthy state of affairs at the club, with a lot of praise being heaped on the manager who, ofcourse, had given the interviews in the first place (nice one, Harry!). These reports were however justified, as Harry had turned fortunes around on the pitch and that is where a club is judged. Supporters, or customers as they are, pay for a product and that is what they see on the pitch. A club stands or falls on its performance on the field and Crewe's resurgence was due to the team and Harry. We, in the background, such as Ken and myself, could only sell the club if that product was satisfactory.

However, the praise reaped on Harry did upset one of our directors and a major shareholder at that. Ken Potts had travelled over from the Isle of Man to attend a board meeting and, in full view of everybody, had tried to take a lot of the credit off the manager for the improved situation that the local press had reported on, referring to the role that he and his fellow directors had played. Unfortunately, because of where he lived, Ken was very rarely able to attend many of the matches or board meetings and I could tell that Ken, trying to score points at Harry's expense, was upsetting the big man- for Harry was six foot plus and about fourteen stone and with a reportedly quick temper which, in his playing days, had been well documented. The board meeting that night had an atmosphere about it, which made us all grateful when it was finally over. Both men had been at each others' throats throughout, Harry criticising Ken for his absence and Ken accusing Harry of "blowing his own trumpet".

It had been well documented in the past that the chairman and Mr Potts had not got on together and so Ken, fortunately that evening, had no support from his fellow directors, who wisely just tried to ride over the confrontation and Harry managed to keep his temper under control.

At the end of that meeting, Harry and myself talked about the incident into the early hours. At least he got it off his chest and returned to the ground the next morning as though nothing had happened, which was so important, as the last thing we needed at that time was to have the boat rocked when, for the first time, we seemed to have it steady.

The forthcoming Centenary season had certainly lifted the spirits of everybody at the club. The chairman was more positive and for once, with a first ever commercial manager and an excellent assistant manager/youth coach on board, improved performances on the pitch over the last two seasons, crowds up by twenty five per cent over the two years, there was quite rightly an optimistic feel about the place. It was therefore decided to celebrate the club's Centenary season with an official brochure. Our club president, David Plastow (now Sir David Plastow) was managing director of Rolls Royce and it was only natural, that being one of the largest employers of staff in the area, that we should approach them to sponsor this brochure. This they agreed to do and so Harry approached two of his press friends, Stan Liversedge and Norman Wynne of the Sunday People, to write the brochure. The brochure was a success and at fifty pence a time, raised us nearly three thousand pounds which, when considering the running costs of the club for a whole year were close to fifty thousand pounds and our gross gate receipts for an average game was just over a thousand pounds, it helped us no end make some inroad into that deficit.

The Football Association also honoured the club's Centenary by presenting us with a beautiful framed scroll which, I presume, still holds pride of place at the football club, as indeed, it should do. For a club like Crewe Alexandra to have existed for over one hundred years, having struggled so long both on and off the field and yet managed to survive, is something to be proud of, just as it was for me to have had the honour of being the club secretary in that hundredth year. Obviously, it would have been nice to have had some of the success that Dario Gradi has since brought to the supporters, many of whom have waited a lifetime to witness such events.

However, the Centenary season of 1976-77 was still to be the most successful one of the decade, resulting in the club finishing in the top half of the Fourth Division, albeit twelfth. This was due entirely to the fact that the club had such an excellent home record that season, which saw us go unbeaten for twenty one League games, before being beaten by Doncaster by the odd goal in three in the penultimate game, finishing off our home fixtures with a goalless draw to Huddersfield to ensure a season of only one home defeat, one of the best in the club's long history. If only our performances on our travels could have been better, we may have reached that elusive goal of promotion which we all wanted so much that season.

Unfortunately, not everybody in the town thought that was the case. Coming up to our home game against Southport on Easter Saturday, we still had an outside chance of promotion and Harry had asked me to prepare a list of the remaining fixtures for all the leading contenders. Enthusiastically, we realised that if we could win half of our remaining away games and maintain our home form, we had a reasonable chance of being in the promotion placings. However, that hope was to all but disappear that day, when we could only manage a goalless draw to Southport, a team well entrenched in the bottom four. Not just had we only drawn but we were so inept on the day.

Some fifteen minutes after the final whistle, I was walking along the old paddock in front of the stand going towards the entrance to the boardroom and dressing room area, when I noticed three men walking towards me but thought no more about it until, when level with me, they accused the Board of Directors of not wanting promotion. Bad enough that but then they accused me of being likewise. Now that really hurt. Already very dejected by the team's performance that afternoon and despite the fact that they were all far bigger than me and also angry and drunk, I told them to come with me and make their accusations to Harry.

This theory of the club not wanting promotion had been ripe in the town following on Crewe's only two other promotion seasons which, for one reason or another, had been followed by instant relegation and a return to the old Fourth Division and subsequent reduction in home attendances.

So, there we were, these three angry gentleman waiting in the Alexandra Club, awaiting Harry's arrival. Not knowing how he would react, I was determined that he should know at first hand what many supporters were thinking. I introduced Harry to them. Their attitude changed so dramatically, being quite polite. Harry's reply was spot on. Rather than answer the question himself, he called over his club captain, Ray Lugg and then, Geoff Crudgington, his goalkeeper and then Paul Mayman, a local lad and the youngest member of the team that day, and just asked them separately, if they wanted promotion. On answering that they did, each was sent away. He then summarised his feelings to those three supporters by saying that they had heard, unprompted, the attitude of the players to promotion and that he was no different to them, in that he wanted to be the manager of a Third, rather than Fourth Division side, and finished off by saying, that all club's destinies are decided by their performances on the field and not in the boardroom and that it would be the players who would determine whether we were good enough for promotion and not the board. With their accusations answered, I had a wry smile at the superb way that I thought Harry handled the situation and could not help saying to them as they left, that they should tell anybody doubting our intentions, what they had been privileged to have been told that day.

Despite the club's relative success, our average home gate of two thousand three hundred was still some twelve hundred short of our break even figure and therefore, the cash flow situation always had to be monitored closely. Unfortunately at times, as our football season is played in winter, games can be postponed due to bad weather. In my spell at Crewe, we lost two home games through the weather and one through an alleged flu epidemic. At our level, however, with our bank balance constantly hovering just below that overdraft limit, the loss of income from a postponed game would inevitably result in a call to the directors to bail the football club out financially.

The first of our home games to be postponed in my spell at Crewe was a secretary's nightmare. The morning of the game had been foggy but the weather forecast was optimistic, expecting the early morning mist to lift. I therefore anticipated no problems and our visitors, Darlington, were allowed to travel. Sure enough, the fog started to lift around mid day and the sun started to break through and so, at two o'clock, with no possible problems envisaged, the turnstiles were opened to let the crowd in. Within half an hour, however, the fog had returned and began to drop so quickly, that with fifteen minutes to go before the scheduled three o'clock kick off, the referee and his two linesman were on the pitch to check on the conditions. We managed to close all the turnstiles temporarily whilst a decision was made but at the scheduled time of kick off, the referee had no alternative but to postpone the match. With several hundred people in the ground having paid and not being prepared for this sudden deterioration in conditions, we had not taken the opportunity of issuing fans with a pass out, which could be used either for a refund or for the re-arranged game. Therefore, hastily returning to the office for a blank set of complimentary tickets, we rushed them over to the two exit gates and made an announcement to collect a ticket when leaving, which could be used for any future League home game. In those days, admission to all the terracing was by cash at the turnstile. Those people requiring a cash refund would have to go to the office and wait for the money to come in. A few supporters ofcourse did that but the great majority just took that hastily prepared pass and returned home as the fog continued to drop.

The second game to be postponed was the local derby game with Stockport County, when the Gresty Road pitch was left unplayable after heavy rain over the previous twenty four hours. The game was called off three hours before the game was scheduled to start by the match referee, Kevin McNally, despite all attempts to get the game played, even in atrocious conditions with rain still falling, simply because I knew that without the gate money from the game we would not be able to meet our wage bill for the week, having been on the limit of our very small overdraft, which the bank was either unable or unwilling to increase.

Sure enough, on the following Friday morning, when I phoned the bank with our cash requirements to pay our wages, in those days everybody was paid in cash, I received the dreaded news that they were unable to meet our requirements because we had overstepped our overdraft limit by five hundred pounds or so, which would have been half of our expected gate receipts from that Stockport game.

With no alternative available, I spoke to the chairman, whom ofcourse had been forewarned. He asked me to first of all contact all his fellow directors to ascertain what money they could loan the football club to get them out of this latest predicament. In the meantime, Ken and Neville Simon, the Alexandra Club manager, had emptied all the fruit machines to see what small amount of money that they could muster. Only the vice chairman, John McHugh, was able to assist with a loan, which nearly matched the deficit. So, I rang the chairman back, as he had instructed me to do, with the updated position. Within half an hour, the problem had been solved, courtesy of the chairman making a further loan to keep the football club afloat. The players received their wages that Friday dinner time a little delayed, which they thought had been caused by the secretary being behind time and were non the wiser with regard to the problems that I had gone through. Harry, ofcourse, did know and had tried to keep them out training longer than normal in order to give me as much time as possible to solve the problem.

Crewe Alexandra certainly owed Mr Rowlinson big style, for despite the criticism he received, to the best of my knowledge, no other person was willing to plough into Crewe Alexandra the type of money that he did in order to keep it in existence.

Our third game to be postponed was just as different as the other two had been. It occurred for a scheduled game against Rochdale. Several of our players had been ruled out by injury and when a further two players phoned in to say that they were sick, we really were struggling to field a team. It was at this point that Harry decided that we should attempt to get the game postponed. In those days, football clubs ran on small squads, ours being just seventeen professionals and one apprentice goalkeeper, but we did have registered a few amateurs which the League could force us to play but whom, Harry believed, were not ready for the rigours of the Fourth Division. Therefore, we had to persuade the Football League that we were unable to raise a team from those players registered. In those days, squads could be this small because only one substitute was allowed. To get the postponement, we had to prove that there was illness at the club and that it had struck so severely that a team could not be raised. Our club doctor, Robert Eason, was therefore asked to call to the ground, in order that we could update him with our problem. Within five minutes of the doctor speaking to the Football League, they asked him to put me back on the phone, whereupon, they informed me that they had agreed to our request to postpone and that I must notify our opponents immediately in order to stop them from travelling. Having already advised Rochdale of our predicament and application to postpone, they were ofcourse waiting on a phone call, which I was so relieved to make.

I could not believe that a game could be postponed so easily. We had abused the system but so did many other Football League clubs in that era and I always had a quite chuckle to myself in later years when I heard that fixtures had been called off due to a flu epidemic, often wondering if the League had agreed, as they had done for us on that occasion, without making any real investigation into the application to postpone a fixture. I was always surprised that they did not possess their own panel of doctors to investigate a club's claims before agreeing to any postponement. The fact that they did not, certainly suited us that day!

Three postponements, all so different but posing headaches for the poor old secretary- some things never change!

In the F.A.Cup, we had drawn once proud Preston North End in the first round, the tie to be played at Gresty Road. Preston had informed me that they expected up to four thousand to make the hour long journey by road to Crewe for the tie and therefore, to try to ensure segregation, I decided to ticket the Gresty Road end, which held that four thousand and send those tickets to Preston, advising them to inform their supporters that admission was by ticket only and not to travel without a ticket. Although unpopular with the home fans at first, the allocation of the area, usually used by several hundred of our more vocal supporters, was necessary in order to keep the rival fans apart. It was a good job that we did this as those away fans that day did so much damage to our ground. Ripping wooden fittings off buildings and hurling them over the boundary wall at traffic passing by, the Preston fans certainly had the local police working flat out!

The game ended in a one all draw, in front of a crowd of just over six thousand, over half being from Preston. A further two all draw occurred in the replay at Preston, this time in front of a crowd of some eleven thousand. A second replay was therefore required, which the Football Association allocated us Anfield, home of Liverpool Football Club and although the gate of eight thousand looked very sparse in that wonderful stadium, an overall aggregate of over twenty five thousand had watched those three games against Preston, which to us, having been used to first round elimination, was the equivalent to getting to the third round and gave the club much needed cash. Unfortunately, at Anfield that night, our

F.A.Cup run was to be over, as we were beaten convincingly by three goals to nil..

As the Centenary season drew to a close, several matters at the end of it were to put a damper on my spirit and enthusiasm for the football club and to make me feel that my future lay away from where I had made so many new friends along the way, all with one common bond, a deep love of Crewe Alexandra. I had worked hard to try to revive local interest something that, being local myself, was close to my heart. This period of time for me, between May and when I finally left at the beginning of October, 1977, was, without doubt, the worst time that I had had in my career up to that date.

The first disappointment for me was when Paul Mayman, whom I had been partly responsible for joining the club and who had impressed so much in his first full season as a professional that many of the top clubs, including Tottenham Hotspur, were close to offering the kind of fee that would ensure our future financially for several years, had decided to call a halt to his career as a full time professional. Being a friend of the family left me with a foot in both camps. I knew that Paul had been unhappy at the club for the last few months, which I believed stemmed from the day when we arrived at Halifax with seemingly only ten fit players but after injections both of our injured players, who only an hour before kick off had hobbled off the coach on its arrival at the ground, were lining up to play in a game, played in miserable conditions, which epitomised our performance on the day, going down to a three goals to nil defeat. Seeing players having to have injections to play would certainly put a damper on any young lad's impression of what the life of a footballer should be like but at Crewe, with such a small squad, things like that had to be done on numerous occasions just to put a team on to the pitch. I am sure from that moment on, however, he felt that was not to be the life for him.

However, the real break came when Harry, who had promised to double his basic wage from twenty pounds a week to forty in order to put it on par with the other younger players in the team, went back on his promise and only offered half. Nobody could envisage the lad's disillusionment at the time when this promise was broken. On turning down Harry's initial offer, no amount of coaxing from the manager, nor increased offer, could change the player's mind and our most prized asset just walked out of the club. Ofcourse, the club retained his Football League registration form for a number of years, as he continued to earn rave review notices by playing in non League with Nantwich Town and Northwich Victoria but continued to decline offers from top Football League clubs to join them.

As well as losing Paul at the end of that Centenary season, the chairman also made his one real crucial mistake. The optimism that he had conveyed at the start of the Centenary season, which had allowed the club to increase its weekly wage bill with the addition of an assistant manager/coach and a commercial manager, was rapidly disappearing and in order to save money, he decided to dispense with the services of Walter Joyce, who, since his introduction to the club in the role of assistant manager/coach, had had such a positive effect on the players, especially the younger ones, who we all hoped would be our lifeline. The club had agreed to take on four new apprentices, taking the number to a record five and yet here we were, sacking the coach who had worked so hard to get them up to the required standard.

Terminating with Walter's services had also meant the finishing of John Tomlinson, who had looked after the reserve team that season and whose infectious spirit had coaxed the junior players to raise enough funds to pay for a week long tour of Scotland, in which Alex Roberts, father of our full back, Ian, and a close friend of Harry's from his Shrewsbury days, had arranged a full programme of friendly games for us. Harry, not being able to go in June for that short tour, left us with nobody in charge. This state of affairs really upset me and I must admit that it made me think that the youth policy that we were running stood no realistic chance of succeeding. Who took charge of team affairs for that tour? The answer was Peter Wainwright, our centre half's father, who did an excellent job in difficult circumstances.

A further setback to dispensing with Walter's services lay in the fact that whilst he was at Crewe, Walter had taken some of the area's promising schoolboy players such as, Ian Butterworth, who was later to sign for Coventry City and enjoy spells playing in the top flight with Nottingham Forest and Norwich City, to play for his junior team in the formidable Warrington Youth League and, ofcourse, also included in Walter's team, was his own son, Warren, who would end up playing a great number of games for Preston North End, who were then a club playing at a higher level than Crewe. By terminating Walter's employment with the club, all hopes of acquiring such quality players had disappeared.

The pessimism that had soon engulfed the club after the end of that Centenary season became evident from the reaction of the fans. Season ticket sales, despite my introduction of a discount which allowed the season ticket to be bought at the previous season's price if bought before a certain date, which had been so successful the previous year, was now a complete flop, with only half the number being sold . It therefore came as no surprise to me when only fifteen hundred and ninety six turned up for the opening home League game of the season, a drop of seven hundred from what the previous season's average had been. The alarm bells were ringing.

Luckily, we won that opening home game against Bournemouth, for I feared that if we had lost that game, the gates would have very quickly dropped to around the one thousand mark.

By this time, the club had appointed Warwick Rimmer, a very

experienced player, who had played with us for the last two seasons, as our new player/coach to assist the manager. Well respected throughout football, having previously played with Bolton Wanderers in the higher Divisions, Warwick was later himself to have a spell as manager but by the time that he took over, I am afraid the decline was in full flow.

All these matters had put the relationship between Harry and myself on a very strained note to say the least. I blamed him for a number of the things that had happened and he, in turn, expected that I should have shown him more support. I had become deeply concerned with what was happening at the club and could only see it rapidly declining.

With the feeling of pessimism growing after the finish of the Centenary season, the chairman began to talk about the possibility of going part time which, in those days, may have had its merits if other clubs would follow suit, but to have competed in a Fourth Division, with all the other teams remaining full time, would have been too much of a handicap.

I began to feel that the writing was on the wall and that we would very soon return to the bad old days of the early part of the seventies, which had seen the club rooted in the bottom four and regularly having to apply for re-election. With this being my gut feeling and with relations strained with the manager, which could only be detrimental to the club in general, I knew that my days at the club, so close to my heart and where I so much wanted to succeed in bringing about a football club that the town could be proud of, were numbered and started to look elsewhere.

My final game as secretary of Crewe Alexandra was on Saturday 1st October 1977, which saw us draw at home to Hartlepools, infront of a crowd of 2051, although, I did spend an enjoyable week working on a voluntary basis, selling tickets for the club's Wembley Play off game against York City in May 1993.

Unfortunately, for the club, my feelings were to be spot on. Only the signing of Peter Coyne at the start of the 1977/78 season, whose sixteen goals out of a pitiful fifty, kept the club out of trouble that season. Peter's transfer from Mossley Football Club being completed by myself travelling to Manchester to sign the transfer forms, after the transfer fee had been raised by supporters of the club, as we could not even raise the necessary one thousand pounds to bring a young, natural goalscorer to Gresty Road, who, as a youngster had already played in the First Division with Manchester United and whose ability reminded me so much of Stan Bowles, another very gifted player who had "gone off the rails" at the other big Manchester club. Just like Stan, Peter was very soon to be sold on for a five figure fee, which represented a very healthy profit to a very hard up club at the time. With regards to support, over half the attendances at home games were to fall below the two thousand mark, with only 1462 attending the home game against Halifax.

The following season, 1978/79, the first full one after my leaving

Crewe, was to be, as I had feared, the one that saw the club plummet to rock bottom, which was then followed by them finishing next to the bottom in the 1979/80 season, before a short respite of just one season, 1980/81, under Tony Waddington, just about escaping having to apply for re-election, before plummeting to bottom and next to the bottom in the next two seasons.

So, in the six seasons after I had left Gresty Road, the club had had to apply for re-election on four occasions. Of the other two, one was the season when I had been there for the first few weeks, the other being when Tony Waddington was manager and had in his side a certain goalkeeper called Bruce Grobbelaar, who was so instrumental in keeping the team out of that bottom four.

Then, in the seventh season after I had left Gresty Road, the start of the 1983-84 season, came a certain Dario Gradi and the rest is just fairy tale stuff. The full extent of the fantastic progress that Dario and the Board of Directors, under the chairmanship of John Bowler, have achieved at Gresty Road, was brought home to me a few years back when I attended a home game in the League against Manchester City. I would never have believed that when I left a star studded First Division, Manchester City, in December 1975, to join perennial Fourth Division strugglers, Crewe Alexandra, that one day in my lifetime, they would be playing each other in a League game - that to me, was pure fantasy!

CHAPTER SIX: BACK TO THE FIRST DIVISION WITH EVERTON.

The summer of 1977 had seen me disillusioned with the happenings at Gresty Road and the growing friction between the manager, Harry Gregg and myself, had, for the club's sake, to be resolved. It therefore became obvious that I should leave, even though the mission that I had set myself when starting at Gresty Road was underway, namely, to make the public of Crewe aware and proud of being involved with the club. The hope and expectation that had existed only twelve months previously, had so rapidly disappeared in just a few weeks after the finish of that Centenary season, a belief that as I say, was to be proved founded over the next six seasons, when only the excellent relationship that the chairman had with the First and Second Division clubs and the sterling work done by Ken Dove, as commercial manager, in raising much needed funds, kept the football club alive.

The first opportunity that arose appeared in a national press advertisement regarding the vacant position of club secretary of Bradford City Football Club. I applied and was selected onto the short list for an interview with the Board of Directors. Unfortunately, I was unsuccessful in getting the job but as fate turned out, this really was a blessing in disguise. Terry Newman, who was appointed as secretary, unfortunately, some eight years later, was to have to face the terrible ordeal that occurred when a fire at the Valley Parade ground, caused by litter gathering under the stand, resulted in the horrific deaths of so many supporters. The ordeal that he, as club secretary, must have gone through must have been a real nightmare and something that I would not possibly have been able to handle, that is ofcourse, if I had still been there after eight years.

Fortunately, three more vacancies were to occur in the close season that were to be offered to me, after informing several influential sources in the game that I was looking to move away from Gresty Road. Each was different but equally appealing. The first interview was at Aston Villa Football Club for the position of club chief accountant. The interview was conducted by the Villa club secretary, Alan Bennett and the club auditors. Alan was very experienced and well respected in the game, holding an official position in the Football League Managers and Secretaries Association. Their offer of three and a half thousand pounds a year, was a thousand pounds more than I was receiving at Gresty Road.

The other two interviews took place the following week. The first had been organised through Norman Wynne, a very good friend of Harry Gregg, who had been responsible for the production of our Centenary brochure. That really summed up Harry. Even though we had been failing to get on, it was due entirely to both of us having different viewpoints on the way the club should be run. I would like to think that Harry, although thinking that I was in the wrong with the way I had acted on my beliefs, respected my opinions and motives, just as much as I respected and admired Harry as a person. I would like to think that that was one of the reasons which led him to contact Norman and arrange for me to have the opportunity of going for an interview to fellow Fourth Division, Southport, for the position of club secretary. Norman arranged for me to meet the Southport chairman, Norman Gillier and team manager, Hughie Fisher, who in his playing days had featured prominently with Southampton. The position was offered to me at the conclusion of the interview but I still had this third interview to attend at Everton Football Club the following morning, so I refrained from giving them my answer until seeing what the Goodison Park club had to offer, whilst still holding on to that offer from Aston Villa.

The interview at Everton was for the position of box office manager and was conducted by the club secretary, Jim Greenwood. The position had become available following the previous box office manageress, Dot Ward, leaving to have a baby.

Both of these positions offered me five hundred pounds a year more than I was earning at Crewe but ofcourse, all of that would have to be absorbed in travel costs, or accommodation, if I chose to live in the area.

With these three to choose from, a decision had to be made and quickly too. In the end, I decided to discount Southport because of their precarious League position and poor crowd potential, gates very rarely touching the two thousand mark. The overriding factor to me against Southport was that the town was not football orientated and those supporters of football had the two Merseyside giants just a short car journey away. Meanwhile, I discounted the offer from Aston Villa because I felt that, with the enormity of the club, the position of chief accountant would be so demanding, that any involvement in the matchday running of the football club would be very rare and that was what I most wanted.

I therefore opted for the offer from Everton. At the interview, Jim Greenwood, the club secretary, had stated that he envisaged my role to be that of box office manager, which certainly allowed me to take an active role in the running of the club on matchdays and which to me, was what working for a football club was all about- the dealing with the fans and in the quieter moments, I would be given added responsibilities on the administration side.

I therefore wrote to both Aston Villa and Southport thanking them for their offers and tendered my resignation to Crewe at the end of August, 1977, in order to commence my new job as box office manager at Everton Football Club at the start of October 1977.

Over the next two years, Aston Villa and Southport were to have contrasting fortunes. Southport, as I felt at the time, were to struggle and it came as no surprise to me, that when they had to apply for re-election to the Football League, they were unsuccessful. Meanwhile, over at Villa

Park, under the managership of Ron Saunders, who had been manager at Manchester City during my spell there in the early seventies, Villa were to clinch the First Division title.

So, it was on Monday 3rd October 1977, that I was to start an association with Everton Football Club as box office manager that would last nearly twelve years, during which time the club were to be involved in their most successful era.

My first week at the club did not, however, go without incident. In those days, the club did not even have a ticket office building. Tickets were sold during non matchdays from the reception window, or a small little office with three windows opening onto the street.

Unfortunately, the main reception window, where we selling tickets for my first game against Middlesbrough in the League Cup, was often having to be opened in order to receive goods.

It was on one of these such moments, that a young lad managed to grab hold of a handful of tickets that were being sold by a member of our staff serving at that window and made his escape. It was therefore obvious that a more secure ticket office was required inside the main building. We already had a good sized ticket office in Bullens Road but, because of its isolation from the main building, it could never be considered secure enough for normal day to day sales but with stewards and police in attendance, it could be used to great effect on matchdays.

We therefore desperately required a similar type office in the main building for selling tickets on weekdays. Luckily, this opinion was also shared by our secretary, Jim Greenwood, who, by the time the season had finished, had arranged for us to use the offices previously used by the Development Association, which had access to Goodison Road. This allowed punters to walk along the road adjacent to the Main Stand, enter a large box office selling area through doors that entered on to the street and purchase their tickets under cover, before entering back on to the street. This would tighten up security and reduce the risk of any more snatches of tickets by opportunists, which had made the Football Club look naive. However, a security risk still had to be overcome. We were always mindful of entry by the backdoor which led into the Development Association, where agents on the day would come in to pay in their lottery takings. That backdoor always had to be locked and a spy hole introduced in order to ensure security was spot on and eliminate the risk of any major losses.

In those days, indeed for the next five years or so, both ourselves and Liverpool Football Club relied on their matchday tickets from a small printing company called Bootle Print, being run by father and son, John and Les Gascoigne. Honest, hard working and totally reliable, they performed a marvellous service for the club. However, it meant us checking over eighteen thousand seat tickets, from a seating capacity of twenty four thousand, the highest in the Football League. This burden was reduced by us deciding to lessen the workload and stop the inconvenience to supporters of having to call at the ground twice, once to buy their ticket and the other, to attend the match, by making admission to the Top Balcony and for away club supporters, the Park End Stand, by cash payment at the turnstile on the day of the game.

Out of these eighteen thousand seats, we then had to be pull out of circulation all the seat tickets that had been sold as season tickets and then we had to check that all the gangways were correct, in other words, a ticket had not been printed where a gangway existed. We would give our printers a list of all seats sold as season tickets, in order that tickets for that seat for a League game could be removed. This would therefore, on average, leave us with ten thousand tickets to sell each game. Checking that the print was correct in order that tickets could be put on sale was very time consuming and, more often than not, two of us would spend a day or two every fortnight checking each home game's ticket print. Although the local printer had done a sterling job, it was a blessing in disguise when the printing of seat tickets for home games was allocated to a computer company called G.M.S from Sheffield, although for all all-ticket games, the printing of all terracing tickets was still done by our local printer, as was the printing of all the club's season tickets, totalling thirty thousand terrace matchday tickets and approximately ten thousand season tickets. When doubled up with Liverpool's order, one can appreciate just how busy John and Les were and how dependent they were on the two football clubs and in return to us at Goodison, how conscientious they were.

One amusing incident however did occur whilst we were selling the tickets supplied by Bootle Print. Over at Anfield, one particular evening, they were staging a World Cup qualifying game between Wales and Scotland, which was a sell out. During the day, we had had a number of travelling Scottish fans call into our ticket office to purchase tickets that we had on sale for our next home League game. I did not think any more about this, thinking that these fans had bought tickets with a view to spending a few days in Liverpool and taking in our home game. Nothing could be further from the truth. That evening at Anfield, they had used the tickets which, being from the same company, had been printed on a similar style of card, same size, colour and lettering etc but ofcourse with different wording to gate crash in at Anfield that evening and it was only when told by Liverpool Football Club the next morning that we realised what had happened. Ten out of ten for ingenuity. That day in the city, was a mass of yellow and blue scarves, as the city centre was taken over by the Scots, as they triumphed in their World Cup qualifier against the Welsh that day and ofcourse boosted our ticket sales for the week!

Our full time staff in the Box Office in those days totalled TWO, a figure that it was to stay at until the successful era in the mid eighties, although, ofcourse, on a matchday, when in those days we did by far the bulk of our selling, this figure was augmented by an additional ten part time or casual staff.

Our casual staff usually came from the Littlewoods Organisation, the owner of which was Sir John Moores, by far the major shareholder at Goodison Park. Sir John had had spells as chairman of the club over the last thirty years and his managing director at Littlewoods was Sir Philip Carter, who was also to become chairman of the club. With several other of the Everton directors also being connected with the Littlewoods Organisation, one could therefore see an obvious link between Littlewoods and Everton.

My assistant in those early days, as she had been to my predecessor, Dot Ward, was Maureen Hawksey, affectionately known by all at the club as "little Mo". Maureen, at the time in her early twenties, was married to Barry and the couple were devout Evertonians, despite living only a stone throw from Anfield, home of our rivals, Liverpool Football Club. Mind you, Anfield to Goodison Park is really no more than a mile apart and so Mo could and did, in those days, nearly always walk to work.

In the first three months of my joining Everton, the team enjoyed an unbeaten run in the League, which led up to an all ticket home game against Manchester United on Boxing Day.

From being with a turbulent Crewe, whose future I really believed was in grave danger, I had been fortunate enough to join a club who, despite having an uncertain start by losing their first game of the season to the future Champions of the League that season, Nottingham Forest, had then gone on this roller coaster run and looked certain to be in the running for at least a placing high enough to qualify for Europe, which ultimately meant a more secure future for myself..

The build up to the game was by far the biggest I had been involved in since Manchester City's League Cup Final appearance. Even the numerous Manchester derby games which I had witnessed paled into relative insignificance, since in those years, neither ourselves or United, were at any time involved in the Championship race. Any game against United ofcourse, because of the fantastic support that United could muster throughout the country, was always a high profile match. Demand for tickets for the game had resulted in myself and our club secretary, Jim Greenwood, keeping open the box office until five o'clock on the Christmas Eve despite the fact that our advertised closing time on that day was originally scheduled for noon, whilst in the boardroom, a small Christmas party was being held for the staff. The party still went ahead but the two of us, being supplied with the odd drop of liquid refreshment and food, continued to sell to the ever flowing customers that made their way to the ticket office. On holiday at home on Christmas Day was just as hectic as numerous friends called around to collect and pay for the tickets that I had obtained for them. If ever anything was needed to make me realise the importance that this game held for the resurgent Everton, this demand more than proved it. Unfortunately, on the day, Everton under performed and were soundly thrashed to the tune of six goals to two.

After that, the season fell away somewhat but the club still managed to finish in a very creditable third place to qualify for the UEFA Cup, with average home attendances hovering around the thirty thousand mark.

As the season drew to a close, with Forest champions, Liverpool second and ourselves in third position, the interest of the fans had been kept alive by the Daily Express newspaper offering a prize of ten thousand pounds to any player who could score thirty goals. It had come to the last game of the season, a home fixture with Chelsea and Bob Latchford, our centre forward, was just two goals short of that target. Everton had gone four goals up and the game was into the second half when Bob claimed his first goal to make it 5-0. Then, with ten minutes to go, Everton were awarded a penalty. Bob, who was not the regular penalty taker, was called upon to take the kick, after all, there was no way in which the crowd would allow for any other player to take that penalty. Up he went to score - 6-0 and Bob had won the ten thousand pound prize with his thirty goals for the season. The forty thousand crowd, nearly ten thousand up on the average home gate that season, went wild with excitement, the likes of which had not been seen at Goodison Park since the 1970 Championship season. I believe that Bob's prize was shared amongst his team mates, which was only right, as the service, especially from our left winger, Dave Thomas, was as good as I had ever witnessed, being one of the best crossers of the ball in the country. Bob's achievement, incidentally, had occurred on the fiftieth anniversary of the legendary Dixie Dean's record sixty goals in a season for Everton.

The following season, 1978-79, was to be Everton's Centenary season. To mark the occasion, the club had organised a Centenary Celebration at the JM Centre, the headquarters of the Littlewoods Organisation. That evening will always remain in my memory and I will treasure the pride that I had in being privileged to attend the celebrations to commemorate a great club's hundredth year. The fantastic tradition that the club had acquired over their hundred years was brought home to everybody by the guest speakers for the night. Many great players from the past were present and great pride and emphasis was placed on the club's tradition in which the supporters had always associated the club as being "the school of soccer science".

An additional extra to me ofcourse lay in the fact that this Centenary Evening had occurred so soon after the Centenary season that I had experienced at Crewe, just one season gap infact, that of 1977-78 and ofcourse, whilst employed by the Football Association, I had also been privileged to attend, as guest of the Football Association, the Centenary F.A.Cup Final in 1972 between Leeds United and Arsenal. Quite a nice little treble, full of nostalgia, which brought home to me how quickly the game of football evolved in this country all those years ago.

Great emphasis had also been placed on the club's Centenary by the new club chairman, Philip Carter, both at the Celebration Evening and at the club's Annual General Meeting. It was hoped that the team would provide the club with a major trophy to celebrate their Centenary.

The manager, Gordon Lee, had sold Duncan McKenzie, a highly talented striker and real crowd favourite to Chelsea. It had been well documented that Duncan was not Gordon's type of player. However, that previous season, Everton had played some excellent attacking football, which contradicted the image of dour, hard working teams that Gordon was supposed to favour and Duncan had been so instrumental in a lot of this. Duncan, flamboyant as he was, was popular with the fans and staff at the club. Articulate, as he has proved to be in his role now in the media and on the after dinner speakers circuit but with one vice, Duncan was to always be seen scrounging a cigarette from anybody who smoked and our poor old assistant secretary, Barry Forsyth and accountant, Brian Lunt, must have supplied him with packets over the few years that Duncan spent at Goodison Park. A pointer to Duncan's popularity came in our home game against Chelsea that season. Working in the box office that day until half time, we had heard such a loud cheer, that we had taken it for granted that at half time we were winning the game by that one goal, only to find out that the goal had been scored by Duncan, for Chelsea- and there were very few Chelsea supporters there that day! After Duncan's sale, Gordon was to be under pressure from the fans, a pressure that I believe could have been avoided by keeping the popular Duncan at the club and playing him on merit.

The 1978-79 season started ironically with a visit to Chelsea which saw us claiming a single goal victory but trouble off the pitch was to result in one of the worst pieces of football hooliganism that I was to ever hear about. At the time, we used to sell rail tickets in the ticket office for football specials, referred to as "The Blue Streak" and on this occasion had sold out a full train with supporters going to the game. Apparently, a huge number of hooligans, wearing Chelsea colours, joined the underground trains taking Everton supporters back to Euston at Earls Court and Kensington High Street, where fighting broke out and many people were badly hurt and had to be taken to hospitals in London for treatment. The trains were badly damaged and therefore, as a result of this extensive damage and the appalling hooliganism that had taken place, the club, along with British Rail, took the decision to finish with 'football specials' trains. Instead, the club decided that coach travel, with good stewardship on the coaches, offered a far safer method for fans travelling to support our club in our away games.

The stories told to us by those fans to whom we had sold tickets to for that eventful visit by rail to Chelsea really sickened us. Young, old and innocent supporters had been trapped up in a mindless attack, which had obviously been planned, and it made us all realise that football had a very big cancer, which unfortunately, was to grow over the next eight years or so and have such damaging effects on the English game and Merseyside's big two clubs in particular.

The team once more enjoyed a relatively successful season finishing in fourth place. The highlight of the season undoubtedly being the single goal victory at Goodison Park over the Champions elect, Liverpool. The goal that day, which would be remembered by all true Evertonians for some years to come, as Liverpool continued to dominate both the Merseyside derbies and football in this country in general, being scored by Andy King, who, by doing so, became something that day of a folk hero to all Evertonians. Andy, a stylish midfield player, with an eye for a goal, was however never able to break into the England set up and as such, never quite made the impression on the game that his undoubted ability warranted.

Our Centenary season had failed to bring us any silverware and to really rub salt into the wound, although we had finished yet again in a respectable fourth position, the Championship had gone to our chief rivals across the Park, Liverpool, something that all Evertonians found hard to bear but which, over the next six years or so, we would have to face up to, as Liverpool were to take a stranglehold on the English and indeed, the European game, but not before Nottingham Forest, under the legendary Brian Clough-Peter Taylor combination, had had their say.

From now on, Everton's performances on the field were to deteriorate rapidly. Five of the members of Gordon Lee's squad, and all very influential players at that, were to leave. Martin Dobson, a classy midfield player, Dave Thomas, who had been the supply line for many of Bob Latchford's thirty goals just eighteen months previously, Bob, himself, Micky Pejic, a dour steady left back, who had been a regular in that position since signing from Stoke City and finally, Colin Todd, one of the finest central defenders that the country had developed under the watchful eye of Brian Clough and who had been talked about as the next Bobby Moore but whom Gordon had, more often than not, played out of position as a right back since signing him from Derby County. Possibly, most of these lads were going slightly past their best but they had formed the basis of teams that had seen Everton hold positions high enough in the League to qualify for the UEFA Cup. What was to follow, was to be a poor shadow of that team, which would see the club struggling to avoid relegation and ultimately cost Gordon his job.

With both the local and national press spreading stories of discontent, it was not surprising that season ticket sales, despite finishing fourth that previous season, dropped by a quarter. During the 1979-80 season, we had signed Asa Hartford, whom I had known from my days at Manchester City, during which, he had on occasions given me a lift into Manchester from Crewe, after having spent a night visiting his old pal, Hughie Reed, whom Asa had known from his days at West Bromwich

Albion. Hughie, ofcourse, had also been a player at Gresty Road during my spell as club secretary. The lack of scoring ability in the team never saw Asa, who must have been one of the most hard working midfield players it has been my pleasure to have seen and yet who, on medical grounds, had a transfer stopped at the last minute because the medical men had discovered a hole in the heart condition, have the influence on the team that his undoubted ability warranted.

The pessimism of the fans, which had been highlighted by the drastic drop in season ticket sales, was well founded and was to also see a drop in attendances, as the team slumped to nineteenth place, just two places above the drop zone, scoring just forty three goals in the forty two games, a far cry from just two seasons previously, when Bob Latchford had scored thirty.

The 1979-80 season also saw the death of the legendary Dixie Dean, who died just a few feet away from where I was standing at the top of the directors box, watching the Liverpool game at Goodison Park, the scene of so many of his triumphs.

Despite a good run in the F.A.Cup in which we reached the semi final where, after a draw against West Ham United, in which Brian Kidd got sent off, we lost the replay in dramatic fashion. In a game, in which we equalised near the end, West Ham went on to get a dramatic winner virtually on the final whistle, scored by Frank Lampard, father of the present Chelsea and England player of the same name.

The season also saw the departure of the tough tackling midfielder, Trevor Ross, who Everton had purchased from Arsenal but more importantly for us in the box office and especially our ex auditor of the club, Harry Bateman, of Trevor's father, Bill. At the end of every home game it was a ritual for the three of us, along with our commissionaire, Jack Gibson, to go across the road to The Winslow pub for a well earned pint or two, after a hard days work. I was box office manager, Harry was responsible for doing the gate book from which the attendance and gate receipts were arrived at, Jack, as commissionaire, was responsible for ensuring peace and order at the queues of supporters purchasing tickets, whilst, Bill was.....just Bill, father of a player in the team, who would involve himself in any number of disputes on a matchday with anybody who wanted to oblige- and in Harry, there was one provocative person. I lost count of the number of times my three friends, all in their late sixties at the time, went into that pub and within half an hour had started an argument with a supporter, that had other supporters joining in and then would walk out of the pub, leaving it in uproar- nobody being any the wiser as to who, or what, had started the argument. Bill and Harry really could start a riot in a monastery.

The 1980-81 season was to be Gordon Lee's last as manager of Everton Football Club. He had been ably assisted in his early years by Steve Burtenshaw, before Steve's move to Arsenal. His first three years had been fairly successful, finishing third and fourth to earn a UEFA Cup place and in his first part season, had taken the team to a League Cup final against Aston Villa and an F.A.Cup Semi-final. Unfortunately, no silverware had been forthcoming and the last two seasons had seen the team slump to nineteenth and fifteenth and more importantly, had seen a rapid decline in attendances.

Gordon's greatest legacy to the club lay in the fact that a good number of young players had been drafted into the first team in the later years of his management. In fact, for an away game at Sunderland, Gordon probably fielded one of the youngest teams ever to represent Everton, when six of the eleven players were aged twenty two or under, namely, Kevin Ratcliffe and Steve McMahon, who were both eighteen, Graeme Sharp, nineteen, Joe McBride, a left winger, who was twenty, Gary Megson, twenty one and Billy Wright, twenty two, four of those six having come through the club's youth policy, the only two exceptions being Graeme and Gary.

As a person, Gordon always came across well to the staff, his total honesty always being very apparent to everybody at the club. He did, however, show to me an example of his uncertainty in making decisions, when a friend of mine at the time, Gary Owen, had been informed by his new manager, Malcolm Allison, who had returned for a second spell at Manchester City, that he did not figure in his team plans and advised him that he would consider any bid from another club for him. Gary, who had been at Maine Road since signing as a junior, was left devastated by Malcolm's views and so with me being at Everton, just a short distance away from his St Helens home, and knowing me from his junior days at City and having done a presentation evening for me in aid of my local bank, naturally, decided to give me a phone call to see if Everton would be interested in signing him. Captain of the England under twenty three team, with a considerable number of First Division appearances already under his belt with City and already living locally, it certainly looked a good proposition to me. I therefore informed Jim Greenwood, our club secretary, of Gary's availability. Jim knew of Gary's pedigree and quickly informed Gordon. Unfortunately, by the time Gordon had made his decision to move for the player and had asked Jim to contact me at home, which he did immediately, the player was already in talks with West Bromwich Albion. I immediately phoned Gary at his home but without success. As it turned out, Gary had that evening travelled down to see the West Brom manager, Ron Atkinson, and had all but signed, leaving us missing out on one of England's best young midfield players at that time.

A second player that I recommended to the club, although not to Gordon but to our chief scout, Harry Cooke, was a reserve goalkeeper with Crewe Alexandra. The season was 1979/80 and to put matters into perspective, Crewe Alexandra, at that time, were hovering at the bottom of the Fourth Division and I was, afterall, recommending to a First Division club, who already had a Scottish international as their first choice goalkeeper in George Wood and even their third choice keeper, Drew Brand, who had in the past spent time at Gresty Road on loan, would be more than welcome at Gresty Road, where he would have been guaranteed the first team spot at that time.

I had decided to spend my Saturday morning, off duty at Goodison Park because the first team were away, watching Crewe Alexandra reserves play Macclesfield Town reserves in a Lancashire League game at Gresty Road, before travelling over to Liverpool Football Club, where their chief executive, Peter Robinson, had arranged for me to have a ticket for their home game with West Ham United. My interest lay in the fact that a number of the lads that I had been instrumental in bringing to Gresty Road were playing for the host club that morning. In the game, however, I could not help but be impressed by the confident Crewe keeper, who was calling for and catching everything thrown at him in the air and then distributing the ball with a throw that resembled a cricketer in the covers throwing the ball in hard and low to his wicket keeper. I just watched in amazement at his awesome presence. Watching the Liverpool game that afternoon meant nothing, as I could not erase from my mind the display of goalkeeping that I had seen earlier in the day.

The following morning, I went on my usual expedition to watch a Sunday League fixture and came across an old friend from my days at Gresty Road, Jack Robinson, who assisted with the reserve team at Crewe Alexandra. On asking Jack who the keeper was, he just pointed to his nose, as if to say that I was being too inquisitive, then proceeded to give me the answer that I was looking for, although the name that he gave me was not quite correct, calling him, "Grovellar" and telling me that he had been loaned to Crewe by Tony Waiters, who was coaching in Canada.

On the Monday morning, I decided to ring our chief scout, Harry Cooke, at the Bellefield training ground and inform him of what I had seen on that Saturday morning in the reserve game at Gresty Road. As I expected, when I recommended the keeper that I had seen those forty eight hours earlier, he scoffed at my recommendation- after all, I was singing the praises of a reserve keeper of a club that lay firmly entrenched at the bottom of the Fourth Division and our first team keeper was Scottish international, George Wood. I was honestly convinced, however, that what I had seen on that Saturday morning was as good an exhibition of goalkeeping that one could have ever witnessed. One could not blame Harry for not taking my recommendation further but if he had, we would have stolen a march on other leading clubs, including our arch rivals, Liverpool, who were soon to be alerted to this awesome keeper over the next few weeks when he started appearing in the Crewe first team.

The following close season, within a few months of advising Harry about him, that keeper had gone on to sign for Liverpool and went on to pick up just about every medal in the domestic game - his name, Bruce Grobbelaar.

They say things happen in threes and there was a third occasion that I was to be involved with possible incomings of players to the club. Paul Mayman, who had played for Crewe during my spell as club secretary, but who had, after making a favourable impression and attracting a lot of interest from the top clubs, decided against a career in football and had decided instead to play semi professional, combining a job in banking with playing football at the time for Northwich Victoria, had impressed our top Non- League scout, Wally Burnett.

Wally had already that season been responsible for three players joining Everton from non League circles. Two of them, John Barton, a right back from Worcester City and Eamonn O'Keefe, a striker or midfield player from Mossley, had gone straight into the first team, whilst the third, John Anderson, a right winger from Stalybridge, had figured on the fringe of first team selection.

A follow up had been done apparently by the coaching staff, who also had been duly impressed, having allegedly watched him play in a F.A.Cup replay at Northwich against Nuneaton Borough. Harry Cooke, our chief scout, phoned me the morning after that replay, as the player in the programme listed as "Mayman", had impressed the Everton contingent. He wanted to know if the player was still of the same frame of mind regarding not wanting to play football at a full time level, for if he were to change his mind, Harry was sure that a deal could be struck.

I had, only the day before that replay, spoken to Paul, who had told me that he would not be fit enough to play in the game. Therefore, I was very surprised on two accounts to receive this phone call. Firstly, that Everton had been following the player's progress and secondly, that Paul had played that night. So, that evening, I rang Paul to find out the score. He informed me that he had not played in that game, being replaced by a reserve player, of similar build it must be said in fairness to our delegation, called David Hall, who had played well on the night and that his viewpoint with regards playing full time had not altered. It does however show how scouting can go wrong, if you do not ensure that the player you are watching is the right one!

The summer of 1981 saw the departure of Gordon Lee from Everton Football Club. His first three seasons had promised so much, with good progress made in both the major two knockout competitions but without a trophy to show, although placings were high enough in the League, third and fourth, to obtain entry for the UEFA Cup. Unfortunately, the next two seasons had seen the team plummet down the League in a constant struggle to avoid the dreaded relegation spots and with Liverpool's continuing success, gates had dropped by nearly ten thousand, to barely the mid twenty thousand mark and to many at Everton Football Club, the change of manager had only been a matter of time.

Jed Hulme, manager of the young Corinthians team.

David Griffin, a player with the young Corinthians who had an England under 18 school boy trial.

They are my comparisons to the first manager and captain of the England football team that I was involved in at the F.A, Sir Alf Ramsey and Bobby Moore. Is grass roots football so much different than at the top level?

Gordon Anderson presenting shield to Kevin Edwards, two people highly instrumental in the history of Crewe Corinthians.

School cricket team with myself second from right back row.

School football team with myself centre of back row.

Gary Owen, Manchester City Midfield Player presenting awards at my bank, the TSB, 5 a side.

Peter Barnes, Manchester City, England, PFA young player of the year doing the favour for me by presenting the awards.

Manchester City squad during Johnny Hart's reign as manager.

Traffic Team

On joining Crewe, with
manager Harry Gregg

First signings, Paul Mayman and
Hughie Cheetham

With the playing staff attending F.A. Commission on Crewe's affairs

The Crewe and District youth team
and

The Crewe Schoolboys town team plus some of our young players which
ensured the continuation of the reserve team at Gresty Road.

The playing squad for the 1976/77 Centenary season at Crewe.

Crewe chairman, Norman Rowlinson, presenting Junior club player of the year award and runners-up to Paul Mayman and Kevin Tully along with an award to Tommy Lowry in his Testimonial year. Tommy still holds the record for the most number of appearances for any Crewe Alexandra player.

With the F.A Cup, Charity Shield and F.A Youth Cup.

The ticket office staff with the F.A Cup, Charity Sheld and F.A Youth Cup

With the Canon League Championship and
European Cup Winners Cup.

The ticket office staff with the League Championship and Charity Shield

The first Crewe Youth Centre Team featuring goalkeeper, Kevin Rafferty, (Back Row) and Colin Chesters (centre of front row) who both went on to play in the football league along with Kevin Westwood far right front row who represented Banger City in the F.A trophy final at Wembley.

Rolls Royce team, with Howard Curran as manager later to become Lord Mayor of Crewe, with their collection of trophies.

The youth centre team in my first and only season as manager.

The youth centre team at Bellefield before playing agianst Everton Youth.

The Corinthians 1000th game

The Corinthians team after winning the Commander Bayley -
sadly to be Gordon's last game.

Corinthians Northern Cup Winners 1999

Corinthians Northern Cup Winners 2005

The Madhatters 7-a-side team which formed the basis of our young Corinthians team.
Photo courtesy of Peter Murphy.

The original four young Corinthians -
(left to right) Jez Tagg, Richard Douglas,
Ricky Barlow and Craig Mayman.

Richard Douglas - so instrumental in the
formation of the young Corinthians team.

With trophies - The Divison Cup and Wrenbury Knockout.

The promotion winning Corinthians team.

The first young Corinthians team - photo courtesy of Des Evans

Goals win matches and these two ,
Jez Tagg (35), Kevin Sharp (37) were some act.

My proudest moment - the handing over of the cheque to the staff
of the local baby care unit - which goes to prove that local clubs can help deserving causes,
whilst helping themselves.

CHAPTER SEVEN : THE KENDALL ERA- AND THE GLORY YEARS AT GOODISON.

The 1981/82 season saw Gordon Lee replaced as manager by Howard Kendall who, as a player, had played for Everton in their last Championship winning team, back in 1970, as part of a formidable midfield trio of Colin Harvey, Alan Ball and Howard himself.

Howard's relative success at Blackburn Rovers had made him a favourite with the fans for the manager's position after Gordon's dismissal. Howard quickly brought in a number of players who had obviously impressed him during his spell as manager of Blackburn. Unfortunately, four of those players were to make little impression at Goodison- Mick Walsh, a central defender, Alan Ainscow, a winger, Mick Ferguson and Alan Biley, both strikers. However, the two keepers that he signed, Jim Arnold and Neville Southall from Blackburn and Bury respectively, whom I had infact watched play non League football for Sandbach Ramblers and Stafford Rangers for Jim and Winsford for Neville, were to prove gems - especially Southall, who, within three years, was to have established himself as not just the best keeper in Britain but probably in Europe too.

Gates continued however to decline to the twenty five thousand mark as Liverpool's success continued to rub salt into the steady progress that Everton were making under Howard Kendall. A mid table position was just not acceptable to the blue half of the city, whilst Liverpool were taking all before them, not just domestically but over the next couple of years in Europe as well. Therein lay the problem that Howard and the Goodison club faced. Fans were not content with the club's steady progress in Howard's first season, where an improvement from fifteenth to eighth was achieved.

Season ticket sales continued to slump in the lead up to Howard's second season in charge, 1982/83.

In coming to Goodison Park, Howard had brought with him his coach, Mick Heaton, from Blackburn Rovers. Mick was a jovial, easy going type, whose nickname ironically was "Easy", basically because of his insistence that every footballing task undergone in training was easy-the only thing however that I found easy to Mick was that he could often get into a financial mess with his tickets, where his kind generosity could sometimes result in him overspending. Well liked, we were not however to see the best of Mick until a future promotion of Colin Harvey to the first team brought the three of them together to form the most successful coaching team that Everton were to ever possess.

It was also midway through Howard's first season that he broke the club's record transfer fee by spending seven hundred and fifty thousand pounds on bringing Adrian Heath from Stoke City to Goodison. Adrian, in his early twenties, was born and bred in the Potteries and had been at Stoke from a junior. He had this ability to play both in midfield or as a striker, where his tremendous enthusiasm and skill, although on the small size, alias his nickname 'Inchy', made him a handful for opponents. Adrian had made his debut at Stoke during the bosses' spell as player/coach at the Victoria Ground and Howard had backed his judgement by making Adrian his and the club's costliest signing. Again with Adrian, his immediate impression at Goodison was to be a bit muted, through no fault of his own but solely because of that roller coaster run that was being enjoyed by our rivals across Stanley Park. Adrian, however, was to be very instrumental in the turnabout in Everton's fortunes and to repay that large outlay that the club had paid for him, with some precious goals and performances- but again, all that was still in the future.

The 1982/83 season saw the departure to Sheffield Wednesday of a wonderful Evertonian, skipper and central defender, Mick Lyons, for whom it was said, that if he cut, he would bleed of blue blood. Mick and Mark Higgins, a young central defender, who had broken into the first team under Gordon Lee, had been the only remnants of the previous manager's team and young Mark was losing a battle to regain fitness, which would eventually see him having to take an early retirement from the game. Such was the mass turnover of players at Goodison in those days, as the club strove frantically for success, driven on by the fans' demands that they should rival Liverpool in the quest for honours.

Into the club were to come two players who would cost little in transfer fees but who were to turn out to be two of Everton's best ever bargains. Kevin Sheedy, a left sided midfield player with a sweet left foot, had moved across the Park, where he had rarely appeared in the formidable Liverpool team and Derek Mountfield, a central defender, was to move from Tranmere Rovers for a modest thirty thousand pounds. Derek, like Kevin, was to play an integral part in forthcoming Everton teams and both were to more than repay their modest fees by scoring many memorable goals that would help to bring such an array of silverware to Goodison. Pound for pound these two players were, without doubt, two of the best, if not the best, that the club have ever bought, although quite a few bargain buys were to be present in future successful Goodison Park teams.

However, back in 1982/83, success was still some time away as the club were to fall to an all time low in November 1982, in a home game against Liverpool. Howard had brought in Glen Keeley, a centre back from his old club, Blackburn Rovers. Unfortunately, both Glen and Everton were to have a nightmare that day as we were beaten, or rather thrashed humiliatingly, to the tune of five goals to nil, in front of our own supporters, with Glen suffering the disgrace of being sent off. That day was the worst day that I had ever spent in football up to then. Losing to Liverpool, at the best of times, was always disappointing but getting humiliated was so much more difficult for the blue half of the city to take. The spirit of all Evertonians that weekend was at an all time low.

Attendances at Goodison Park continued to decline, with an all time low of 12872 attending our home game with Coventry City. This was despite the fact that our League position was still a healthy seventh but because of Liverpool's phenomenal success, in which they claimed their fourteenth Championship and the European Cup that season, Everton's position faded into irrelevance, with attendances struggling to reach the twenty thousand mark.

The following season, 1983/84, has to be one of the most remarkable seasons that Everton Football Club have ever experienced with regards to contrasting fortunes.

In the build up to the season, Howard had sold the popular local midfield player, Steve McMahon, to Aston Villa and had brought in as a replacement, Peter Reid. Peter had been very impressive during his early spell at Bolton but injuries had started to hinder his performances. Allegedly, to finance the Peter Reid transfer, the club had had to switch its bank from the Midland to the Trustee Savings Bank in order to get the increased overdraft which was required to finance the transfer. Also bought in that close season were Alan Harper, a utility player from Liverpool who, like Kevin Sheedy, had failed to make an impression in the Liverpool first team but who, like Kevin, was to play an integral part in the club's future success and a very gifted right winger/midfield player, Trevor Steven, from Burnley who, over the next few years, was to become a gem and figure prominently for England.

The season started quietly with goals being in short supply - only seven being scored in the first ten games. It was at this point that the chairman gave the public vote of confidence in the manager. Normally, when this was done, it was usually done tongue in cheek and more often than not was a timely warning from the chairman to the manager to improve or face the consequences. However, this vote of confidence was genuinely meant, which proved that there was always a first time for everything in the world of professional football. Later events at the club were to be a just reward for a chairman, in our case, Philip Carter, for his confidence in the manager to achieve the kind of results that the club were seeking and keeping his nerve, when a lot of supporters were losing their's.

November 1983, was to see the signing of one of the most influential players that the Goodison Park club have ever had. Andy Gray joined the club from Wolverhampton Wanderers and on signing, simply told the press that he had joined Everton, 'to win things', which, because of Liverpool's success, had resulted in the press being somewhat sarcastic towards his comments. It was, a few years later, to be Andy's experience and determination to win, which would influence his team mates so emphatically.

Until the end of 1983, things continued to go from bad to worse. A dour goalless draw at home to Sunderland on Boxing Day saw cushions hurled onto the pitch in derision at the final whistle, an action that was to lead to the Board of Directors implementing a ban on the sale of cushions at all future home games. The situation even worsened at the next game, when the team went down by three goals to nil at bottom of the table, Wolverhampton Wanderers.

Morale was at an all time low at the end of 1983 and cost cutting exercises were being put into place throughout the club as attendances continued to decline. I received a memo in writing from our chief executive, Jim Greenwood, telling me to reduce my staff in the ticket office to either one full timer, or two part-time staff. At the time, we had two full time, Dot Williams and Harry Bateman and it was mutually agreed that Dot would do the mornings, with Harry the afternoons. However, this was never to come into force as the fortunes of the club on the field were to improve dramatically at the turn of the year. In fact, all our part-time staff, some eight in number, were working not just full time but also burning the midnight oil, as the team made quite remarkable progress in the two Cup competitions.

A new year, 1984, was to herald in the birth of a new era at the Club, which was to see unprecedented success over the next few years. It started with an excellent 2-0 win at Birmingham City, followed by another win by the same scoreline at Stoke in the F.A.Cup, when the following on the terraces that day was incredible. We had been allocated six thousand terrace tickets to go with some four thousand seat tickets for the tie. Almost immediately, demand was so high that the instructions that we had received from above to reduce our staffing levels were, for the moment in time, impossible to implement. More than half the eighteen thousand crowd that day were from Merseyside and the vocal support that the team received made it feel more like a home fixture, which was even more incredible bearing in mind, that only two weeks previously, the team had been booed off the pitch, accompanied by the throwing of cushions from disgruntled fans in the stands. The tide was turning and just how quickly it turned was to take everybody by surprise.

The team then had a rather unconvincing win against Gillingham in the next round which, ironically for me, took three ties to resolve, just as it had done during my spell at Manchester City (in City's case against Walsall and then against Norwich, which eventually was to culminate in them reaching the Final at Wembley on both occasions). Fate was to repeat itself, as Everton were to go on to Wembley in that year for the F.A.Cup Final. Firstly, however, that win against Gillingham had taken us into the fifth round, where a home tie against Shrewsbury Town lay ahead.

The team from Shropshire were, during the eighties, one of the best run clubs in the country, holding their own in the old Second Division with gates barely touching five thousand. Shrewsbury were more convincingly seen off than Gillingham, to put the club into the quarter finals, where an away tie at Notts County awaited.

At the same time as our F.A.Cup run, the team were also enjoying a run in the League Cup. It was at Oxford United that lady fortune was to smile on us. Oxford, under the chairmanship of Robert Maxwell, had already accounted for some big scalps in their League Cup run, including that of Manchester United and had, as the competition gone on, hiked up the admission prices at games staged on their ground. This had caused a fair deal of animosity amongst away fans but reluctantly our fans had quickly swallowed up our allocation of tickets for the evening game at Oxford. On a frozen surface, we were very fortunate, on the run of play, to be only one goal down at the time, when a pass back, which was to become infamous in the history of Everton Football Club, by the Oxford midfield player, Kevin Brock, only succeeded in finding Adrian Heath, who expertly took his chance to give us a very fortunate draw. That goal by Adrian was to be one of the most important goals ever scored by an Evertonian. As for the pass back by the unfortunate Kevin Brock, an excellent midfield player in his own right, well, all that Evertonians can say is, a big thank you, for what was the most important of passes. That equaliser had come at a time when even the most hardened Evertonian present that evening must have really believed that we were going out of the League Cup.

In the replay at Goodison, the team made no mistake and convincingly disposed of gallant Oxford, to set up a two legged semi final tie with Aston Villa.

A crowd of forty thousand were present at Goodison Park to see us record a 2-0 win in the first leg, courtesy of goals by the two Kevins- Sheedy and Richardson, against a Villa side, who had in their ranks, Steve McMahon, an Evertonian from a boy, who had been at the club from his junior days. The departure of Steve from Everton had, for many of us in the staff, been tinged with a touch of sadness. Obviously, in football, you soon come to accept the fact that players move on at a fairly rapid rate but Steve, I believe, had even been a ballboy at Goodison, before being signed as an apprentice professional. His aggressive, non stop performances soon earned him recognition at an early age in the first team under Gordon Lee and for many people at the club, he was the traditional Evertonian. His younger brother, John, also no mean player, was a regular in the reserve team at either full back or midfield and to link the club even stronger with the McMahon's at the time, John was to marry Nicky, the daughter of our souvenir shop manageress, Muriel Clinton, whose husband, Tommy, had played for many years at Everton. It was therefore with a certain amount of disgust that we saw how just a few so called Evertonians, who we always believed to be true sportsmen, reacted towards Steve in the second leg game at Villa Park, where we managed to retain our advantage, despite losing by a single goal, to go through to the final, courtesy of a 2-1 aggregate scoreline. Our opponents in that final were to be...Liverpool, thus setting up the first ever Merseyside final in a major competition after over ninety years of attempts.

The excitement of meeting Liverpool in a final at Wembley really started to get a grip of the city. Everton were on a roll, albeit just three months into its infancy, but could they give their more illustrious neighbours and rivals a surprise? The good thing about the League Cup Final, as opposed to the F.A.Cup Final, as far as I and my staff in the box office were concerned, lay in the fact that the competing club's allocation of tickets was far greater and, therefore, more in line with possible demand. The great chunk of tickets that have to be distributed to all the County Football Associations for the F.A.Cup Final would be allocated to the two competing clubs. It made our final that day, a game for the two sets of supporters as opposed to what is, for the F.A.Cup Final, a day for football in general, where many fans of the two competing clubs often lost out in the distribution of tickets to persons 'who knew somebody'.

On the pitch, the dream of beating the formidable Liverpool team was not to be however. Although, at Wembley, the team had thoroughly deserved their goalless draw and had proved to many Evertonians, and also a few Liverpudlians, that the recent upsurge in playing performance was no flash in the pan and that they could now start to compete with the best, that first trophy was still to prove to be elusive, as Liverpool went on to win the replay at Maine Road, the home of Manchester City, the Red's goal being scored that day by Graeme Souness.

The motivation and confidence that the team and management had received from the League Cup run was to see them succeed in the F.A.Cup that season. A win at Notts County, witnessed by close to ten thousand travelling Evertonians which, just like the third round tie at Stoke at the start of the cup run, had made it feel more like a home tie, saw us paired with Southampton in the semi final to be staged at Highbury.

A very late goal by Adrian Heath was enough to see the club through to its second Wembley final in a season.

Adrian, by the fact that he had scored that goal, had probably scored the two most important goals in the club's history, the goals certainly being the catalyst to the great things that were to happen to Everton over the next few years and, ofcourse, repay that record transfer fee many times over. The fans had had their doubts early on as to whether his ability would win through but his success had been merited by both himself and his mentor, Howard Kendall, who had shown so much faith in him, by paying that large fee in his first season as manager, back in 1981/82.

The transformation had occurred so quickly and everybody at the club had no doubt whatsoever that the promotion of Colin Harvey, who had put together a string of impressive results for the reserve team with a number of the lads who had started that 1983/84 campaign in his reserve team, had been instrumental in the club's new found success on the field. Players such as goalkeeper, Neville Southall, defenders, Derek Mountfield and Gary Stevens, midfielders, Peter Reid and Trevor Steven and striker, Graeme Sharp, had all come through Colin's reserve team to become the nucleus of the first team. The staff of Kendall, Harvey and Heaton had masterminded such a total and sudden recovery of a once great club's playing performances that they really could start to compete with their rivals across the Park.

So, to the second appearance at Wembley for a final that season and this time, one which we could believe that we realistically had a good chance of bringing the club that first elusive piece of silverware which Howard, on his joining, had stated was so important and which he felt would lead to more trophies finding their way into the Goodison Park boardroom. Not for the first time, we in the box office were to burn the midnight oil in order to sell tickets for our second appearance at Wembley for a final in a year and not forgetting also ofcourse that final replay held at Maine Road- all just four months after that memo asking us to reduce our staffing levels in the ticket office!

The final against Watford was, to all who attended, to be one of the most friendly, family occasions that it has ever been my pleasure to attend. Under the chairmanship of Elton John and the excellent management skills of manager, Graham Taylor and secretary, Eddie Plumley, Watford had become the leading light in trying to bring about a friendly, family based club in football, something that everybody in the game admired and some of us would try to copy in order to try to beat the ugly image of the football hooligan that was starting to rear its ugly head again and which, very shortly, was so nearly to damage the English game beyond repair.

Goals by Andy Gray, who had been a revelation since his signing from Wolverhampton Wanderers and Graeme Sharp were to give us that first elusive trophy on a day football was the real winner.

Although, for the neutral, the game had not been a classic, to those present, the friendly atmosphere that had been created by both sets of supporters made it a very special day. The wonderful way that the Watford supporters accepted defeat was to be a credit to them as they enjoyed their day on the biggest occasion that their small club had ever had.

Howard had also written himself into the record books that day by becoming not just the youngest player to appear in a F.A.Cup Final, a feat he did with Preston, playing against West Ham but now, some twenty years on, he had also become the youngest manager to win that coveted trophy.

The success of the club during the season had not just been restricted to the first team. The youth team had also clinched the F.A.Youth Cup. Everton had always had a vibrant youth policy, with three members of that F.A.Cup winning squad having come through the junior ranks- skipper, Kevin Ratcliffe, defender, Gary Stevens and midfielder, Kevin Richardson. A youth policy that was so well managed in those days by the club's youth development officer, Ray Minshull and his coach, Graham Smith.

The youth team had been beaten by Norwich City in the final the previous year and had now found itself up against Stoke City in a two legged final, the first game being held at Goodison Park. Although we did not sell tickets for this game, making it cash admission at the turnstile on the night, I had obviously decided to stay over for the game. A gate of five or six thousand was expected but, inspired by the success of the first team, the support on the night was more than double that figure. With large queues forming, it was absolutely essential to open more turnstiles and quickly. With this in mind, Alan Storey, who doubled up his role as head groundsman with that of chief steward, asked me if I had ever operated a turnstile. I said that I had on a couple of occasions- once at Gresty Road for a reserve game and once at the old cricket ground in Earle Street when on the local club's committee. I was therefore ushered off to open a turnstile. What I was to witness that night operating that turnstile was astounding. Although, the admission price was a nice round pound and indeed, very cheap, I have never witnessed so many people jumping over, or crawling under the turnstile in order to avoid payment. When I eventually managed to close my turnstile and bring in the cash that had been tendered by the honest ones, I told Alan of my experiences. He just gave a wry smile and remarked that now I knew what it could be like working a turnstile. No wonder that stewards had to be placed inside the ground by each turnstile to try to stop this gate crashing. Incidentally, the youth team triumphed against Stoke City to add the F.A.Youth Cup that season to that of the F.A.Cup, the first trophies that the club had won since their championship winning team of 1970, which had featured both Howard and Colin Harvey as players.

The following season, 1984-85, was to be the most enjoyable one that I have ever witnessed. However, March 1985, was to be a very sad personal moment for me, as my mother, Christine, who had been diagnosed with cancer of the bowel, was very quickly, after just four months, to lose her battle against this illness and pass away at the age of seventy.

Season ticket sales had been buoyant as optimism had grown amongst supporters throughout the summer of 1984 and it had been further fuelled when a solitary Graeme Sharp goal had seen us lift the Charity Shield in front of a one hundred thousand sell out at Wembley Stadium against of all teams....Liverpool.

Confidence was sky high, the whole club was buzzing. It was difficult to believe that only eight months previously, morale was at its lowest ebb and pessimism from director down to supporter level was common place. The players, coaching staff and manager had turned it all around. All the experts started to put forward their reasons for the up turn but for whatever the reason, it was happening, or so we thought. However, the one certain aspect about sport, is its uncertainty and sure enough, the first two League games of the new season were to bring us down to earth. Our first home game saw the players parading the F.A.Challenge and Youth Cups to an adoring Goodison crowd. Unfortunately, the jubilation had soon disappeared, as a rampant Tottenham side inflicted a four goals to one drubbing on us. This was followed by a second consecutive defeat at West Bromwich Albion and a comment which I made to our chief travel steward, George Hogan, on getting onto the coach that evening to travel back home, basically stating that that second defeat had ruled us out of any realistic Championship hopes and only left the Cups to play for- how wrong I was!

The team went on, however, to win their next game, a televised away game at Chelsea on the Friday evening and then went on a fantastic run of success, which saw them beat Liverpool at Anfield for the first time for a good number of years, courtesy of a spectacular shot by Graeme Sharp on the volley past my old friend, Bruce Grobbelaar, who had by now established himself in the Liverpool team after his days at Crewe- the goal quite easily winning television's "Goal of the Season". A further masterful performance saw us destroy our rivals, Manchester United, by five goals to nil at Goodison, with some of the best football that it had been my pleasure to watch which, in those early days of video recorders, actually prompted me to purchase the video of the match.

This winning run in the League saw us head into pole position and along with the team also enjoying a successful start in their attempt to retain the F.A.Cup and also making good progress in their European Cup Winners Cup campaign, in an attempt to bring to the club its first European trophy, had put everybody in an optimistic mood.

The only setback to the season came about as a result of our elimination from the League Cup at Goodison Park against lowly Grimsby Town, whose scorer that day, a young England under twenty one international, Paul Wilkinson, was to later sign for Everton and be the source of the most bizarre phone call that I was to ever receive at Goodison Park.

We were working late in the box office one evening and the main switchboard had been put through to our office, when I received a call from Paul who, unbelievably, had tried so late at night and ofcourse, under normal circumstances, the call would not have been answered. However, on this occasion, he was in luck and proceeded to explain to me how he had travelled down that day to join the young England squad but had forgotten his boots which, ofcourse, he would need for the following night's game and wondered if I could get them down to him to play in. I told him that there was nothing that could be done until the following morning, when I promised that I would immediately notify the boss of the situation. Howard's reaction, the following morning, was to laugh - typical footballer, he and I thought. Some things do not alter. To this day, I do not know whether Paul received his own boots to play in. Incidentally, that Grimsby defeat had come after such a convincing win in the previous round at Old Trafford, in front of a sell out crowd of fifty thousand plus.

One could not take it away from Paul, however, that up to May 1985, he had scored the one goal that had stopped Everton having the opportunity of winning all four trophies.

In the European Cup Winners Cup, a comfortable win had been achieved against the Irish team, University of Dublin. The visit to Ireland was one of the most enjoyable trips possible, with the Irish hospitality for the Everton party and its following second to none. Inter Bratislava and Fortuna Sittard offered little resistance in the next two rounds and this brought up the formidable West German team, Bayern Munich, in the semi-final.

Meanwhile, in the F.A.Cup, comfortable wins had been achieved against Leeds United and Doncaster Rovers in the third and fourth rounds respectively to set up for me, not necessarily to all Evertonians, a memorable fifth round home tie against non League, Telford United. Telford had drawn their fourth round tie at Darlington and were awaiting the replay to be held at their Bucks Head ground, when the draw for the fifth round paired the winner of this replay with us, the game being scheduled for Goodison Park.

Included in the Telford United team was Paul Mayman, whose family I had remained in close contact with ever since our first meeting, when Paul had joined Crewe Alexandra in December 1975.

I had travelled to Telford's second round tie at Preston on the train with Paul's father, Frank, where we had been guests of the host club and sat in the directors box, close to where the legendary Tom Finney was sat, witnessing probably Telford's best ever performance, as they beat their illustrious Third Division opponents to the tune of four goals to one. I had also travelled down to their Bucks Head ground with Frank for the third round tie which had seen them dispose of Bradford City, who featured in their team that day, a young midfield player, Stuart McCall, who was later to command a high fee from ourselves to secure his signature and who, at the time, was instrumental in Bradford's lofty position in the Third Division.

So, to me, an Everton versus Telford United fifth round tie was real fantasy and here it was, just one game away- a replay at home to Darlington, who were then near the top of the Fourth Division.

I therefore arranged with Frank to go in his car for the replay, taking with me the tickets for the forthcoming fifth round- hoping that it would be Telford United who would be picking up those twelve thousand tickets to sell to their fans.

The boss also travelled down to that game and we were to witness three of the best goals scored by Telford that one could ever hope to see. So good infact, that the Darlington goalkeeper, Fred Barber, gave such a flawless display that evening that he was shortly after that game to sign for Everton. Fred, however, could do nothing about a free kick from Eddie Hogan, that Kevin Sheedy, who was probably regarded as the best free kick specialist in the country, would have been proud of and a spectacular volley by Dave Mather, which was reminiscent of Graeme Sharp's "Goal of the Season" against Liverpool, flew past him that night as Telford deservedly earned the right, courtesy of a 3-0 win, to come to Goodison Park to play the Champions elect and present holders of the F.A.Cup in the fifth round.

With the exception of Liverpool's tie at York, all the other scheduled fifth round ties were postponed and so, with our underground heating system working, the tie against Telford went ahead in full view of the television cameras.

Over forty eight thousand attended that game, including a good twelve thousand from Shropshire and a few hundred that I had sold to Paul and his team mates, many of whom were from Merseyside, including the Telford manager, who was probably one of the best ever Non- League managers, Stan Storton and the Telford United centre-forward, Ken McKenna, who was later to become manager of Welsh Champions, TNS, who would play against European Cup holders Liverpool in the European Champions League. Ken was such a devout Evertonian that he had a tattoo of the club on his body and so naturally, after getting to know him, I arranged for him to have tickets for our home games when he was able to attend.

As a special treat before the game, I had decided to arrange for a meal for Paul's wife, Diane, her mother and father, Nora and Ken, her sister, Carol and her husband, Kevin, along with Paul's mother and father, Joyce and Frank, and Joyce's sister, Pat and her husband, Alan. Right at the last minute, a phone call came from a previous manager of Paul's- Paul Ogden, who had been responsible, whilst manager of Northwich Victoria, for signing Paul, to see if I could accommodate him with a meal and ticket for the game. I offered him the opportunity of joining Paul and Diane's families at the game and not only did he just join them but he footed the bill for the meal and drinks, which I had intended to do. A superb gesture and it is lovely to see Paul, some twenty years on, still have that enthusiasm to be manager of his home town club, Leek Town. Paul's desire to be there that day, being a former manager of young Paul, showed to me the great spirit that existed in the non League circles and if any proof was needed, one only had to look at the cost of the bill that day!

On the pitch, Everton eventually ran out three goals to nil winners but not before a minor set back, when at half time, the game was still goalless. The reward for Telford United that day was a cheque to the tune of fifty thousand plus pounds, which would more than cover their season's expenditure, in addition to the television fee that they acquired, plus ofcourse, the great experience and the memories that came from the day. Everton's reward was a quarter final home draw against Ipswich Town.

After a few alarms, Ipswich were disposed of, the game at Goodison being notable for the death, whilst watching the game in the directors box, where just before the legendary Dixie Dean had died, of Harry Catterick.

Catterick had been the manager of the last Everton team to win the Championship in 1970 and had recently been given a testimonial by the club. It was to be the first of two testimonials that we were to be involved in at the box office during my spell at Goodison Park but, unlike the second, that held for our young centre half, Mark Higgins, who had been forced to give up playing professional football through injury after having just established himself as a regular in the team, the Catterick testimonial offered no thanks to either myself, or the box office staff, who put in extra work. In Mark's case, both Mark and John, his father, who had been a defender in the Bolton Wanderers team of the fifties, went out of their way, as did Tony Book, when I was involved at Manchester City, to thank the staff for the extra work that they had put in, alas no such thanks were forthcoming from Messrs Catterick and his agent, Gordon Brown, whose only contact I had, was when a bundle of two hundred tickets that I had given to Gordon for him to sell had gone astray. Almost immediately they were found, just as I was ready to issue duplicates. I was never even to meet Mr Catterick, never mind receive any thanks for the efforts of our box office staff. Although I appreciate that we can never demand gratitude as a right, it does go a long way towards getting the best out of people. No doubt, gratitude was expressed at a higher level but it never, on this occasion, filtered down to the box office.

On the pitch, the club were now in two semi-finals and riding high at the top of the League. We had been drawn against Luton Town in the semi-final of the F.A.Cup and had been given the honour of Goodison Park staging the other semi-final between Manchester United and Liverpool. In those days there was no Sky TV and very little live football on television so therefore, both the games were scheduled to kick off at the same time. This meant, ofcourse, that none of our staff could go to our semi-final at Villa Park and it would also lead to the most hectic time in the box office that we had thus far experienced. Being the staging club, we were entitled to a small percentage of tickets for the Liverpool-United game, which we allocated to our season ticket holders along, ofcourse, with their priority for our tie at Villa Park.

Unfortunately, around this time, my mother had passed away and living at home, it had left a big void which the sheer volume of work certainly helped to ease. Even on the day of the funeral, I was duty bound to return to the ground to prepare for those big games. It was difficult to do but somehow it helped to take my mind off matters more depressing at the time, which, with the passage of time, certainly eased. I was also very fortunate in that my brother and sister were so supportive of my father at that sad time.

The League Championship was virtually sewn up courtesy of a 2-1 win at Tottenham, avenging that opening day defeat. Spurs had been our main challenger that season and that game at White Hart Lane had been memorable for a wonderful save made by Neville Southall, who had fast become, just like Everton, one of the best in Europe and certainly the best in Britain. Neville going on that season to receive the coveted Football Writers Player of the Year award.

In the F.A.Cup semi-final at Villa Park, after an early hiccup when Luton scored first, an equaliser was soon followed by a late winner from centre half, Derek Mountfield, to put us into the F.A.Cup final for the second consecutive year and an elusive chance to complete the double of winning the League and Cup in the same season, a feat that even with Liverpool's dominance over previous seasons, they had failed to achieve.

Derek, the goalscorer on that day, was a quiet, unassuming lad, whose eye for a goal from set pieces had brought Everton much success but none more so than that day, when his winner paid back all of his thirty thousand pound transfer fee that the club had paid our near neighbours, Tranmere Rovers, in what was undoubtedly the bargain of the decade- making Derek, for me, the best pound for pound player that the club had ever signed, or indeed probably were ever likely to.

However, hopes of the first ever all Merseyside final failed to materialise as Manchester United overcame Liverpool to set up a final with ourselves.

In the European Cup Winners Cup, our semi final had seen the two strongest sides left in the last four paired against each other. The visit to the Olympic Stadium for the Bayern Munich tie was certainly the most memorable trip I had been on. In a game that featured the eventual West German and English Champions, Everton gave a very professional performance to secure a goalless draw in the magnificent setting. The match really was devoid of real action- that was to be left to the second leg at Goodison Park. It was a game of cat and mouse, as both sides were very aware that day of not losing, which was a policy that was to rebound on the Germans.

The demand for tickets for the second leg, with all to play for, was tremendous and resulted in a near fifty thousand capacity crowd - the only unsold tickets being in the area of the stadium allocated to the German fans. The atmosphere at Goodison that night was, without doubt, the most electric I had ever witnessed at the famous old stadium- a feeling that was also supported by many long standing Evertonians. The Germans took a surprise early lead but in a wonderful comeback, backed by a vociferous crowd, Everton scored three goals in an awesome second half display, which rocked the star studded German team, to take the Blues into their first and, at present, only European final.

April 1985, had seen the club virtually clinch the First Division title and reach the finals of both the F.A.Cup and European Cup Winners Cup, just sixteen months after those all time low performances against Sunderland at Goodison Park and at Wolverhampton Wanderers. The upsurge had happened that quickly. The whole club were on a roller coaster ride and we were enjoying every minute of it. The work load regarding tickets was fantastic, as the history books looked like being rewritten. The "double" was definitely a distinct possibility- the League Championship virtually sewn up and an F.A.Cup final against Manchester United, who we had already beaten three times that season convincingly, twice being at Old Trafford, awaited. It was also noted ofcourse that Liverpool, despite their fantastic run of success in the seventies and early eighties, had still to achieve the "double", it only having been done since the turn of the century by the two North London giants, Arsenal and Tottenham Hotspur.

The League Championship was clinched and later presented to the team at our home game against Queens Park Rangers on 6th May 1985, some fifteen years after Howard Kendall and Colin Harvey had been players in the last title winning team. That day was more like a festival than a competitive game of football and one could feel for Queens Park Rangers, who really were there just to make up the numbers. Fortunately, they did not spoil the party, as Everton turned on the style to win yet another game, enabling the club to win the title by a double figure points margin. Task one of three duly completed for that historic treble, which no English club had ever achieved.

Wednesday 15th May 1985, was to herald the day that Everton were to win their first European trophy and complete stage two of the treble, by beating Rapid Vienna in Rotterdam.

Thousands of Evertonians made the short journey across to Holland for the final and the club chartered a plane to take the staff and player's wives or girlfriends on the morning of the game to the Dutch city. The flight took just one hour and after lunch we were left to our own devices to sample the atmosphere in the city pubs, where both sets of supporters mingled happily with each other, just determined to enjoy the day. How different from what was to happen just a few days later, when Liverpool and Juventus fans were to show the ugly side of the coin, with crowd troubles that would have such far reaching effects on the lives of so many Italian families and cast a real shadow over English football for so many years to come. That day in Rotterdam, however, saw rival fans drinking and playing football in the streets together and fans wearing the colours of both sides. The local police just stood back and smiled and no doubt admired the behaviour of two wonderful sets of supporters.

The game itself turned out to be a fairly comfortable win for Everton. After a goalless first half, which Everton had controlled, the goals soon flowed in the second half to see the Blues clinch their second trophy, to the tune of three goals to one.

The flight back to Liverpool after the game that night will always remain in my memory, as the team, management and directors returned on the plane with our party of staff and player's wives to land at Speke Airport in the early hours of Thursday morning, to be welcomed by thousands of cheering Evertonians.

Approximately sixty hours later, the team would be having to walk out again on to the pitch, this time at Wembley Stadium, in front of one hundred thousand, to try to achieve that elusive "treble" and ofcourse, become the first of the Merseyside clubs to do the domestic `double'.

The ticket selling for the Manchester United F.A.Cup Final unfortunately brought into play the ticket touts for the first time in my eight years at Goodison Park. Although they had been present at all of the Merseyside derby games, they had not really caused us much trouble.

How different for this game, so much so that I have dedicated a whole chapter about the problems that we faced and the dangers that they posed for the game.

On the field, the dream of the treble was broken, as a tired Everton team, both mentally and physically, lost out to Manchester United. This must have been one of the very few occasions that Liverpool supporters had ever wanted United to win (in order, ofcourse, to ensure that Everton did not become the first to do the `double', or `treble' with the European trophy thrown in for good measure).

Despite previous convincing successes against United, and with United only playing with ten men after Kevin Moran was sensationally sent off, Everton just did not have it in them that day to overcome a ten man United team, who destroyed thousands of blue hearts, when Norman Whiteside scored an extra time winner.

Nobody will ever be able to persuade me, or any true Evertonian, that the short respite between those two finals, less than seventy two hours, was not responsible for Everton failing to beat a ten man United team that day.

The team had been superb throughout the season. Very nearly the same eleven players had played in every game, a fact that had also happened across at Anfield during Liverpool's success. In those days, it was often boasted that a programme editor could print a team at the start of the season for the last match of that season at Anfield and that it would show little or no changes- that could now be said about Everton.

Today, there would have been a national outcry if a team would have had to have played two finals in three days using the same eleven players for both games. Fixture lists had to be strictly adhered to but ofcourse, we did not have the tremendous demands (or, ofcourse, the money) placed on the authorities by Sky Television, who virtually control the game at the top level today. The game then was run for the benefit of the supporters. They paid their money and called the tune and club sponsors knew their position in the pecking order and accepted the importance of the fan. Television had to go along with this, or do without.

The Everton team of the 1984/85 season has quite rightly gone down as the club's best ever side. For a team that had been described for much of that season as a "team without stars", the awards that individual players received that season made very impressive reading. Neville Southall was made "Football Writers Player of the Year" with the other major award, `Professional Footballers Association Player of the Year' going to Peter Reid. In addition to this, the boss, Howard Kendall, was naturally voted "Manager of the Year".

However, within two weeks of all of this success, the chance for the team to prove themselves as the best in Europe, by taking part in the European Cup, lay in ruins, through no fault of their own. The story of Hysel, with its tragic deaths, has been well documented but the resulting ban imposed on all English teams, as a result of those mindless few Liverpool hooligans that day, was to have far reaching results on the English game and more particularly on Everton Football Club, who suffered far more than most.

The start of the 1985/86 season saw the departure of Andy Gray, who had joined the club in November 1983, at probably the club's lowest point. His infectious, competitive spirit had soon had the desired effect on his team mates and enabled him to became an integral part of the club's success, which had proved what he had said, which at the time had been scoffed at by the media, that he had signed for Everton "to win things"- now, a League Championship, F.A.Cup winners and runners-up medal and a European Cup Winners medal in slightly less than two years, he was leaving, having proved a point. His replacement was to be a young Gary Lineker, a record signing from Leicester City, who had just broken into the England squad.

The summer leading up to the 1985/86 season was a hub of activity for us in the box office, as season tickets soared to a record high. Although only twelve thousand, which surprisingly does not compare favourably with today's figure, for what is basically a shadow of the team that the 1984/85 Championship team were, it was, at the time, a vaste improvement on previous seasons.

The Charity Shield, to be played at Wembley Stadium, offered us an opportunity to play in front of a full house and the team acquired their first trophy by beating United 2-0 . However, in a season of " so near yet so far", this was to be the club's only piece of silverware.

Unfortunately for Everton, soccer was taken off the television screen after the two sides- the Football League and the television companies-had failed to agree on a deal, not returning until the New Year. During this time, I was to witness, what was for me, the best "derby" game of all for pure excitement, although we were to lose. In a pulsating game at Goodison Park in September, we found ourselves three goals down but pulled two back and in a frantic finish, just failed to get what would have been a much deserved equaliser. The two clubs, Everton and Liverpool, were soon to make it a two horse race for the honours that season, with the result that day having such an influence on the destination of the Championship.

In the F.A.Cup, wins over Exeter, Blackburn, Spurs and Luton had set up a semi-final with Sheffield Wednesday, whilst Liverpool had also progressed to be one of the other semi finalists. Therefore, not for the first time, the opportunity arose for the first ever F.A.Cup Final between the two Merseyside giants, just two years after they had competed in the first ever final - the League Cup.

In the League, a defeat on the notorious synthetic surface at Luton gave Liverpool the advantage, whilst in the F.A.Cup, goals from Alan Harper and Graeme Sharp gave us a 2-1 win over Sheffield Wednesday and with Liverpool also winning, it set up, for the first time in the history of the F.A.Cup, a final between Everton and Liverpool and both clubs still had the opportunity of converting that into the elusive "double", as the two had pulled well away from the remainder of the field for the League Championship.

This was the game that the whole of Merseyside wanted tickets for. The city was alive with football fever, with such slogans as "Merseyside Unites" being introduced, as pride throughout the city grew as a result of the dominance of their two football clubs. For being so long in the shadows of Liverpool, Evertonians now had pride. The club, even in the early days of Howard's management, had comfortably held a position in the top half of the League, a position today and over the last decade, that would have been very acceptable to present day Evertonians but in those days, it had not been. Now, football in Merseyside had touched a new height.

This was my third consecutive F.A.Cup Final at Everton, a feat in the game that had only been equalled once before since the turn of the century when, in the early seventies, Arsenal had appeared in three consecutive finals. Each of the three finals had been different. The first against Watford, was a nice starter with regards to ticket demands, with our allocation of twenty five thousand tickets being fairly comfortable to nearly meet the demand of our regular fans. However, because of demands made by outside sources, the next final, that against Manchester United, was probably the second hardest final that one could have regarding ticket distribution, only to be made harder by our third final against Liverpool, where the same allocation would be deemed to be totally inadequate.

Letters flooded into the ticket office with requests for tickets but one letter in particular was quite remarkable. A relation of an Everton season ticket holder, who had fallen ill, had been using his ticket when, unfortunately, the season ticket holder had died. The season ticket holder's dying wish was that all his Everton souvenirs, including that season ticket, were to be buried with him. As the supporter had been using his relation's season ticket, he had never had the need to buy a ticket and therefore did not possess a voucher or ticket stub, which may have qualified him for a ticket for the final. He had therefore written to us at the box office to enquire about whether there was anything that we could do to help him acquire a ticket for the big game. The letter went around the club, being far and away the most bizarre application that we had received and was even mentioned by the manager, Howard Kendall, in one of the interviews for television that he had given in the build up to the game.

The all-Merseyside F.A.Cup final also gave me the opportunity to make small television appearances, as I was interviewed by both the main television companies, who were so keen to get stories in the prelude to the big occasion on the fans search for tickets for this momentous event. The one thing that I really did notice about those television interviews was the length of time, usually an hour or more, that was required just to create a few minutes interview, which made me realise just how much work went into just getting a half an hour programme like "Football Focus" on the air each week.

Incidentally, the person who had been using his sick relative's season ticket book, had, by doing so, broken a condition of sale that related to the purchasing of Season Tickets that the club had at that time, which basically stated that tickets were not transferable. I was always led, however, to believe that the gentleman in question did in fact receive a ticket from a source within the club. His efforts certainly deserved to be rewarded, although his feelings towards his relation, who had just died, were somewhat lacking in compassion, perhaps, being more concerned with the probability of missing out on a ticket. I am sure that he did not really wish his letter to come over that way but it just did to us!

To allocate the balance of tickets after the sale to season ticket holders, fund raising agents, sponsors, players, directors and staff, we had allocated either a voucher at the cash turnstiles, or asked seat ticket holders to retain the stub of their ticket from a previous home game. By then using the last numbers on these, we would be able to select enough holders to be able to sell the remaining balance of tickets. Our staff therefore had to be very vigilant on checking for alterations or forgeries, as we had worked out the proportion of vouchers issued to that of the tickets available, and any mass forgery would have caused us severe problems and not a little embarrassment.

On this one occasion, a member of our staff had spotted a very obvious alteration to the figure on the voucher. I had been called over, after the person had become argumentative after being refused a ticket and, despite having a police presence, was holding up the queue by his refusal to accept my staff member's decision that the voucher had been tampered with. I immediately took his name and address and wrote "void" on his voucher and returned it to him so that he could not try again to get a ticket. At this point, he became very aggressive and threatened me. Luckily for me, there was a re-inforced glass window between us, as he really did dwarf over me and even that police officer inside the building, who was there to look after us against such aggression. His threats at the time were, as far as I was concerned, to be taken seriously enough, that I decided to report the matter to our chief executive, Jim Greenwood.

His advice to me was to contact Fred Peacock, an elderley season ticket holder, who held in his name a number of three and five hundred club season tickets which I knew that he often loaned out to many of his business contacts. Fred was a wonderful old Evertonian but of no physical build and I admit that I was not too confident with the solution that Mr Greenwood had offered to the threat that I had received, which I was certainly taking seriously. No need to worry though. I phoned Fred and told him of the incident, giving him the man's address, which I had obtained off his voucher. The next day, to my utter disbelief, the gentleman concerned, who had been so aggressive to me the previous day, was one of the first in the queue, but with a completely different attitude, being so apologetic for his previous behaviour.

After that, it certainly gave me a feeling of comfort to be able to know that the club had people around such as Fred and his contacts, if ever again a violent threat was made against any of us.

Meanwhile, the chase for the Championship continued. Despite that defeat on the synthetic surface at Luton, if we won our last four games we would retain the Championship. However, things were to go wrong. A goalless draw at Nottingham Forest on a hot May Saturday afternoon, was followed by the most disastrous result possible, a single goal defeat at lowly Oxford United, ironically on the very ground where, just two years previously, Everton's successful run had really started to take off. This had therefore given the advantage to Liverpool, who went on to claim the title, courtesy of winning their last game of the season at Chelsea.

It was therefore Liverpool who would be approaching that F.A.Cup final between the two Merseyside giants going for that elusive "double" and it would fall on us, their biggest rivals, to try to stop it from happening.

Needless to say, as the history books tell us, Liverpool went on to win that Cup Final, courtesy of a 3-1 win, with Ian Rush, an Evertonian in his younger days and so often a thorn in Everton's side in the past, again being the match winner with his goals, after Gary Lineker, who was to be playing his last game for the Blues, in what was his one and only season, had given us the lead.

The 1985/86 season had been one of those` so near, yet so far away' seasons- runners up to Liverpool in both League and F.A.Cup but ofcourse, with that ban on English clubs being imposed after Hysel the previous year, both clubs had been frustrated in their attempts to prove themselves in Europe.

The 1986/87 season started with the departure of the popular Gary Lineker. Perhaps the writing was on the wall for future years, as his move to Barcelona for a record transfer fee would allow him the opportunity to play in the European competitions that had been taken away from our players and which would cause so much frustration to the nation's better players over the forthcoming years. Ironically, despite Gary's own personal success, it was to be the one season in three that the club did not win any of the major domestic honours. Using some of the money from the sale of Gary, the boss bought Dave Watson from Norwich City and Ian Snodin from Leeds United and complimented this with the marvellous acquisition of long time Manchester City servant, Paul Power, who was to play such an important role as a versatility player in the forthcoming season.

The signing of Ian Snodin for seven hundred and fifty thousand pounds was of particular interest to me. As a young junior player with Doncaster Rovers, he had broken into the team, under the management of Billy Bremner, where his impressive form had earned him selection for the England youth team. Needing his passport fairly urgently, Ian had reason to have to travel to the Passport Office in Liverpool with his club secretary, Roger Reade. I had known Roger since my days at Manchester City and he had, on my last day at Crewe, attended a Junior Club meeting as my guest, bringing with him the Manchester City and England under twenty one international midfield player, Gary Owen. I was therefore very grateful to Roger for that day and so, when he informed me that he had to travel to Liverpool with Ian for the passport and enquired as to the possibility of them calling over to Goodison Park for a meal and a short tour around the famous old stadium, I was only too pleased to be in a position to return the favour. Roger compared young Ian's ability to that of Gary's- no mean judge of a player. My parting gift to a young Ian that day was a home match programme against Chelsea, for during our meal, he had admitted to being a fan of Chelsea, along with a soft drink and the meal. Now, here he was returning as a first team player for seven hundred and fifty thousand pounds, in a career that would see him stay for eight years, picking up both a League and F.A.Cup winners medals and but for injuries at the height of his form in 1989-90 would, almost certainly, have received full international recognition.

On the pitch the season started with, what was becoming, our annual trip to Wembley Stadium for the Charity Shield, which was billed as, "Merseyside Unites", the two clubs, Everton and Liverpool, having completely dominated the previous season's football. Quite predictably, the honours finished even, with the two club's sharing the Charity Shield, courtesy of a 1-1 draw.

In the League, a thirty five thousand gate, a couple of thousand higher than the previous season's average, saw our opening day's victory over Nottingham Forest. However, by the time that we played Liverpool at Goodison Park in November, the recession, that had started to hit Merseyside, had seen gates drop to around the thirty thousand mark.

Therefore, in order to try to improve our attendances, the club introduced, what was later to become their popular, family club enclosure. From the time that we had played Watford in the 1984 F.A.Cup Final, Everton had been impressed with Watford's commitment to the family and quite rightly saw that the way forward was to encourage family attendance.

The Family Club had been a natural progression from the Junior Evertonians, which we had introduced in order for juniors who, on the payment of a small membership fee, were given a membership card, which allowed them reduced admission to the Gwladys Street terracing.

Many years previously, Everton, like Liverpool, had partitioned part of their terracing for reduced admission for juniors but this had resulted in problems, such as bullying, which the stewards had found great difficulty in dealing with. The so called "Boys Pen" was therefore abolished and for a good number of seasons there had been no concession for juniors. We all felt that this policy would result in the demise of Everton Football Club in future years if not rescinded in some way and so the Junior Evertonians membership card was introduced to enable us to fill the vacant gaps on the terracing. With Liverpool's continued success in the seventies and early eighties, their gates were virtually assured of being a sell out at Anfield but our gates in this same period barely saw Goodison Park half full to its fifty three thousand capacity. Therefore, although the two Merseyside clubs in this era had always had a similar price structure, there was less need for the Anfield club to rectify the situation with regard to concessionary admission prices than ourselves.

The natural progression from the Junior Evertonians was ofcourse to offer the facility of half priced seats to juniors which, although at the time was a step in the right direction, was only offered to them provided that they were accompanied by an adult, who paid the full price. I knew from my own experience that, in my days as a junior, I would have had great difficulty finding the full admission price to watch my first Football League games and for many years argued that point with several members of the staff, but to no avail, until the introduction of the Junior Evertonians. Now things were moving in the right direction which, with the success on the field, would ensure Everton's growth, despite the recession that was hitting Merseyside.

Unfortunately, the area that was chosen by the powers that be, the terracing infront of the Main Stand, popularly known as the Goodison

Road Enclosure, was more liable to be affected by adverse weather than the Bullens Road Paddock on the opposite side of the ground, with the first few rows being most at risk. Typically, the nightmare scenario happened on the first occasion that the area had been sold out, for a home game with Manchester United. Fortunately, the heavy rain had reduced the gate to a below average twenty six thousand, for what was normally one of the better attended fixtures on our calendar and therefore, we were able to allocate disgruntled fans in the saturated Enclosure with alternative seats in the Main Stand. However, moving and relocating them together took some time for our over worked match day stewards and resulted in a fair degree of aggravation, which was vented against us in the box office after the end of the game. Fortunately, the team won convincingly, to at least lessen their anger. From that moment on, however, a warning was to be printed on the tickets to state that the first few rows could be affected in the case of adverse weather. If only, as we had suggested, the Bullens Road paddock would have been chosen as the designated area, perhaps I and my staff, would have been spared the anger of those fans that day.

The first "derby" game that season between the two Merseyside giants took place in November at Goodison and earned me a rebuke for a slight indiscretion. The game was refereed by Crewe based referee, Neville Ashley, who, at the end of the game, through knowing me from local football in which he still refereed, offered me a lift home, which I was only too willing to accept. Little did I realise the folly of my ways in accepting that lift at the time but it was soon to be brought home to me several days later by several high ranking people at the club. I can honestly say that neither myself, Neville or the guests that he also had in his car that day, had envisaged any such problem when I had accepted his offer. From that moment on, however, I was always very careful not to place either myself or Everton in that predicament again, especially as Crewe in those days had two other referees on the Football League list, Don Shaw and John Lovatt, not to mention Peter Harding and David Farrall on the League's linesmen list, making a total of five - an unprecedented number for the area, which will probably never be equalled.

Despite injuries, the team continued to climb the table, so much so, that by April and the return fixture with Liverpool, a victory would see us pick up our second Championship title in three years. Unfortunately, a 1-3 defeat and a goalless draw with Manchester City at Goodison, saw the team still require two more points from our last two fixtures at Norwich City on the May Bank Holiday or in the final home game of the season against Luton Town.

The day out at Norwich, although long and tiring involving approximately a five hundred mile round trip, was fairy tale material, as a season's work for the players and staff was once more rewarded by the title, for the second time in three years, courtesy of a goal by Pat van den Hauwe.

Pat, the hero that day, was a real character. Nicknamed "psycho" by the fans and almost everybody at the club, for obvious reasons. My experience with Patrick is rather amusing now but was just the opposite at the time. During the whole of my twelve years at Goodison Park, I had commuted by rail from my home in Crewe to Liverpool, usually on the early morning 7.35am train. On one occasion, however, I saw Pat sat on the train and joined him for the hour long journey to Liverpool. The previous evening, he had been playing for Wales and was travelling back home and we talked before going our separate ways. On arriving at Goodison Park, I went as usual to get our mail from the reception and just happened to be there at the same time as the boss, Howard Kendall. More out of polite conversation than anything else, I mentioned that I had travelled in that morning on the train with Pat. Not noticing, nor expecting any reaction from him, I never for one minute gave it another thought, until our assistant secretary, Barry Forsyth, rang down to me later that morning to tell me that I had inadvertently placed Patrick into trouble with the boss. Apparently, Patrick had been told to travel straight back home after the international. Barry, however, really stirred it up. He told me that Pat was "looking for" me and when Pat was "looking" for somebody, that usually meant trouble.

With a home game on the Saturday and after two days of anxiety, as the players arrived at the ground on the matchday, a good hour before kick off time, I decided to "bite the bullet" and made a beeline for Pat. I could tell from one or two remarks that Barry had let several of the players in on what had happened. I approached Pat with my offer of a sincere apology for my loose tongue, which had, I was led to believe, given him so much aggravation from the boss. Pat, on hearing my heartfelt apology, just gave a wry smile (I am sure that was the only time I ever saw him smile- come to think of it, neither did many players) and just muttered, 'that's o.k. lad, don't let it happen again'. I smiled but needless to say, I did not.

Although a long journey back from Norwich that day, the thousands of Evertonians there had made the day, and more especially the journey back, that bit special. Instead of going home to Crewe, I went onto Liverpool to flavour the beer in the city pubs, on an evening which will always remain in my memory. I was, however, determined not to have too much to drink, as I so desperately wanted to be able to savour every minute of the occasion. Evertonians just painted the city a mass of blue and white that evening. Two League titles in three years and in that intervening season, a well earned runners up spot, the club really were top of the tree and the supporters certainly let all and sundry know it. The success that Howard, his players and staff had brought to Everton was beyond anybody's wildest dreams such a short time ago and I, just like all

Evertonians, kept having to pinch myself to make sure it was not a dream-but it was real, so very real.

The title that season, unlike the previous one two years ago, had seen the club having to use twenty three players because of injuries to several key players, which had made this even more rewarding for the management, especially when one considers that Aston Villa, when they won the title in 1980, had only used fourteen (incidentally, as a slight on today's football, very nearly all of them were English born and they followed that by winning the European Cup - where have we gone wrong?).

So, on Saturday 9th May 1987, Everton were presented yet again with the League Championship trophy at a packed Goodison Park for the visit of Luton Town, who just happened to be there that day to make up the numbers and offered little resistance, as the Blues chalked up yet another win to finish off a superb season in style. It was ironic that it should have been Luton who were the visitors to Goodison that day, as it had been they, on their artificial surface, who had been one of the main reasons why Everton had not made it a hat-trick of title wins, as they had thwarted us in the run up to the end of that season by beating us, and thus allowing Liverpool the opportunity to pinch the title on the closing day of the season, after it had looked likely to come to Goodison.

From now on, however, things were never to be as good. Within six weeks of picking up the title, the worst scenario happened. The date of 19th June 1987, should figure as one of the blackest days in the history of Everton Football Club. That date heralded the departure of the most successful manager that the club had ever had.

In the six seasons that Howard Kendall had been with Everton, two Championships, one F.A.Cup, a European Cup Winners Cup, two Charity Shields with one shared, along with an F.A.Youth Cup trophy had been brought to the club and in addition, Everton had finished runners up in the League once, the F.A.Cup twice and the League Cup once. Even in the so called bad days at the start of Howard's reign, they had never been outside the top half of the League.

Now, possibly because of the ban on English clubs in Europe but for whatever personal reason, Howard had decided that his future lay away from Goodison Park and was to try his managerial skills in Spain with Athletico Bilbao.

The disappointment felt throughout the club that the Board of Directors had been unable to keep him in order to try to continue this success was immense. Just as things were really on the up- only Everton could do this, or so we felt, as many of our older supporters recalled how the 1970 championship winning team, which ofcourse featured Howard as a player, was allowed to break up so quickly.

Like the true gentleman that Howard was, he invited all the staff up to the boardroom during their lunch break for a champagne lunch but the event was tinged with sadness, as many of us realised that this was the end of an era, the likes of which we would probably never see again. He said his farewells and thanked everybody for their efforts but Everton Football Club would never be the same again.

Although disappointed at the board's inability to keep Howard, full credit should still go to Philip Carter, the then chairman, for giving the proverbial "vote of confidence" in Howard's managerial ability and meaning it, sticking with the manager, when many in the press and amongst our own supporters, would have sent for the taxi for him. The taxi story relating to how, in the past, John Moores, the then chairman, had sacked Johnny Carey, a previous manager, during a taxi ride, thus creating the myth of sacking a manager by calling for a taxi and which, during Howard's earlier days, had seen a broken down old taxi left outside the Goodison Park entrance with a large note left on it, stating that it was hired out for Howard- how he had made those critics eat their words!

Credit should go to Howard and his staff, Colin Harvey, Mick Heaton, reserve team coach, Terry Darracott, youth coach, Graham Smith, physiotherapist, John Clinkard, youth development officer, Ray Minshull and chief scout, Harry Cooke, all deserving a special mention and ofcourse, the wonderful set of players that he assembled for the club over that three year period, from the F.A.Cup win in May 1984 to the second championship title collected in May 1987. Their success had resulted in a hectic time for us in the box office, which had seen our staffing levels grow to nearly having a team of our own, a good one, which the club and its fans deserved.

Only Howard and the chairman will ever know his real reasons for going but I have no doubt that the ban enforced after Hysel on all English clubs was probably a major factor, as it later resulted in two of Howard's team, Trevor Steven and Gary Stevens, both regular members of the England team, leaving the club at the peak of their career, to try their luck with clubs that were still allowed to play in Europe. So, it was only natural to believe that the feeling of being exempt from playing in Europe was to influence the dressing room and who more so than the boss, who still only forty or so at the time, had years on his side to prove himself, not just the best in England but in Europe. Unfortunately, that opportunity was no longer available at Everton but perhaps he could have chosen to go to a more fashionable club than Athletico Bilbao, having become the best English manager on the scene.

Everton were never really to recover from that ban, losing the revenue from two European Cup runs, a Cup Winners Cup and a UEFA cup run over the next few years and also ofcourse, the prestige that it brought.

The 1987/88 season saw the popular Colin Harvey appointed as manager to replace Howard Kendall, as Everton attempted to copy the philosophy that had been used so successfully by Liverpool of appointing from within the club, just as the Reds had done with Bob Paisley, Joe Fagan and Kenny Dalglish to name just a few.

Colin, a true Evertonian, had, like Howard, been a member of the 1970 Championship team, before working through the coaching ranks to become first team coach at the end of 1984, a promotion which resulted in the upsurge in form of the first team to their present heights. Therefore, he was quite rightly the obvious and popular choice of all concerned, directors, players, staff and supporters, who we all hoped would succeed in following the hard act that Howard had achieved. Well respected, likeable, honest and a stickler for hard work were characteristics that probably described Colin best of all.

Colin immediately brought in two Evertonians to support him in Terry Darracott and Mick Lyons. However, it was only Colin's opening game, the annual pilgrimage to Wembley Stadium for the Charity Shield, this time against Coventry City, that was to bring him his one and only trophy to Goodison Park, courtesy of a Wayne Clarke goal. After the Charity Shield success, the spirits of the fans and those of us in the club had been lifted by the success of the team in picking up that early season trophy and we all began to hope that the club could continue with the success that Howard had brought it, under his able lieutenant, Colin Harvey.

Colin was soon to stamp his mark on the club, when he broke the club's record transfer fee, by paying out a fee of two million pounds for Tony Cottee, a prolific goalscorer with West Ham United. However, despite Tony making a dream start by scoring a hat-trick in his first game at home to Newcastle United, in a convincing four goals to nil win, on the opening day of the season, he failed to make a real impression in that first season. Other big signings, such as Stuart McCall, a midfield player, from Bradford City, whom I had watched as an outstanding teenager play for Bradford at Telford in a F.A.Cup tie two years previously, Neil McDonald, a full back from Newcastle and Pat Nevin, a top class winger from Chelsea, had also been bought to add to the strength of the squad.

Wins over Liverpool and Manchester City set up a two legged semi final in the League Cup against Arsenal and with Sheffield Wednesday and Middlesbrough both beaten in the F.A.Cup, this had paired us with Liverpool in the fifth round, the tie to be played at Goodison Park.

Success in the League, however, looked distinctly remote as Liverpool looked to be moving towards the title.

Unfortunately, the season fell apart for Colin, when we lost all three of those crucial ties and petered out in front of only 22445 for the final game of the season at home to Arsenal.

Everton had finished in fourth position, very creditable in today's standard, but not acceptable in those days to supporters that had been fed on the success of the last three seasons. As a result of this downward trend in results, coupled with the fact that it had been Liverpool who had won the Championship and with the recession in Merseyside continuing, it was not surprising that season ticket sales that close season showed a downward trend. For the first time in four years, we were not involved in the Charity Shield. It began therefore to hit us all at Goodison - had the bubble burst, or was it just a blip?

The 1988/89 season was to be my last at Goodison Park. The old team had started to break up as Gary Stevens, Adrian Heath, Derek Mountfield, Alan Harper and Peter Reid were to move on .

The season, by Everton's previously high standards, started disastrously, as only one league win was acquired in the months of September and October, during which time, the club were dumped out of the League Cup, quite unceremoniously, by lowly Bradford City at the Valley Parade.

It was now becoming quite apparent that the bubble was bursting quickly. Although the ability in the team that season enabled us to be in with a shout in the cup competitions, the necessary quality for a continued push for the Championship was missing.

It was   on 18th February 1989, that I ended my twelve year association with Everton Football Club.

My lasting memories of the club were, ofcourse, the successful times on the field from 1984-87 but most of all, the marvellous staff that I had in the box office during those days.

The staff, all part time, with the exception of Dot Williams, whose husband, Eddie, ironically, was a devout Liverpudlian and possessed a season ticket for the Kop. However, over that four year spell, their hours were often longer than full time employees in other walks of life.

Our team, just like the one on the field, was the best around and comprised of several members of the same family, all with a common bond, a true love of Everton Football Club. Dot Ward, who had vacated her position in charge of the ticket office when she became pregnant, had returned after the birth of her son, Christopher, also had her mother, Eileen Vivyan, working for us. Tina Storey, who was married to Alan, our head groundsman, and whose father-in-law, Ted, had also been head groundsman before his retirement, had in their family over seventy plus years of service at the club. Our assistant secretary, Barry Forsyth's wife, Mary, also worked in the box office, as did Elsie, the daughter of our commissionaire, Jack Gibson, whose link with the club went back forty years, as did Harry Bateman, who, shortly after the Second World War ended in 1945, rejoined his accountancy firm, where he was club auditor until his retirement in 1977, when I persuaded him to work part time for us in the ticket office.

So, one could see tradition everywhere in our staff and with it went loyalty and honesty.

Other members of our staff, such as Maureen Hawksey, had been at Everton before I arrived and had looked after ` the ship' between Dot finishing and my arrival, along with Christine Kelly. Then there were Arthur

Adams and Tommy Garnett, two retired gentleman, who for many years had been tried and trusted turnstile operators on matchdays, who doubled up in the week, by working part time in the ticket office. Infact, the only one to join our staff since my arrival twelve years previously, was the eighteen year old niece of Dot Williams, Janice deGeir. That staff remained throughout my twelve years at the club and several of them still remain at Goodison today.

A box office manager, like any other manager, is only as good as his staff and they were the best. They had been put to the test over that hectic three year spell, between 1984 and 1986, in which we equalled the record number of consecutive appearances by a club for the F.A.Cup Final in the twentieth century, only being equalled by Arsenal in the seventies.

The bitterest disappointment to me came in 1987, after our second Championship win. For the first success in 1985, all the staff at Goodison Park had received a financial bonus, being based on their personal wage. However, the second time around, the Board of Directors decided regretfully that only heads of departments, such as myself, would receive this bonus. I must admit that this really did disappoint me and resulted in my losing a lot of affection for the club. Probably the staff were not as upset as me about it but I really felt that the club had shown a lack of appreciation by that act. For me, from that moment on, things were never to be the same again. I know that several members of my staff knew how disappointed I was with the club's apparent lack of gratitude towards them with regard to this bonus payment. However, nobody could ever envisage how much, over the next eighteen months, it would eat away at me, resulting in uprooting myself and leaving a club, I had for so long, twelve years in fact, been regarded as part of the furniture- but that was exactly what was to happen.

Despite all those fabulous times, by the winter of 1988, I was determined to leave Everton, realising that I must start to look elsewhere for motivation.

In late November of that year, an advertisement had appeared in the national press asking for applications for the vacant position of club secretary of Blackpool Football Club. I therefore decided to contact the present secretary of the club, David Johnson, whom I had known from my days as club secretary of Crewe Alexandra during which, David had held a similar position with Tranmere Rovers, in order to find out more. David had decided to move on and advised me to send in my application, which I duly did and I was selected to attend an interview in early December.

The interview with the board of directors was held in the absence of the chairman, Owen Oyston, and went well and along with two other candidates, I was invited to attend a second interview. We were informed that on the three of us meeting Mr Oyston, in the presence of his fellow directors, a final decision would be made.

At this meeting, I was asked by the director conducting the interviews to give, for Mr Oyston's sake, a brief description of my career to date and the reasons why I felt that I could do a good job at Blackpool Football Club, if I was to be chosen as club secretary.

No sooner as I had started to talk when, to my surprise, Mr Oyston stood up and began to walk to the coat stand to take his coat off. I was taken aback by his actions and disgusted by his rudeness and apparent lack of interest in what I had got to say. I left that interview very angry and, needless to say, the interview talk did not come over as well as I had hoped. Infact, throughout my talk, I had considered the possibility of informing Mr Oyston of my opinion towards his behaviour and storming out of the interview in mid stream. I had decided against this, however, because all the way through that interview, I kept thinking and trying to convince myself how much I wanted the job.

I was asked at the end of the interview to wait whilst the directors, or rather Mr Oyston, pondered on the appointment.

One of the other two applicants attending that afternoon, Dave Capper, I knew as the assistant secretary of Stoke City Football Club. At the end of the afternoon, we were summoned into the room individually, where I received the expected news from the apologetic director who had conducted the interview, whom I am sure felt for me after my ordeal with the rude Owen Oyston. David had travelled by car from his home in Stoke to the interview and offered me a lift home, which I gratefully accepted, during which, he informed me that he had been offered the job but expressed doubts about whether to accept. Perhaps, he too, had been surprised by Oyston's antics. He told me that he would telephone me next day to inform me of his decision, just in case, I was still in the hunt. True to his word, David did ring me to tell me that he had decided against taking up their offer and would be remaining at Stoke City. The board did not, however, come back to me but re-advertised some weeks later, with a curt note asking for those who had previously applied, not to apply again- not that I would, one meeting with Owen Oyston was enough- two!

The second opportunity arose for me courtesy of Roger Reade, who had by now moved on from being secretary of Doncaster Rovers to working as chief administrator to the Professional Footballers Association in Manchester.

Roger had known of my disillusionment with Everton and a job had come available for the position of regional administrator to the Community Programme in Professional Football.

The interview took place at the PFA Headquarters in Oxford Court, Manchester and was conducted along with Roger by Brendan Batson, the chairman of the Professional Footballers Association and its secretary, Gordon Taylor.

The interview went as well as I could have hoped but, as Roger explained in his letter, I had been unsuccessful, `having been thrown in at the deep end, my experiences in work of that type being far less than some of the ex players who had worked in the system' and they were also applying, ofcourse, as existing members of the PFA.

Third time lucky, however, as far as interviews go, when, as a result of another advertisement in the national press, I answered an advertisement placed by Leeds United Football Club, who were looking to appoint a box office manager.

At the time, Leeds United were languishing in mid table of the Second Division but were still playing infront of gates of over twenty thousand which, when compared to the gate on the final day of the season in which Everton had finished in fourth place of just over twenty two thousand for the visit of Arsenal, showed the vaste potential that a successful Leeds United had.

I therefore decided to apply and was invited down to Elland Road for an interview on 2nd February 1989, being interviewed by the club secretary, David Dowse, administration manager, Alan Roberts and the club's chief executive/director, Bill Fotherby.

I was offered the job that afternoon, at a salary of twelve thousand pounds a year, some two thousand pounds more than I was earning at Everton, who were some thirty places above Leeds United in the Football League. I immediately accepted their offer and we agreed a starting date of Monday 27th February 1989.

The next morning, I went into see our chief executive at Everton, Jim Greenwood, to hand in my notice, thus terminating an association with the club that had lasted close to twelve seasons, during which time, I was very honoured to be at the great club's Centenary celebration dinner and was also fortunate to be at the hub of the most successful period in the Club's long history, those glory years of the mid eighties during which, under Howard Kendall, so much silverware had ended up in the Goodison Road boardroom.

As well as the highs and lows on the football pitch, the twelve years at Goodison Park had also had its embarrassing moments .The first of these occurred when our underground heating system was given its first real test for a League Cup tie against high flying Ipswich Town, managed at the time by Bobby Robson. Overnight snow had left the pitch with a covering of some three inches or so but the experts had told us that this would not be a problem and that the snow would have cleared by kick off time that evening to give a good playing surface. We had been advising all and sundry of this fact, including hundreds of Ipswich supporters making the five hundred or so round trip to Merseyside. Imagine our embarrassment, when just three hours before the scheduled kick off time, the match referee inspected the pitch, only to find it still covered deep in snow and unplayable. Game postponed and hundreds of irate Ipswich supporters to apologise to- what a night!

The second potential embarrassment occurred shortly after we had moved away from GMS Computing Services, who did our match tickets, to install our own ticket computing system. On its first game, the system crashed for several minutes and it was only the skill of the experts, who had been sent down to oversee the first game, which saved us from the acute embarrassment of having to suspend ticket sales.

My time at Goodison Park had also given me the opportunity to meet my boyhood hero, the legendary Liverpool manager, Bill Shankly, who, after finishing at Anfield, made several excursions to Goodison to attend matches, which on most occasions, usually meant Bill recalling a footballing story in order to collect his tickets. The passion with which he could tell those stories left me in admiration of the great man..

Before closing the chapter on Everton Football Club, it would be amiss not to mention some of the marvellous Evertonians that I got to know who lived in the Crewe area and travelled the eighty or so mile round trip to every home game to Goodison Park to watch their beloved team and were more than willing to help me in any way that they could. People like Bob McClintock, who worked, as my father did at the end of his working life, at Rolls Royce Motors and Griff Jones, who was manager of the local Menzies bookstore at Crewe Railway Station, both of whom, were extra kind in regularly taking me into Liverpool on a Sunday morning by car, when the train service was totally inadequate, which allowed me to be able to sell tickets on that day for many of the big games that we had to sell for. To Les Linnell, Alan Buckley and Glyn Osborne, who shared a car with Griff and who, often at night games, waited patiently for me to finish my work, before travelling home with them, where the full journey was always spent discussing the merits or otherwise of the Everton performance . To David Oakes, probably the oldest Evertonian that I had known, whose ashes I arranged to be scattered on the Goodison Park pitch. To three lads who travelled the length and breadth of the country watching Everton, Dave Cattermole, Martin Smith and John Cliffe, who was affectionately known as, "Womble", their dedication to the Blues cause in those days knew no bounds, often going a whole season without missing a game. Just to prove how being an Evertonian goes through the family, Mark Jones, who I remember as a young fifteen year old going regularly to watch Everton by train, who now takes his two sons to the club's home games, although taking both together may prove rather expensive, such is the pity of today's pricing structures that they have to take it in turn to attend.

To all of those people, along with all the many wonderful people I either worked with or knew at Goodison Park, thanks for the memories that helped make my time at Everton so special.

My biggest disappointment, other than ofcourse the mistake of leaving Goodison, was that the team never in fact beat that record of consecutive F.A.Cup Final appearances in the twentieth century, only equalling it with three, the villains being Wimbledon, who defeated us on their Plough Lane Ground in the winter of 1987.

CHAPTER EIGHT: THE EVIL CALLED THE TICKET TOUT.

Throughout the eighties, Everton and Liverpool had dominated football in this country. In those days, the only unfortunate things that we suffered from were the ticket touts and in the later years, the ugly head of the football hooligan had, once again, started to reappear.

Fortunately, because of excellent segregation at Goodison Park and virtually full houses at Anfield, the problem of the football hooligan in Merseyside was not so noticeable. At Goodison Park, we allocated the whole of the Park End Goal Stand, with a capacity of two thousand three hundred seats and four thousand terracing, to the visiting club, which on very nearly every occasion would suffice, ensuring that adequate policing and stewarding were also in place. Segregation worked well at Goodison Park and violence on the terracing was kept to an absolute minimum. At Anfield, virtual full houses ensured that because of being so vastly outnumbered, the few visiting supporters that could be allocated tickets would be very foolish to contemplate causing trouble.

Although the two grounds were generally trouble free, one could not give the same guarantee to the surrounding streets but this was an area that the two clubs could do little about. We were only held to be liable for the behaviour of the fans inside the ground and to that extent, both clubs had excellent records.

Success on the field, however, had brought with it the ticket tout, a person who basically exploits the economic rule of supply and demand for his own financial gain. When tickets for a particular game were in short supply, or sold out, the value of his supply would increase and make him his profit. All tickets for matches under Football Association regulations carried a condition of sale to state that they should not be resold for more than their face value. This gave the Football Association power against any offender. Unfortunately, clubs continued to ignore this condition because the recording of the sale of each ticket in order to identify any misuse was always considered to be too time consuming. Therefore, the only time that the Football Association insisted on the purchaser's name and address being recorded was when the club were playing in the F.A.Cup Final.

League games at Goodison Park rarely caused any problems with the touts. Very few games were ever sold out, the exceptions being the local "derby game" against Liverpool or perhaps for the visit of Manchester United. For the "derby" game, the local tout was always out in force, often profiteering from his fellow Liverpudlian. However, for semi finals and finals, the bigger and far greedier national touts were present.

I always regarded there as being two types of touts. The first, I would refer to as "Johnny Spiv", who was usually local and would get his hand on a bundle of say, twenty tickets, often complimentary or concessionary priced , usually issued to people as a privilege for work done for the club and who had no particular use of the ticket, would pass on or sell the ticket on to the tout, who would then attend the game and, even though there was often no shortage of tickets, he would sell on this ticket for a profit. The price that he obtained was often below the face value but because he had acquired it for nothing, or very little, he still made his neat little profit at the expense of the club, who would lose out on a full paying customer because they had acquired it below the going rate from our little spiv. This type of tout was present outside the ground at every game, his cheek even allowing him to have the audacity to stand in front of the box office to sell his goods, before we would become wise of his presence and have him moved on, only for him to return at the earliest opportunity. This type of tout was more of a nuisance than a threat, although it did cost the club a few thousand pounds over a season in gate receipts. It was just a pity that privileges were being abused by ungrateful people within the club but I am afraid that this happened at almost all football clubs.

The real threat however came from the bigger touts who would only be interested in games where there was a shortage of tickets and they could exploit the economic rule of supply and demand to their advantage. They would only be interested in large numbers of tickets for the games that were assured of being sold out and which had fans wanting tickets and willing to pay well over the face value in order to obtain them.

My first recollection of seeing this type of tout in action was during my spell at the Football Association when I attended the Arsenal versus Liverpool F.A.Cup final in the early seventies. On this occasion, touts selling tickets outside Wembley Stadium were set upon by Liverpool supporters and had their tickets taken off them and distributed amongst the many fans in need of tickets who had come down to the ground without a ticket. I will always remember how the Police that day ignored the events that were going on, allowing the tickets to fall into the hands of those deserving fans.

The spiv's techniques had certainly improved however, some fifteen or so years later, when I returned with Everton for our F.A.Cup final with Manchester United. The spivs around the stadium no longer had the tickets on them but took customers to a central point, where the transaction was carried out in safety.

Ticket touting affects all sports and it is therefore very obvious as to where the supply of tickets that the spiv can get his hands on to sell comes from. All sports have one body of people, the competitors, whom the organisers have to look after. For many years, it was regarded as a perk of the job, with the old excuse that their careers were only short and that they had this right to look after their futures in whatever way they could, even if it meant allowing the touts a good living out of their privilege of an allocation of tickets for a big sporting event.

The Football Association, in the eighties, had strict guidelines regarding the maximum number of tickets that could be allocated to any one individual. This maximum was set at thirty, whether it be chairman, manager, club secretary or star player. Allocations of tickets would then be reduced accordingly throughout the club. That figure was very realistically arrived at, being based on estimated demands made by family and close friends and if that maximum figure could have been kept to, it would have meant very few tickets finding their way into the greedy hands of the touts. The figure of thirty was still more than generous, as I could count on one hand the number of times that a player or official had purchased more than that number for a normal game. I know and appreciate that for a big game, such as a F.A.Cup Final, how long lost relatives suddenly appear out of the blue but most members of staff in the club knew that they had no alternative but to be unable to supply and the same philosophy had to apply throughout the club.

However, greed and fear that players would under perform in big games, often led to clubs not adhering to the rule on the maximum allocation. It therefore became common knowledge inside the game that the allocation of tickets for first team players was several times greater than the maximum permitted. This would therefore allow a vaste number of tickets to be available to the touts.

Players greed had always tried to be justified by claiming that their careers were short and that they had to maximise their earnings at every possible opportunity. Against this theory, however, is the fact that I know of a great number of players who, having finished playing , have gone on to earn an excellent living and have never, in fact, come across any footballer, who, having finished playing, has not been capable of earning a living in another occupation.

The blame for this abuse of the privilege that staff had regarding ticket allocations must, in my opinion, be placed firmly on the shoulders of the Football Association, who were so ineffective in their checks on the methods of competing clubs distributing their ticket allocations. Their regulations stated that every ticket sold had to have recorded against it the purchaser's name and address. These records then had to be kept for investigation, if necessary, by the Football Association for a length of time after the game, or sent, as in the case of allocations to staff, players and directors to the Football Association headquarters prior to the game, so that if a ticket had been reported to the Football Association as having been purchased on the black market, an immediate check could be made regarding whether it had come from one of these allocations. This forwarding of a list of where allocated tickets had gone ensured that clubs would be unable to tamper with records in order to ensure that important members of the club could avoid disciplinary action. Over the years, a number of senior club officials had received bans on ticket allocations as a result of having one of their allocation of tickets reported as being purchased from a tout.

The remaining balance of tickets, totalling all but a thousand of the club's allocation, were therefore never audited by the football authorities and ofcourse, this was where the additional allocations would come from, finding their way into the hands of the touts, all under false names and addresses.

It was at this point that I believe that the Football Association were negligent in their duty. Throughout my time in football, which included those three consecutive F.A.Cup Finals, the Football Association never asked for a breakdown of how the allocation of tickets were to be distributed. If they had and had taken the trouble to travel down to the two competing clubs to check the figures, which quite easily could have been done within a day, the loophole that existed for the distribution of tickets to outside sources would have been blocked. I am sure that everybody in football knew that this was the simple solution to a problem that nobody really seemed to want to tackle.

Instead, the Football Association only took action if a ticket was reported to them as having been purchased on the "black market", in which case they would contact the offending club regarding that ticket and take action against the culprit. This, ofcourse, was the easiest option for the football authorities, who should shoulder much of the blame for not detecting the source of the tickets and ensuring stricter control of ticket distribution.

To safeguard the club against the abuse of selling tickets at an enhanced price, all clubs competing in finals ensured that persons receiving a ticket from an allocation did so, by signing a written understanding that the ticket was for personal use and would not be resold. This therefore ensured that it would be the individual, rather than the football club, who would be held responsible for any irregularity if the ticket had been reported as being sold on the 'black market' and this in turn would mean that any ban received would be against an individual, rather than the club, which would have been disastrous in the event of the club getting into any future finals.

The pleasing outcome to all of this was that, in three consecutive F.A.Cup finals at Everton, involving first of all Watford, then Manchester United, who were such a powerful drawing power and finally, Liverpool, in a game that the whole of Merseyside wanted to watch, not one ticket was reported to me as box office manager by the Football Association as having been bought at an enhanced price, a fact that everybody at Everton Football Club should be proud of.

Further blame should also be placed on the shoulders of the Football Association for the derisory allocation of tickets to the two competing clubs. Originally, back in the fifties and sixties, allocations to the two finalists had only totalled twelve and a half thousand each, out of a Wembley capacity of one hundred thousand. This had, however, because of adverse publicity in the national media, been nearly doubled by the time that we had reached those three consecutive finals in the mid eighties but with our home gates averaging thirty thousand, was still short of the tickets that we could sell, leaving real fans without the possibility of getting tickets from the correct source - the club that they supported. The problem for our two opponents, Manchester United and Liverpool, was even worse, as their average attendances were far closer to fifty thousand.

In the eighties, to keep football trouble on the terraces in check, great emphasis had been placed by the Police, with full support from the Football Association, on segregation between rival fans, a policy that hitherto, in the fifties and sixties, had not really existed, when the allocations to the two competing clubs had been so derisory. By its allocation policies, the Football Association was making segregation between rivals fans virtually impossible because half of the tickets being sold for the final, were not being done by the two competing clubs and so supporters would be mixed. Fortunately, the old style sportsmanship still existed in finals, as supporters just wanted to enjoy the day and were not looking to cause trouble.

Ticket allocations, as governed by the football authorities, were to be held, in my opinion, responsible for two of the greatest disasters ever to hit the British game, resulting in the deaths of so many innocent fans at Hysell and Hillsborough.

In both cases, allocations to our rivals across the park at Liverpool Football Club were totally inadequate to meet the demand, resulting in fans either travelling to the game and purchasing tickets from incorrect sources, or being unsuccessful and then gaining entry to a section of the ground already full to capacity. In both cases, innocent people suffered because of the inflexibility of the football authorities to bring their allocation system up to the required standard to meet the demands of the two clubs. In those days, nobody could ever make sense of a ticket allocation that gave Liverpool the same allocation of tickets as Forest, when support for the Anfield club was double that of Forest. Trying to be fair in order to ensure equal support for both teams could be justified but it could never be achieved when so many tickets were not even allocated to the two competing clubs.

The Football Association were in those days, as they always have been, the best ally the touts have ever had. It was their policies that enabled a breed of people whose greed knew no bounds, certainly caring little for segregation or the safety of fans, to prosper at the expense of so many innocent lives. The Football Association were always to remain aloof from the problems, always looking to put the blame of touts onto the two competing clubs, instead of being strong enough at its council meetings to arrive at the conclusion that ticket allocations had to be more in line with the two competing club's fan base at the expense of the non competing club's and County F.A's allocations. The football authorities had the real opportunity to eradicate the problems that occurred at Hillsborough. They failed because self interest was always given preference to the good of the game and the real fan.

At Everton, the 1984 F.A.Cup Final against Watford had caused very few problems regarding tickets but all this was soon to change the following year with our final against Manchester United. The problem with playing Manchester United in a final, where tickets were at a premium, lay in the fact that Manchester United had such a large fan base, many of whom were unable to obtain tickets from Old Trafford due to the miserly allocation of tickets, which totalled less than half of their average home gate. The pressure was therefore on everybody at the club having an allocation of tickets, as friends of their families put pressure on them for tickets, brought about more by people who supported United than Everton. That was just how big United were at the time and that was without them winning the Championship for close on twenty years. There is no in between with regard to Manchester United, fans either love or hate them but for the touts they were mega profit, always were and always will be.

The first problem that occurred for us with our allocation of tickets for that Manchester United final lay in the fact that, in those days, Wembley Stadium was not all seated. Thus, our allocation of tickets comprised of both seats and terracing tickets. Unfortunately, and I know that this was an even bigger problem with United, who had a far greater number of season ticket holders than ourselves, our majority of season ticket holders, some eighty per cent, were seat season ticket holders, many of whom, because of the allocations made out by the Football Association to the two competing clubs, were unable to be offered a seat ticket. Only being able to offer seat season ticket holders of the two competing clubs a standing ticket was yet another example of the way that the football authorities failed to look after the interests of the fans!

Over twenty per cent, some two thousand in total of our seat season ticket holders, many of whom were elderly and really struggled to stand for any length of time, were unable to be offered seat tickets for the biggest game that their club could play in. The system of choosing the lucky ones to have a seat ticket had to be done on selecting serial numbers, as no other method could have possibly been devised in such a short period of time. It always left a nasty taste in my mouth when I heard of people that had received a seat ticket for our Cup Final through an outside source within the Football Association allocation system, whilst many of our elderly season ticket holders, who struggled to stand and had seat season tickets at Everton, were forced to endure to stand at a game featuring their club.

Segregation at the F.A.Cup Final against Manchester United was almost non existent. Areas designated for our supporters, due to the allocation system, saw numerous United followers in those areas, having received their tickets from the allocations made by the Football Association to its various bodies. Fortunately, on the big day, sense prevailed amongst the fans, as they aimed solely to enjoy a trouble free day, no thanks due to the ticket allocations from the governing body.

The lengths that the touts would go to in order to obtain their tickets for the Manchester United final were soon brought home to me.

We had been working late during the selling period leading up to the game and with daylight still present one particular evening, I left the Goodison Road box office to walk down a small side street which led on to the main, Scotland Road, where I was eventually to catch a bus that took me back to Lime Street Railway Station, from where, I caught my train back home to Crewe. I did all of this without noticing anything untoward, when suddenly, just as I was about to open the front gate at home, there was a tap on my shoulder. Looking behind me, I saw a large gentleman, who was waving a bundle of ten pound notes in front of my face and proclaiming that he knew who I was and that if I could supply him with two hundred seat tickets for the Cup Final, he would give me four times the face value in cash, so that I could just replace the tickets with the cash and nobody would be any the wiser. Two hundred tickets at twenty pounds each, being the top price, would have given me a profit of twelve thousand pounds, in a year in which my annual gross salary at Everton was ten thousand pounds.

I can honestly claim that I was never tempted by the offer but what did worry me was the fact that he had managed to stalk me over a hundred or so yard walk from the ground to the bus stop, a bus journey to Lime Street, the train journey home and finally the mile long walk from Crewe Railway Station to my home, without my noticing him and that he now knew my home address and that if he was prepared to go to those limits with myself, what level would he go to in order to pester my staff, who all lived locally and had access to those same tickets, for which he was willing to pay so handsomely. On him taping me on the shoulder, I did react quickly enough to ask him for a telephone number in which I could contact him and pretended that I would give him his answer then, knowing only too well that I had no intention of accepting but at least, if this number was correct, I could at least get him of our backs. Unfortunately, he was too wise for that and just stated that he would contact me again in the very near future.

The next morning, I went to see our chief executive, Jim Greenwood, to tell him of my experience the previous evening. We immediately put into operation a system to carefully control the tickets by ensuring that every ticket sold had a valid voucher to accompany it. This would ensure against any temptation being placed on our members of staff, although it would greatly increase the workload by having to balance tickets sold to vouchers, which would now be done independently. It was well worth it in order to ensure that all the tickets earmarked for the true fans were safeguarded. It was agreed never to mention the stalker incident to the staff, as being mainly women, we did not want to worry them unduly but I did reiterate the temptations that could be offered and to report anything untoward. The staff that we had were of the highest quality - dedicated, honest and capable and I knew that there was no reason to worry but that stalker incident just went to prove the levels that the touts would go to in order to obtain tickets.

Incidentally, he did come back for a reply but was given short change and told in no uncertain terms where to get off.

On the funnier side, if that is possible, are two stories that went around in football. The first concerned the goalkeeper of a First Division team, who had travelled down to London with the tickets that were to be handed over to the touts, only for him to have them allegedly stolen out of his car. The Police, ofcourse, were not called because of the embarrassment of what had gone missing and where they were at the time - many miles away from his club's ground.

The second story, concerned a young gullible player who had placed his whole allocation of tickets into the `pot' for distribution to the spivs, forgetting even to keep some tickets back for his family, thinking that these would be given to him separately. The rest of his team mates, rather unsympathetically, allowed him to do this, knowing that they would reap the financial benefits of his mistake. It was only when he approached the day of the game and summoned up the courage of asking his club secretary, that he was told that he had already received his full allocation of tickets. Feeling sorry for the lad at his stupidity, the staff had a collection in order that at least a few of his family could watch him in the Cup Final but not as many as he would have liked and he had some explaining to do to those who missed out.

One example of ticket touting that did cause me some embarrassment occurred at one of our `sell out' games at Goodison, when I overheard, in the corridors leading to the player's entrance, one of our opponents, an established international, saying to a chap, whilst brandishing a handful of tickets that, ` he wanted his holiday money out of the sale of the tickets'. Without being able to see the tickets, I immediately came to the conclusion that they were tickets for that days' game. In anger, I went up the stairs to the boardroom to seek out his club secretary to report what I had just heard and seen. This I did and to that club secretary's credit, he did have the decency to phone me back a few days later, to tell me that the player openly admitted that he was looking to make money on tickets but that the tickets were nothing to do with the game against Everton that day but a forthcoming fixture that he was to be playing in, which already was a guaranteed sell out, with tickets going on the "black market" at many times their face value.

Touting was an evil in the game but it had been allowed to grow by the outdated, selfish policies of the Football Association. Policies that were dangerous and were to lead to innocent fans dying at Hillsborough, when proper ticket distribution of allocations more in line with the average attendances at Liverpool and Nottingham Forest, would probably have averted the disaster.

CHAPTER NINE: LOCAL FOOTBALL AT CREWE YOUTH CENTRE AS A MANAGER- THEN TO ROLLS ROYCE.

During my time at Crewe Alexandra and Everton, I had become involved at the local youth centre in Mirion Street, just a few hundred yards or so away from my home in Earle Street.

The connection with the local youth centre came about as a result of my father working at Rolls Royce Motors and meeting Norman Lyon, who was also a part time youth leader at the centre. Norman, along with another colleague, Peter Scarratt, was keen to re-introduce a football team into the centre, after it had allowed its football teams to disappear a few years previously.

The set up at the youth centre was ideal for football, having two full sized pitches just behind its main building on a piece of land which the locals referred to as the `Raza'. In addition to this, a small floodlit court existed which could be used for training purposes, along with a good sized indoor hall. This little floodlit hardcourt pitch made the centre's facilities excellent, as in those days, astroturf pitches were still a thing of the future.

The first Crewe Youth Centre team was set up at the start of the 1976/77 season in the Crewe and District Regional Sunday Football League. However, my involvement was not to commence for a further twelve months, as my position as club secretary of the town's Football League club made it imperative, I felt, to remain neutral as far as the local footballing scene was concerned. I still, however, continued to support football at the centre, wherever possible, giving as much encouragement as possible to the venture, as I knew that Crewe Alexandra could reap the benefits from the centre's football, as they were committed to playing young players, who I felt that we could tap into for the benefit of all concerned.

In that first team at the centre, there were two players who would go on to play professionally in the Football League. Kevin Rafferty, a young fifteen year old goalkeeper from Sandbach, who was to go on to play twenty plus games for Crewe Alexandra in the Football League and Colin Chesters, a striker, who was to play a number of games in the First Division with Derby County, before moving to Crewe Alexandra, where he figured regularly in their first team as a centre forward but once, actually started a Football League game in goal for the club and in doing so, became the first and only outfield player ever to have to start a League game in goal for Crewe Alexandra. Colin, after finishing at Gresty Road, went on to play for Northwich Victoria in two F.A.Trophy finals at Wembley Stadium, where he played against two other local lads from the same era, Paul Mayman of Telford United and his own cousin, Kevin Westwood, with Bangor City, who, incidentally, also played regularly in that first ever

Crewe Youth Centre team.

With the youth centre fielding a young team, average age of nineteen, it was only natural that a number of them, with my connections at Gresty Road, were to start to feature prominently with the reserve team at Crewe Alexandra. Players such as defenders Roy Sheen, Duncan Davenport and Paul Young were all drafted into the reserve team, where they acquitted themselves well but without being able to break into the first team squad.

The team finished a very commendable mid table in the Second Division in that first season and were also runners up in the Divisional Cup.

At the start of the 1977-78 season, following my move away from Gresty Road to join the ranks of Everton Football Club in the October, I was able to give more of my time and effort in assisting with football at the centre.

It was at the start of that season that we signed Jimmy Quinn, after Peter and myself had watched Jimmy give an outstanding display in playing for a team which featured our coach, Roy Broughton, in the Sandbach Knockout, at the end of the previous season.

It really was a pity that Crewe boss, Harry Gregg, did not admire Jimmy enough to bring him into the Gresty Road set up as I had pushed for, as the player was later to prove himself at the highest level by playing for Northern Ireland on numerous occasions, just around the time when Crewe were languishing in the Football League basement.

Jimmy was to stay at the youth centre for just one season, before moving on to play for fellow Sunday Regional League team, Hunters Lodge, under their coach, Tony Waddington, the son of the then Stoke City manager and Jimmy Pepper. Moves then followed to clubs, such as Whitchurch Alport, Congleton Town, Nantwich Town and Oswestry, where his impressive performances were to see him graduate to play for a host of leading clubs in the Football League and pick up all of those international caps.

The 1977-78 season saw the team win their first trophy by beating Horse Shoe in the Divisional Cup final and were also to finish as runners up in the Second Division to Gordon Haley's young Socialists team, with whom they were to have some epic games over the next few years as the two teams grew up together. Crewe Youth Centre's ability to run Socialists close was shown to be an outstanding achievement when Socialists picked up the Crewe F.A. Sunday Cup by beating Oddfellows, who had completely dominated the rival Cheshire and Border Counties Sunday Football League, in the final.

The youth centre were also to link two ex Traffic stalwarts, Graham Swallow and Roy Broughton, to form a coaching double that was without peer in the local area and which to me, now at Everton, put the flagging Gresty Road coaching scheme for youngsters into a shameful second place. Both Graham and Roy were Junior schoolteachers and had passed their F.A. coaching badges. Both had played at the top level in the amateur game and knew the local football scene inside out, something that was lacking at Gresty Road, where one or both should and would, if I had remained at the club, have been brought in, for in those days of very tight financial control, the reserve team at Gresty Road had to comprise virtually of all local players.

The 1978-79 season saw Crewe Youth Centre win their biggest trophy yet, when they beat Betley Black Horse, then managed by the old Stoke City goalkeeper of the fifties, Dennis Herod, after a replay in the Crewe F.A.Sunday Cup at Gresty Road, following up this with the Divisional Knockout, by beating League champions, Fox Vics, in the final.

The following season, we retained the Crewe Cup by defeating Willaston White Star on Gresty Road, then a regular venue for both the District Football Associations two major trophies, with the League being won by Roy Boffey's, Leopard.

The 1980/81 season was, I believe, the best ever for local football. Not only at the youth centre did we win our first ever League Championship, winning seventeen of the twenty two games played, we also won our League Cup by beating Parkside, who only the year before, had, under Joe Cotton, become the first team to win the Crewe Vase, open to all Sunday League teams in the area outside the top Division of their respective Leagues, an innovation for teams outside the top division to win a major local trophy that hitherto had not existed and was a real step in the right direction for local football. However, all that glory was nothing compared to the fact that, infront of a crowd of two thousand plus at their London Road ground, Nantwich Town, with at least four local lads, Ted Neale, Ted White, Kevin Everett and Kevin Westwood, had, by beating Hyde United, claimed for the first time, the Cheshire League title. Local football also in that season possessed in Neville Ashley, Don Shaw and John Lovatt, three Football League referees and in Dave Farrall and Peter Harding, two League linesmen, which meant that it was at an all time peak as far as match officials went. Unfortunately, however, not at Gresty Road, where the Alex, I am afraid, languished again around the re-election places, as they did in four out of the five seasons leading up to the appointment of Dario Gradi in the summer of 1983.

The 1981/82 season saw Crewe Youth Centre retain the Championship by winning seventeen of the twenty games played, whilst the cup competitions were dominated by Willaston White Star, who defeated us and Nantwich Boys Club in the Divisional and Crewe Cups respectively. A new team appeared for the first time at the centre, when Youth Centre Rovers had joined the existing Youth Centre Rangers and ourselves, to mean that three teams were now operating from the centre in the local Sunday Football Leagues. That season saw Rangers finishing third and Rovers ninth in their first season in the Third Division.

1982/83 season saw, what I believe to be, the highest number of teams that this area had ever seen operating in local Leagues. There were three divisions of twelve teams in the Regional Sunday League, three divisions- two of eleven and one of ten operating in the Cheshire and Border Counties Sunday League and two divisions of twelve and fourteen respectively in the newly formed Crewe and Nantwich Sunday League, making a total of ninety four clubs and over one thousand players playing football every Sunday in the area.

It was also at the start of the 1982/83 season that Norman Lyon decided that football at the centre was no longer representative of the age category of "youth". A team, which had been running for six years, had now aged so much that most of the players were well into their early twenties and in some cases, even older, and the name of Crewe Youth Centre was looking decidedly out of date. Norman therefore decided that an under seventeen team had to be formed to ensure that youngsters were catered for in football. With this in mind, he contacted Keith Timmins, who, for the last few years had managed the successful Crewe Royals team in the Lads and Dads local Junior Football League.

Crewe Royals had competed the previous season in the under fifteen League and the next step up had to be entry into the local Sandbach and District Youth League, which had an age limit of under seventeen. This meant that all players had to be under the age of seventeen at the start of the season, a date of the 1st August being chosen to comply with the school year. This would basically mean that the Royals would be coming to the youth centre and would be able to compete in this League for two seasons and in doing so, would become one of the younger teams in the League.

Keith readily agreed to this proposal of Norman's and his team arrived "en bloc" and with a few additions of youth club lads who expressed a desire to play, formed the basis of a new Crewe Youth Centre team.

I had always fought shy of taking an official capacity with a local football team because of my commitment within professional football. So when, in July 1982, Norman asked me if I would be the manager of the new team, with Keith to assist me, in order to ensure that it was not just Crewe Royals under a new name but was Crewe Youth Centre and open to all, it was a major step for me. Eventually, I agreed to commence my first and, as it turned out to be, last spell as a manager.

It was left to Keith, Norman and myself to gain us entry into the Sandbach Youth League- who, during my days as secretary of Crewe Alexandra, had made me a honorary life vice president. Entry to the League was therefore virtually guaranteed for the lads and so it was proved, gaining our admission at the League's Annual General meeting.

We were a comparatively young team, with an average age of fifteen, playing against lads a year older and as anybody who has been in this predicament will tell you, a year is a lot to concede in junior football and most teams who do, usually end up by struggling.

As manager, I decided that the only way that I could do the job was to adopt a professional attitude. Training sessions were set for every Wednesday evening for one hour and any player not attending, without an excellent reason, would not be picked for that weekend's game. In the build up to the season, training would also been held on a Sunday morning. This would culminate in a series of pre-season friendly games, after which, the squad for the season would be selected. The final part of our pre-season training was to be a short weekend tour over the late August Bank Holiday visiting and playing against teams from Glasgow, similar to two previous tours that I had arranged for Crewe Alexandra youth and a youth centre team a few years previously.

I therefore contacted my old friend from Glasgow Rangers Boys Club, Alex Roberts, who kindly arranged two friendly games for us against Possil YMCA and his own team, the first of the games to be played on the Saturday evening with the following game twenty four hours later, allowing us then to travel back on the Monday, after spending two evenings in a nice little hotel, The Burnside, just outside Glasgow.

The lads were taken for their training sessions by Roy Broughton and trained with the senior teams, which helped them to become physically stronger.

However, the Scottish tour was to be a rude awakening. After a strenuous pre-season, in which eight friendlies had been played during August, I was now sure of my squad. By fundraising and a small charge of five pounds per player, on Saturday 28th August 1982, we set out by mini bus, driven by Norman Lyon and accompanied by the youth club's chairman, Frank Baldwin, for our three day long weekend tour of Glasgow and those two games.

Possil YMCA, managed by Bob Dinnie, a close friend of Alex Roberts, were far too strong physically for us. On a red ash surface which, in those days because of a shortage of grass pitches, was very common in Glasgow, we were hammered to the tune of nine goals to one. Our lads had been beaten before the start on seeing the surface that they were having to play on. Nobody fancied it and the Scottish lads certainly made us pay. Players, whom I had thought had a future in the game, were to show a complete lack of heart for the physical game on that surface, as the speed, strength and desire of the Scottish lads made us look grossly inferior on the day.

Fortunately our second game, twenty four hours later, was to be played on grass. Mr Roberts had congratulated himself on obtaining such a surface- such was the rarity of grass pitches in the inner city and following on his comments, we came to the ground that day expecting to see a pitch like Wembley. However, when we turned up, we were confronted with probably the narrowest pitch that I had ever come across.

An area of a field had been converted into as many pitches as the minimum length and width of a football pitch would allow. The pitches were so close together that supporters found themselves literally on the touchline, such was the lack of space between each pitch, with players often overrunning onto the neighbouring pitch and ofcourse, the ball doing likewise. However, it was grass and more in keeping with what our lads were used to playing on. These facilities, or rather lack of them, really brought home to me the toughness that was required by lads from the inner city of Glasgow if they wanted to achieve anything in football. Even at that early age, their physical and mental attitude was far superior to that of our players, whose comfortable backgrounds made it harder for them to achieve success in sport. We were once again beaten heavily, this time to the tune of five goals to nil.

Back at the hotel after the game I was presented, quite unexpectantly, with a gift from the tour party for taking the trouble to organise the tour, which rounded of a weekend of mixed emotions but one from which I had learnt a lot.

The next day, Bank Holiday Monday, on what was the hottest day of the year, saw us travelling back to Crewe in a rather uncomfortable mini bus, tired but hopefully ready for the season.

Unfortunately, all our pre-season build up did not have the desired effect. Our first game had seen us paired with Red Rovers, who were managed by Howard Curran, later to become Lord Mayor of Crewe and somewhat of an expert in local history. I had known Howard from his days as manager of Traffic Football Club, during their successful period in the seventies, knowing only too well that any side he ran would be formidable - and so it proved. We lost that first game by the odd goal in five but were later to gain our revenge when the scoreline was reversed, which was to inflict on Red Rovers their only defeat in a season in which they acquired the League and Cup "double".

Confidence was soon restored, however, in the Staffordshire Youth Cup. Norman Lyon, who acted as our secretary, had somehow managed to gain us admission to this competition, despite ofcourse being based in Cheshire, who, unfortunately at that time, did not hold a similar competition. We had been drawn away at Cellarhead, where we came away with a convincing four goals to nil victory, courtesy of goals from Robert Morgans, whose father, Jeff, had been a professional footballer with Crewe Alexandra, Phil Lomas and two from Paul Jones, both of whom were to have spells in the Cheshire League with Nantwich Town, along with another player who played that day, Anthony Benfield. A further player in my team that day also had strong football connections. Our goalkeeper, Kevin Mailey, was the son of Willie, who I had watched and admired as probably the smallest but bravest goalkeeper I have ever seen when he was custodian at Crewe Alexandra in the sixties. A Scottish schoolboy international, Willie had joined the Alex from Everton. In the future, Kevin, then a highly promising keeper, was to join Bolton Wanderers but, after completing his apprentice professional contract, left the club to make a living outside football.

Our run in this competition was to end in the next round when, on a Sunday afternoon at Mirion Street, we were beaten by Richmond by four goals to two. In that game, we were not helped by the fact that two of our key players, Phil Lomas and Anthony Benfield, had played in an open age Sunday League game that morning, which had only ended eighty minutes before our scheduled kick off. Therefore, in what was a difficult game against good opposition, they understandably tired near the end and were unable to perform to their normal high standard.

I was fairly confident that the amount of ability I had seen in the League would allow for a representative team from within the League to be tested against Football League opposition. With his in mind, what better opposition than my own club, Everton?

I therefore arranged with our youth development officer, Ray Minshull, to bring a representative team down to the Everton training ground at Bellefield to play against his under fifteen team. In order to allow us to be an affiliated team, we played under the name of Crewe Youth Centre but incorporated several highly promising players from other teams. Our team was an under seventeen one and as such had a two year advantage over the Everton team, although at least half of our players were under sixteen and as such just a year older, with our goalkeeper, Kevin Mailey, being the same age as the Everton lads. The date of the game was fixed for 23rd December 1982 , after which, we had arranged for a short tour of Goodison Park and then a Christmas lunch in the Royal Blue Restaurant. Unfortunately, overnight snow forced the game to be cancelled and so instead, we arranged for a series of five a side games to be held on the astroturf indoor pitch.

In order to take advantage of the school holidays, the fixture was rearranged for the following week when, unfortunately, we went down to a five goals to one defeat, although three of those goals were to come in a five minute spell just before half time. We had also had to field a somewhat weakened side after it was found out that three of the players I had selected, Kevin Mailey, Paul Jones and Phil Lomas, had been invited to spend a week on trial at fellow First Division club, Stoke City.

In view of this, Ray and myself arranged for a third visit to Bellefield, which was fixed for Sunday 17th April 1983. To ensure that the lads felt the importance of the occasion, I had managed to hire the Everton first team coach and its driver, Jimmy, to take the lads from the youth centre to Bellefield, striking a good deal with the owner of Eavesway Coaches, Arthur Eaves. Two players, Nigel Oakes and Henry Flanagan from Sandbach Town were drafted into the side to replace Glen Kelly and Phil Edge from Red Rovers, who had been included in the side for the first game to strengthen our team. This had been done with the assistance of

Nigel Oakes' father, Colin, who at the time was manager of Sandbach Town and who has continued, over the last twenty years, to give sterling service in support of youth football in the area. Although, we lost the game by six goals to two, our goals coming from Paul Jones and Nigel Oakes, it was a very creditable performance against an Everton team that fielded two players who went on to become England youth internationals, one of whom, John Ebbrell, going on to make numerous appearances in the Everton first team, whilst the other, Neil Rimmer, went on two years later to represent England against Yugoslavia in a youth international.

The performance the team gave that day quite deservedly resulted in three lads, Kevin Mailey, whose father, Willie, whose attendance that Sunday at Bellefield, on the very same training ground that over twenty years previously he had started his professional football career, was so full of nostalgia, Neil Timmins, who was later to emigrate to Australia and become involved in the organisation of the Sydney Olympics and finally, Paul Jones, who was to end up playing a lot of local football, playing with teams such as Nantwich Town, were all invited back to play in games for Everton at the end of that season, although, I am afraid nothing materialised from those invitations.

In view of the relative success of staging those attractive friendly games, I decided to arrange one more before the end of the season, this time against Crewe Alexandra's youth team. The game was arranged for Wednesday 3rd May 1983 and, on an atrocious evening of weather at Dane Bank College, the same side, which just two weeks previously had played against Everton, played an enthralling game against the Crewe Alex youth team, just losing out by the odd goal in nine, our goals coming courtesy of a hat-trick from Colin Davies and one from his fellow striker, Andy Alcock.

My view had been vindicated that there was sufficient talent in the area, still unaffiliated to Football League clubs, to play at a higher level, given the chance. We had given Football League Clubs, at opposite ends of the scale, a testing.

It therefore came as no surprise to me that several of the lads went on to play in a good standard of non League football - Phil Lomas, Anthony Benfield and Paul Jones with Nantwich Town and John Timmins with Congleton Town, with Kevin Mailey going on to sign apprentice professional forms with Bolton Wanderers.

Other lads in the squad, such as Dominic Connolly, went on to make his mark in life by becoming a barrister in London, whilst other good club lads, such as Dave Watson and Stuart Cheetham, continued to play locally for a good number of years. Our regular full backs, Dave Stubbs, now a local postman, who I often see regularly on his round and Darren Gallimore, later became, I believe, the last manager of the Crewe and District senior schools team.

The young Crewe Youth Centre team competing in the Sandbach

Youth League finished a creditable third behind the older Red Rovers and Sandbach Town teams. Unfortunately, by strengthening the side by two players at the exclusion of a couple of our own players in order to play those prestigious games, I had upset the hierarchy at the youth centre, who decided that I should be replaced as manager by my assistant, Brian Cornes, who had, during that first season replaced Keith Timmins, who, because of work commitments, had struggled to be available for many of our games.

My viewpoint had always been that only by strengthening the side in order to play those games, could I be confident of those lads who played doing themselves justice and having the opportunity of a lifetime. Although nothing came of those games, I hope that those who took part will remember the experience even today, many years on.

I was offered the secretary position, which I admit that I was probably more suited to. Pride would not, however, allow me to accept and so I left with a certain degree of ill feeling.

The following season, with the withdrawal of the two older teams who had finished above us in the League, Red Rovers and Sandbach Town, the team, as I had expected, went on to win the League.

In the meanwhile, I was very shortly to revert back to being associated with the senior youth centre team who, in the summer of 1983, would be moving to Rolls Royce "en bloc" to become one of the most successful Sunday League sides that the area has ever known but who, that previous season, for the first time since their formation, had failed to win a trophy.

The first season under the Rolls Royce banner, saw us finish third in the League and start off with a trophy, by winning the Divisional Cup.

The following season was to see the team win all three knockout trophies, beating Weston White Lion by four goals to nil in the Crewe F.A.Sunday Cup and Willaston White Star in both the Divisional and League Cups. The League was won by Malpas, who have since switched to playing on a Saturday, by progressing to the Mid Cheshire League..

The 1985/86 season saw Rolls Royce finish as Champions, scoring twenty nine more goals than any other team, culminating in a phenomenal ninety eight goals in just twenty two League games. In addition to this, the team also retained the Crewe Cup by beating Wellcome by the single goal. The season also saw the emergence of teams such as Salvador, Willaston Villa, Faddiley and Wrenbury to join along with one of Crewe's oldest football clubs, Willaston White Star, where they still form the basis of today's Regional Sunday League.

For us, however, the real importance lay in the Cheshire Sunday Cup, which no team had ever won from the town. In April 1986, we had found ourselves pitted against a team from Altrincham, called Brooklands, in the semi-final at Congleton Town. Ironically, in our team that day were the very experienced Martin Scholes, who was assistant manager at

Congleton and his team mate at Booth Street and probably, one of the best midfield players I have ever come across in the local Sunday League, Graham Harrison. Unfortunately, despite an heroic effort, we went down by the odd goal in three.

At that time, however, Cheshire possessed in Avenue Football Club, from the Wirral, without doubt, the best team ever to play in the county on a regular Sunday basis. In the final, Avenue totally overwhelmed Brooklands, winning by three goals to nil and, for good measure, added the English F.A.Sunday Cup to their list of honours, by defeating Glen Sports by a single goal in the final. The Avenue team consisted of a number of players who played on a Saturday in the Alliance League, later to be known as the G.M.Vauxhall, which was, ofcourse, the highest standard of football outside the Football League. To prove their quality, they were to re-appear in the English F.A.Sunday Cup Final the following season but failed to retain the trophy, losing to Lodge Cottrell.

Try as we did over the following years to win that coveted trophy, we were to have no success but to have succeeded, especially with Avenue on the scene, would have been a phenomenal achievement.

The team played together for two more seasons under the management of Steve Bache, after Roy Broughton had decided to retire from the local football scene, winning the League in both of those seasons in order to achieve, what was then, a first hat-trick of title wins, from 1986-88 inclusive. This was later equalled by Malpas (1992-94) and more recently bettered by Bentley Motors, whose championship wins since 2000 has only been interrupted by a title success in 2003 by Willaston White Star.

However, the teams' three consecutive Crewe F.A.Sunday Cup triumphs, between 1985-1987, still remains unequalled in the forty years that the competition has been held.

In the fourteen years that the team had been together since starting as Crewe Youth Centre, under the managership of Peter Scarratt and Roy Broughton and finally, Steve Bache and Micky Hill, the team had won eighteen trophies, seven under the banner of the Youth Centre and the other eleven under the name of Rolls Royce, being both five times Champions and winners of the Crewe Sunday Cup, League Cup winners four times, Divisional Cup three times, with a Division Two Cup winners trophy thrown in for good measure during their early days. Real success locally but the big one, the coveted Cheshire Sunday Cup, remained outside both ours or indeed any other team from the area's grasp.

As the lads grew older, more and more decided to call it a day and stopped playing. A number of players, such as full backs, Roy Sheen and Duncan Davenport, defender Tony Lewis, strikers Neil Ridgeway, Neil Larvin and, although he joined from another youth centre team, Tony Hales, had formed the basis of the team throughout. They were supplemented for many years by the likes of utility player, Peter Beasley and for many years at Crewe Youth Centre by Robert Ryan, whose father, Vinny, had looked after the old Vine Rovers Saturday team, who had been one of the best local young sides to have graced the local Saturday football scene and featured so many lads, such as Ted Neale, Kenny Moulton, Mick Meachin and Rob Wheeler, who had progressed to play in the old Cheshire League. Many of these lads had also played under the managership of John Fleet at Crewe Ham United, who along with Traffic, had dominated the local Sunday football scene in the early seventies, with some epic battles being staged between these two giants in front of big crowds.

So many good players over the last forty years or so have passed through the local Sunday football scene. Back in the early days of the mid sixties, Sunday football, which had hitherto been banned by the Football Association for religious reasons, had been regarded as a poor substitute for the Saturday game. The Crewe and District League, which has a very proud history, was dominant up to the late sixties but by which time, players who featured in the Saturday League and also players who performed in a higher League, such as the Mid Cheshire or even the Cheshire League, were starting to play on a Sunday, at first in the Cheshire and Border Counties and then in the newly formed Crewe and District Regional Sunday Football League. This started to ensure that the Sunday football scene started to outstrip the Saturday game to such a point now that the number of players playing on a Sunday far outweighs the number of local players playing on a Saturday, although both now are worryingly starting to show signs of a reduction in numbers.

To try to collate all the best players that I had seen in the Regional League would in itself be enough to fill a book, especially with some of the tales that go with those characters.

I thoroughly enjoyed my time spent watching Crewe Youth Centre and then Rolls Royce each Sunday morning, even though at the time, I was often working so many hours extra at Goodison Park following Everton's tremendous success from the mid eighties onwards that, unfortunately, I had to miss some of the games. Despite this fact, I was always made to feel part of the set up and every season, to show their gratitude, a gift was always presented to me for my continued support, the value of which to me would be as high as any of my other souvenirs from the world of professional football which I treasure so much.

It is good to see, some twenty years on, two of our old Youth Centre players, Graham Harrison and goalkeeper, Dave Farmer, still performing for Willaston Villa/Peacock and Salvador respectively but more especially, for grass roots football throughout the country urgently requiring more referees, to see our old centre forward, Neil Ridgeway, who went on to play Cheshire League football with both Nantwich Town and Congleton Town, along with Dave Bloor, who played in goal with one of our other Crewe Youth Centre teams, putting something back into the game after they had finished playing by refereeing.

Football for me at that time really was a twenty four hour, seven days a week job but I enjoyed every minute of it, at both ends of the football scale.

CHAPTER TEN: LEEDS UNITED- AND AN END TO A CAREER IN FOOTBALL AND INTO BUSINESS.

Monday 27th February 1989 marked my first day at Elland Road, after close to twelve years as box office manager of Everton Football Club, during which time the club had their best ever period of sustained success in their one hundred year plus history, culminating in two Championship wins, a European Cup Winners trophy, a F.A. and F.A.Youth Cup triumph and finally, winning the Charity Shield on two occasions, all done during a four year spell. Leeds United, even under the great Don Revie, had failed to match that kind of success and although I realised that Leeds United were a sleeping giant and could achieve the top honours, to have equalled that kind of success was virtually out of the question.

From 19th June 1987, the day that Howard Kendall had been allowed to leave Goodison Park, Everton had started to show signs of decline. Although still in the top six, some thirty places above my new club in the League, I could sense that Leeds United were on the way up to where they belonged, the First Division.

Leeds, despite being in mid table of the old Second Division, which to their fans was mediocrity, were still the best supported team in the division, with an average gate of twenty three thousand, more than had watched the last home game of the previous season at Goodison Park when Everton had played Arsenal to finish in fourth place in the First Division.

I felt that if Everton had suffered the indifferent run that Leeds United had, gates at Goodison would have been far less, drawing on the fact that only 12872 had turned out for the Everton home fixture with Coventry, in a season which saw the club finish in a respectable seventh position in the League and had to ask myself what sort of gates would Everton have been receiving if they were in mid table of the Second Division?

Although wages were never a vital part of my decision to move from Goodison to Elland Road, I had been somewhat flattered by Leeds United's offer of two thousand pounds a year more than what I was getting at Everton. A further point that had influenced me at the interview at Elland Road was the superb way in which Messrs Fotherby, the managing director, Dowse, company secretary and Roberts, administration manager, had managed to portray the Elland Road club, so well in fact, that I agreed to join them that afternoon.

I started at Leeds United on Monday 27th February 1989 and two days later, on the Wednesday, we had a home fixture against local rivals, Bradford City, attended by a crowd of thirty three thousand, which quickly brought home to me the potential of a successful Leeds United, attracting a crowd far and away the best so far in the Second Division that season and bigger than any of the attendances up to that date at Goodison Park.

The result, a disappointing three each draw, only went to prove that Leeds United's problems lay firmly on the playing side.

Joining Leeds United had seen me renew acquaintances with Ian McFarlane, who had been assistant manager to Tony Book during my spell at Maine Road. Ian, popularly known as "The Big Man", was now chief scout at Leeds United.

On the field, the team's performances continued to be that of a mid table Second Division side, certainly not good enough for the support which the club were receiving from their devout fan base, being one of the best ten or so supported clubs in the country.

Just before the transfer deadline, at the end of March, Howard Wilkinson made three important signings, one of which to me was extra special, bringing the experienced Gordon Strachan to Elland Road from Manchester United. The other two, the signings of Carl Shutt and Chris Fairclough, would, along with Strachan, help him in the near future to take Leeds United back to their rightful place in the First Division.

Already at Elland Road was Gary Speed, a young midfield player, who was making real headway in the reserve team and established in the first team was a young David Batty, who was showing signs of becoming a top class midfield player. So, the basis was starting to take shape of a midfield quartet of Strachan, Batty, Gary McAllister, whom Howard was to very shortly sign and Speed, which would be the equal for Leeds United that the wonderful quartet of Steven, Reid, Bracewell and Sheedy had been for Everton in their Championship successes a few years earlier.

Another player that I was to get to know at Leeds United was Glyn Snodin, the elder brother of Ian, who was ofcourse at Everton. Glyn was to give good sterling service for the Elland Road club as a left back in those days and was, ofcourse, one of a rarity, brothers playing top class football in the same era.

However, Leeds United, not for the first or the last time, had got themselves into serious financial problems, by defying the old concept that Yorkshire people were very careful on how they spent their money. They had spent heavily in the transfer market, one major signing in particular, that of Peter Barnes, whom I had known well from his Manchester City days, had not really worked out and had therefore incurred a heavy debt with the bank.

In order to solve this problem, the club had taken the unprecedented step of selling their Elland Road ground back to the Leeds City Council. They in turn, rented it back to the football club but unfortunately, also hired out the ground to Hunslet Rugby League Club, so that every second Sunday or so, the Elland Road pitch was subjected to a game of Rugby League and suffered as a consequence, with only a handful of spectators present to compensate.

At the time of joining Leeds United in February 1989, I was fully aware of the football hooligan problem that the club were facing. Leeds United had become notorious for their band of away followers that were causing trouble in their travels to the smaller grounds that they were visiting since their relegation from the First Division.

At my interview, to the absolute credit of Messrs Fotherby, Dowse and Roberts, it was very obvious that the club were very committed to trying to resolve the problem and part of my job as box office manager was to administer the membership card system that the club had introduced with regards to selling tickets to those fans who wanted to support Leeds United on their away travels.

However, in an away game at Plymouth Argyle, on Sunday 9th April 1989, all was to take a turn for the worse. The game had been changed from a Saturday afternoon to a noon kick off on the Sunday, solely to ensure that as few Leeds United supporters travelled to the game as possible. The long journey and change of times that Plymouth had hoped would deter the Leeds following from attending, only appeared, however, to act as a challenge, as demand for the tickets was relatively high.

To purchase a ticket, a membership card had to be produced. This was then fed into the computer to ensure that fans could only buy one ticket. The club then arranged for their own stewards to travel to these away games, where fans would have to show the Leeds United steward their membership card and ticket before entering the ground. This ensured that every Leeds United fan at that away game was in fact a member and any trouble that occurred would result in the culprit's membership facility being withdrawn.

The system of selling tickets for our away games had greatly increased the work load of the box office and ofcourse was highly instrumental in my appointment.

The incident that was to sicken everybody at the club occurred when a group of thugs, travelling without membership cards, were stopped by a conscientious steward from gaining entry to the ground. In the argument that followed, the diligent steward was violently attacked and stabbed. The culprits somehow managed to escape either into or away from the ground, as startled Leeds fans watched in horror at what had happened. That incident certainly set the club back a long way and was a real body blow for our efforts to rid the club of its notorious hooligan element.

The Government, under Prime Minister Margaret Thatcher, were trying to introduce a compulsory identity card system for all football supporters in England and Wales after the horror of Hysel. This would have required all supporters to buy an identity card, complete with a photograph, if they wanted to attend a match. On matchdays, they would then have to queue, and we all knew inside football that if the computer system linking everybody in the country that had been registered, broke down, there would be absolute chaos, either at one or every ground in the country at the same time. Even if the computers were working normally, there would still be a good chance that somebody in the queue would have a card that would cause a delay. It would then be left to the ticket office to take control of this unworkable system.

At Leeds United, we already realised how much extra burden was placed on the administration of a club just by introducing this membership card system for away games, when support totalled no more than two or three thousand, compared to the twenty plus thousand for a home fixture.

Everybody in football knew, as I believe did most politicians, that these proposed identity cards would not stop the hooligans that had attached themselves to the game. It was like using a sledge hammer to knock in a nail. The football authorities had had endless talks with Government officials about the hooligan problem. The Government had been upset at the image created throughout Europe of the English football hooligan. The football authorities tried to defend itself with the fact that it was not just a football hooligan but a hooligan and that the problem that existed was one of law and order, thus throwing the ball back into the court of the Government. The Chairman of the Football Association reportedly, on being asked on the subject of the so called "football hooligan", cleverly rephrased the question to ask the Government, what they intended doing about "their hooligans damaging football", stating the fact that the person did not just become a hooligan at kick off time on a Saturday but was causing trouble in the streets throughout the week, a fact backed by many Police officers that we had dealings with on matchdays.

In those days, many law abiding supporters would have been greatly inconvenienced by a scheme, designed by a Government that did not either appear to care or understand the game of football and the people who loved it so much.

If the membership card scheme, which the Government saw as a solution to the problem of the football hooligan, would have been implemented, it would, because of its costs, ruined many of our smaller clubs and deterred so many innocent people from attending games.

However, it was what happened at Hillsborough on Saturday 15th April 1989, that was to have far more reaching consequences for everybody in football, especially myself . On that particular day, Leeds United were at home in a mid table Second Division clash against Brighton and Hove Albion. As the news began to filter through that the semi final between Liverpool and Nottingham Forest, scheduled that afternoon for Hillsborough, had been delayed by crowd problems, followed within minutes of news filtering through of the tragic events that were taking place, the horrible reality began to stun everybody. Suddenly, the game at Elland Road started to be meaningless.

That afternoon, because of Everton's involvement against Norwich City in the other F.A.Cup semi final at Villa Park, I had decided to keep my ear to the radio to hear about how my old club were going on in their game. With my connections with the two Merseyside clubs, I had managed to obtain a few tickets for various people for the two semi-finals and suddenly began to worry about the safety of those fans that I had obtained tickets for at Hillsborough. The game at Elland Road just appeared to drag on for ever that afternoon. All I wanted to do was to get home and find out about their safety. However, what I was to witness on the train journey home, was to turn me off professional football for a long time to come and make me feel sick at heart at the mentality of the yobs who had affiliated themselves to our Football League clubs.

My train journey home from Leeds required changing trains at Stockport. Whilst waiting for the Crewe train to arrive, I noticed a few drunken yobs, wearing the colours of Manchester United, waiting on the same platform as myself. They had been at Old Trafford that afternoon witnessing United being beaten by Derby County.

As the train pulled in to Stockport Station, I entered into a compartment to find it full of shell shocked Liverpool supporters travelling back from Sheffield. Incredibly, I found a seat directly opposite to a man that I knew from local football, who had taken a young girl to that fateful match. They had been in the Leppings Lane end of the ground and had experienced the traumas of the day. The man openly admitted that he had lost the girl in the crush that followed. The anxiety of not knowing of her safety for some considerable time, as the whole horrific episode unfolded, must have been very traumatic. He went on to tell me of the relief that he had on finding out that she was safe. As he was telling me about his ordeal, I began to think of the people that I had been able to obtain tickets for. Luckily, I was to later find out that they were all safe. However, so many were not, on a day which will forever haunt British football.

Meanwhile, all we could hear in the background were the mindless chants of those drunken yobs who had boarded the train at Stockport. The chants became personal against the Liverpudlians and under normal circumstances would have resulted in them being forcibly quietened. On this occasion, however, everybody in the packed compartment was just too upset to do anything. Their mindless chanting made me totally sick that I could possibly be involved in football at that level.

I had moved to Leeds United at the end of February in the hope that it would re-kindle my enthusiasm for the job. The first two weeks spent at the chairman, Leslie Silver's hotel, had been like a life of luxury and had made my settling down period at Leeds most enjoyable. However, after that, I had had to try to find alternative accommodation and had been moved from pillar to post. The better accommodations being some distance away from the ground and being reliant on public transport, became inconvenient. Whereas, those accommodations nearer to the ground were far less comfortable. I am sure that I could have handled the constant moving about searching for suitable accommodation until I was successful but the last thing that I wanted that afternoon, was to witness the sick state which existed in football with the yobs. It made me realise that the compulsory identity card system, which we all felt in football was totally impractical, was now inevitable. The future, as we knew it, of professional football in this country was now in doubt. Valley Parade, Hysel and now Hillsborough, three tragedies within a space of four years, demanded that urgent remedies were now required and that they would be forced upon the football authorities by a government, who neither cared for or knew about the game.

After long and hard soul searching on the Sunday, I went into the club secretary, David Dowse's office on the Monday morning, to tell him of my decision to finish in professional football and the sad reasons which had been so instrumental in arriving at that decision.

A career, which had lasted nearly twenty years, was over in a weekend, which was incidentally, also the worst weekend that the English game had ever experienced. What had hit me personally was the fact that I felt that I could not deal with, nor stand to see, the type of sick mentality shown by those yobs that weekend, whose behaviour had been so totally repulsive.

I agreed to stay the week, finishing with Leeds United on Friday 21st April 1989, after just fifty four days at the club, slightly more than the legendary Brian Clough- but not a lot longer.

I must say that I was pleasantly surprised to receive from Leeds United an ex gratia payment of fifteen hundred pounds, who, no doubt, sympathised with my feelings. The payment was certainly never expected but more importantly to me, were the kind words in the letter of thanks which accompanied the cheque. This proved, even though none was really required, that football had numerous gentlemen, whom it was both a pleasure to know and work alongside. I felt for them with how the game was heading.

David Dowse was a young club secretary, who was friendly and supportive of his staff and very enthusiastic and Howard Wilkinson, as manager, on the occasions when I met him, came across as having a very dry sense of humour. He was the first of what I can only describe, for use of a better term, as a `clip board' manager- one who took notes during the game, from which he would give his team talks to the players. All the other managers that I had come across were never seen to use a pen to take notes with, relying on passion and memory work to give their half time or after match briefing- but each to their own method.

I had also struck up a good working relationship with the new Leeds United commercial manager, Arnie Todd, who had joined the club, just before my arrival, from Sunderland, where he had held a similar position with the Wearsiders. Being both newcomers to the area and in lodgings, we spent several evenings talking about football and Leeds United in general, discussing ideas about how things could be improved upon at

Elland Road.

One of the things that I would have liked to have seen introduced was the formation of a Family and a Junior Club, in order to try to get away from this "hard" image which the club had found itself tarnished with throughout the Football League. These ideas had worked well at my previous clubs and had given supporters an understanding of the values of sportsmanship and an extra loyalty towards their club. With Leeds United's excellent fan base throughout the country and the problems that they were facing from a mindless section of its travelling support, I could honestly see the idea being of excellent benefit to the Elland Road club.

Unfortunately, time would not permit me to put forward my proposals but I am sure that Bill Fotherby, who was then chief executive, had that ability to listen and pick up on good ideas and would have looked on them favourably.

Leaving Leeds United on Friday 21st April 1989, it was to come as no surprise to me that the following season, under Howard Wilkinson, who had bought wisely over the summer of 1989, the club were to finish as Second Division Champions but what was to really surprise me, was that the improvement had been so rapid, that they followed this success with the ultimate prize of all, the Football League Championship, in their first season back in the top flight.

It had proved my initial assessment of Leeds United, in which I had been quoted in both the local Leeds press and their match day programme on my joining the club as saying, ` that it was only a matter of time before Leeds United took their rightful place amongst the elite of English clubs'.

Their potential was far greater than that of Everton because of the loyalty of an excellent fan base, which gave them such excellent gates, far higher than many contemporary high ranking clubs could have hoped to have mustered in times of playing mediocrity.

I just wished that I could have stayed there long enough to have seen my assessment come true and enjoyed that success, for having tasted it at Everton, it was certainly worth savouring.

The last few weeks of the season saw me attend only one more game of football but it turned out to be an occasion which helped to restore my enjoyment of the game.

Telford United had succeeded in getting through to the F.A. Trophy Final, where they were to play Macclesfield Town at Wembley Stadium.

I attended the game with Paul Mayman's parents, Frank and Joyce and his wife Diane's parents, Ken and Nora and together we took Paul's son, Craig, then three and a half years old, to his first game of football at a football ground- and they don't come any better than at Wembley Stadium.

The day was marvellous, as both sets of supporters, making up the twenty thousand plus gate, enjoyed the game together. After all the hassle which football had gone through, most of which had been brought about by hooliganism, it was such a pleasant change to be present amongst people who enjoyed the game in a very friendly surrounding, with not a hint of trouble between the two sets of supporters. On entering the famous old stadium that day, young Craig had been given a plastic bucks head, the emblem of Telford, which he had let slip from his hands during the game. It had landed a few rows forward from where we were sat, amongst some Macclesfield supporters, with whom we had been having friendly banter with during the game. On going with Craig to retrieve his mascot, not just did they retrieve it for him but also gave him their own plastic silkworm emblem and were so friendly towards us.

That was what football should be about and the enjoyment I received from the atmosphere at that game was, at the time, priceless in restoring my interest in football.

From that moment on, I have continued to watch two or so games most weekends in the football season, one on a Saturday afternoon and one on a Sunday morning, although in all of this time, the number of Football League games which I have attended could possibly be counted on my fingers.

The summer of 1989, saw me as a gentleman of leisure, as I searched for my next job. I had, over the last few weeks at Everton, contemplated purchasing a business but instead had made the move to Leeds. Now, this idea started to come through as a good proposition and I started to look at various businesses that were up for sale in the area.

In the meantime, however, I offered my services on a voluntary basis to Lancashire County Cricket Club. I had, over the years, because of favours done for the club, been forwarded a complimentary pass by their secretary, Chris Hassall, whom I had first met during his days at Preston North End, when we, at Crewe, had met them in the F.A.Cup. Chris had also been the club secretary at Everton before I had joined them. So, with the Australians visiting Old Trafford for a Test match that summer, the offer of my services was accepted and I spent an enjoyable period of time checking that all the seats, some twenty four thousand in total, were correctly numbered, in order that no problems with seating could occur on the days when all tickets had been sold for the Test match.

The autumn of 1989, was to see me finding a business which I felt would provide me with a future. I had been alerted to a newsagents shop in Edleston Road, Crewe, owned by a young man who had played for Crewe Alexandra's reserve team during my spell as club secretary at Gresty Road. I agreed with that young man, David Cooke, to buy the lease on the shop for twenty one years which, at thirty nine years of age, would take me up to the age of sixty, at which point, I would, with help from my Football League pension payments which made provision for retirement payments to commence at that age and by taking up a further private pension plan, be fairly confident that I could meet that retirement date.

Unfortunately for me, it was around this time that newspapers and magazines, which had previously been a monopoly held by the retail newsagent, were offered to all, with the big supermarket chains getting their hands on this nice little earner at the expense of the small newsagent. Sales declined and an urgent replacement for the lost revenue was required.

Dave, a keen Manchester United fan, knowing of my knowledge of football, mentioned the idea of supplementing the shop with the sale of Manchester United merchandise, which sounded an attractive idea and certainly more in line with my working experiences.

I therefore contacted the club secretary of Manchester United, Ken Merrett, who arranged for Dave and myself to meet their marketing department. They came down to Crewe to assess the potential of the shop and our ideas and ability to provide a successful outlet for their merchandise and gave us their approval to start selling United souvenirs, which we would be supplied on very attractive terms direct from Old Trafford. The shop was quickly reorganised with all the new fittings put in. Shutters were installed to protect the windows from vandalism at night and to lessen the possibility of a hatred towards the shop, we decided to refer to it as the `Football Shop', rather than just the `Manchester United shop' and I arranged through Peter Robinson, the chief executive of Liverpool Football Club, who originated from the Crewe area (Willaston to be precise) and had, like myself, been a previous club secretary of Crewe Alexandra, to be able to sell certain items of Liverpool merchandise. The third club that I would like to have involved was our local club, Crewe Alexandra, who, unfortunately, declined our offer, citing that the shop, being only a mile from the ground, would not increase sales sufficiently to warrant them supplying us with goods at a discounted price. To be loyal however to the local club, I did carry a Crewe Alexandra scarf in the window and my viewpoint as to Crewe's wisdom was only strengthened by the fact that so many people, on seeing that scarf, came into the shop in the early days wanting to buy Crewe souvenirs which, unfortunately, were not available. Although redirecting them to Gresty Road, except ofcourse during the many hours, such as on a Sunday, when we were open and they were not, led me to believe that they had made a mistake in not allowing their products to be sold at the shop. However, it was a decision I could appreciate and was done genuinely in what they thought were the best interests of the club.

For the official opening of the shop, we invited two of Manchester United's local stalwarts, Frank Blunstone, who, during Tommy Docherty's spell as manager at Old Trafford, had been the club's assistant manager and Ronnie Cope, who, in the years around the Munich air crash in 1958, had played on numerous occasions at centre half in the first team.

In its first year, the football side of the shop really prospered and so we started a local Junior section of the Manchester United Supporters Club, courtesy of the secretary of the local branch, Andy Ridgeway. We soon had several hundred youngsters flocking to become members, offering them, for a nominal membership fee of a pound, a membership card, a quarterly meeting and discounts of ten per cent off all products of United merchandise bought from our shop. In addition to this, we also put on for them at Dave Cooke's club, Jesters, in High Street, an afternoon Christmas party, along with a summer coaching session held at the local Shavington Sports Centre, together with organised tours around Old Trafford.

Just as things were looking rosy, disaster occurred. The tenants of the flat above the shop had suffered a fire and as a result, the fire brigade had soaked the place. The outcome saw the ceiling of the shop badly damaged and all the products were affected by the smoke. The sight on that Sunday morning, when I first entered the shop to find large parts of the ceiling's plastic tiling lying on the floor in a mess and the smell of smoke, made one realise that things would never be the same again. Even though the insurance paid out for the damage that had been incurred, the loss of trade which resulted from the shop being unable to trade in the United products for a good number of weeks was something that we were never able to recover from. This, coupled by the fact that the local Birthdays shop had also started to sell United products for Christmas and had a far better display of available goods than ourselves, was to be the final curtain for the shop. Some loyalty from our patrons, whose children had become Junior Club members, remained, which allowed us to take orders for Christmas, which Dave travelled down to Old Trafford to collect and allowed us to make a small profit but not enough to sustain the shop. That fire had resulted in the momentum being broken of the one thing that could have kept the shop trading. The sale of Manchester United merchandise had fallen away and it came as no surprise to us when United told us that, due to low sales figures brought about as a result of lost sales during the recovery period, they would be unable to continue to offer us goods at a preferential rate and instead passed us on to one of their agents, whose discounts were far less than what we had been receiving from United.

From now on, it became my objective to try to get somebody to take over the remaining eleven years of the lease of the shop. My enthusiasm had been destroyed by the fire. I could see no way out but to try to get somebody with money to invest in rebuilding the shop with new lines and walking away from the sinking ship.

At this point, Tony Owen entered onto the scene and started to rebuild the shop. Unfortunately, that spell lasted just three months, before the opening of a superstore directly across the road, which sold all the same products but on a far greater scale, saw Tony pull out of the deal to take over the lease and once more, me having the problem of the shop.

There was no alternative but to bite the bullet and agree a compensation fee for lost revenue on his rent with Dave Cooke and close the shop down, which I duly did in the early part of 1999.

Financially, I had a lot to thank my brother, Alec, and his wife, Connie, for during this period of time. Going into business had been an interesting but costly exercise but like everything in life, I was pleased to have at least tried it. Some very enjoyable times had been had, especially during the times of the 'Football Shop'. However, luck had just ran out with that fire, just as the shop looked like turning the corner. I had, however, met some nice customers, like Arnie and Jean Jones, who still keep in contact.

My life in local football had still continued during my ten years or so in charge of my own shop but I was always looking for the opportunity to get back into professional sport and it was around the time that the shop was struggling, that I decided to answer an advertisement in the local evening paper, in which Port Vale Football Club were looking to employ a ticket office manager. With my credentials, I was obviously selected to attend an interview, which was conducted by the Vale club secretary, Bill Lodey . Unfortunately, the millstone of the shop kept arising at the interview and as such the position could not be offered to me, as my commitment would always be in doubt.

The same thing was to happen to me at Lancashire County Cricket Club when I attended an interview for the position of shop manager, which had been arranged for me by the club's marketing manager, Ken Grime, whom I had known since the days of Chris Hassall, being secretary of Lancashire County Cricket Club, although Chris had by then moved on to become chief executive of Lancashire's arch rivals, Yorkshire County Cricket Club.

My advice now to anybody thinking about signing a lease, would always be never to sign too long a one, as one never really knows what lies around the corner.

It was also during my spell at the shop that I spent a fortnight helping to sell tickets for Crewe Alexandra's first ever visit to Wembley Stadium in May 1993, when they played York City in the promotion play offs. With having great experience of selling tickets for Wembley games whilst at Everton, I felt it only right to offer my services on a voluntary basis to my local club on their first ever visit to the grand old stadium. This had gratefully been accepted by the club secretary, Gill Palin, and I spent a very enjoyable and nostalgic time working in the very same club offices, where I had been some sixteen years previously as club secretary.

Unfortunately, for Crewe, on that occasion, the club missed out in the play offs but were successful second time round against Brentford.

My second little venture into the world of football occurred as a result of the landlord of the shop, Dave Cooke, being appointed as manager of Nantwich Town Football Club and asking me to attend their Annual

General Meeting. David had informed me that the club's existing secretary, Joe Davies, wished to relinquish the position and had asked me if I would be interested in the job. Having started to miss the involvement of being involved at a club, I was vulnerable and willingly accepted what I believed to have been an offer.

I was taken to the Annual General Meeting by Dave but was horrified when the position of secretary came up for discussion. My name, as I had expected it to be, was put forward and seconded. Then, to my surprise and anger, a further recommendation was put forward by the floor, when Malcolm Hughes, who I had known during my days at Crewe Alexandra, having appointed him onto the Junior Club committee and who had, over the years after I had left, worked diligently for the club's youth system, was also nominated. Never, for one minute, did I expect to have to go into a vote for the position. I was angry to have been brought all the way down to a meeting, thinking that the club wanted me as secretary, only to find that no such feeling existed and that they were infact looking to appoint a secretary from the floor, of which, I was just one of two candidates and they were even asking for further nominations. It was at this point of time that I stated that under no circumstances would I allow myself to be voted on by the floor and withdrew my nomination in anger. Ironically, so did Malcolm who, like myself, must have believed that it was a foregone conclusion that he was to be appointed secretary at the meeting, only to find out that other factions on the committee had arranged for an alternative candidate. So therefore, Nantwich, instead of having two candidates, had neither of us take on the position and poor old Joe Davies, who wanted to relinquish the job, had no alternative but to remain. If only the powers that be at the time had consulted together, I am sure that embarrassing episode could have been avoided and Nantwich Town Football Club would have had a secretary installed that evening. However, that was a long time ago and is now water under the bridge.

It was during my spell at the shop, in November 1991, that my father died. He had been knocked down by a car on a pedestrian crossing in Earle Street. Although, at the time, the injuries were not considered serious, repercussions of the collision were to lead to him getting pneumonia, from which he was to die from a few days later. The death of my father resulted in the selling of the family home in Earle Street and my purchasing a bungalow in Fuller Drive, Wistaston.

So, what do I think of today's professional game?

Football today owes much to two major factors that have brought about significant improvement but from which, the benefits could have been made better use of for the game of football as a whole. The Chester Report, brought about after the disasters of Valley Parade and Hillsborough in particular, demanded that all stadium in the top divisions must be made all seated. As a result of this, many grounds, which had seen little or no improvements made over the last thirty years, now had to see major upheavals, which would force them up to a twenty first century standard. Grounds that at best, in the mid eighties, could be described as very basic, were to be brought up to an excellent standard almost overnight and those that could be aptly described as slums were made neat and tidy. Now, I honestly believe that this country can boast to have more excellent club stadiums than probably any other country in the world.

A lot of the necessary finance came from the emergence of the other most influential gain that the game was to benefit from over the most recent years. The emergence of Sky television has provided football with the sort of revenue that, prior to the late eighties, it could only ever dream about.

Unfortunately, the downside to all of this has been several fold. Admission prices, over the last fifteen years or so, have spiralled from an average six pounds to sit or just three pounds to pay for a place on the terraces, to on average twenty five pounds for a seat.

Top players' wages from a high of two thousand to thirty thousand and transfer fees from two million to thirty million, which when worked out on percentage annual increases, far exceeds the wildest dream that the average man could possibly obtain in his own wage packet.

Despite all of this money being thrown into our top player's pockets, it has not resulted in any increased success on the field for our top clubs in their quest for European glory. In fact, just the opposite is true. The magnificent achievements of Aston Villa, Nottingham Forest twice and Liverpool on three occasions, to win the European Cup, in a ten year period between 1976 and the ban in 1985, far outweighs the efforts of our overpaid and overrated players of today. All this goes to prove that money thrown at players from throughout the world does not necessarily bring success at the top European level.

The nationality of our leading teams has also been reversed and now, unfortunately, this trait is beginning to be seen even in the lower divisions of the Football League. Teams, that in the eighties comprised of no more than two foreign players, are more likely now to see that figure represent the number of British players in their team. The fantastic success of the three teams that triumphed in the European Cup in the seventies and eighties, Liverpool, Aston Villa and Nottingham Forest, was achieved with teams that were made up of British players, with just the odd exception. It will be this reduction of English born players performing in our Premier League that will, in the non too distant future, see the demise of the England team.

The real danger is that this country will end up a second class footballing nation with a first class domestic competition, probably the most entertaining in the world - the benefit of which will be reaped by the many foreign players playing in our league.

The game has certainly changed over the years, whether for the better - let us just say that the jury is still out on that.

CHAPTER ELEVEN : INTRODUCED TO THE CORINTHIANS.

The one disadvantage of having to commute to work over the years had, ofcourse, been the many wasted hours spent travelling.

From April 1989 to the summer of 1995, I watched numerous non League or local games, with just a few Football League games thrown in for good measure, without an allegiance to any one club, as the running of the new shop venture had to take preference. All that was to change however in the Summer of 1995.

I had always enjoyed cricket and on two previous occasions had served on the committee of the local cricket club. The first occasion was as a seventeen year old at the now defunct Crewe L.M.R., whose ground in Earle Street was just a few yards away from my home and whose success in the old North Staffordshire and District League and then in the newly formed North Staffs and South Cheshire League, especially in the years under their professional, Dennis Cox, had been so phenomenal. My memories of seeing some of the world's best cricketers perform against Crewe in the early sixties in front of thousands of supporters will always remain. Later, in the early nineties, following their amalgamation with Crewe Vagrants and subsequent move to their Newcastle Road Ground, I was to serve for one year as club secretary.

Cricket had though, from the time that I joined the Football Association, taken a back seat and my season watching could only run during football's close season.

In the summer of 1995, young Craig Mayman had started to take an interest in cricket and most Saturday afternoons would see me batting or bowling tirelessly at him, whilst getting a glimpse of the cricket that our group, Graham Dutton, Les Linnell, Jimmy Wright, Dick Brereton and Mary Walker had gone along to watch. I bowled some overs that year in the vaste open spaces which surrounded the Vagrants cricket pitch and coming up to the age of forty five and not having bowled for close to twenty five years, believe me, the aches and stiffness told the day after but I battled on and soon the aches the following morning did not seem to be so bad. It was not long before the powers that be at the Vagrants, secretary, Carl Ward and youth coach, Dave Long, started to take note of our practice sessions and it wasn't me that they wanted to promote into one of their teams. Craig was invited to play in the club's under eleven team for the rest of that season, a team which had been in existence for two years without winning a game.

At the end of that cricket season Messrs Long and Ward, knowing of my footballing background, approached me with a view to helping out with a football team which they had planned to start in order to keep their cricketers together during the long winter months and help with team spirit as well as keeping people fairly fit. With Craig's involvement at the club, he was promised the captaincy of the team for the following year, which he duly accepted, I felt duty bound to accept and promptly arranged with Jeff Minshull, the secretary of the Crewe Regional Sunday Football League, who was himself an ex Vagrants cricketer, to have a League handbook and set of fixtures, in order that I could arrange friendly matches for the team.

It was to be a fixture against Carl Ward's own team, Crewe Nomads, that was to have a major bearing on my football for the next ten years or so. The game itself was a fairly non descript affair in which the only memorable moment was, I am afraid, Carl throwing a bit of tantrum when substituted by Dave Long. Fortunately, after the game was over, the incident was quickly forgotten, as Carl had to act as host to his Saturday side, having invited them all back to the Vagrants Club, where he had arranged for a Christmas buffet to be put on for the two teams. The buffet, put on so expertly by club steward, Roy Preece, along with Roy's wife and mother-in-law, Betty and Elsie Platt, soon had everybody thoroughly enjoying the evening and the beer soon started to flow. During the course of the evening, I got talking to the Nomads' long serving officials, manager, Les Ashcroft and secretary, George Davies and the season ended with me watching most of their remaining home fixtures.

The highlight of the Nomads' season were probably the two fixtures which they played against local rivals Crewe Corinthians and so it was only natural that I should attend both those games in that first season. The Corinthians were run by Gordon Anderson and the two club secretaries had donated a cup, named after themselves, which the two sides competed for on an annual basis, the winners being decided by the aggregate score over the two games. When I arrived at the game, I found a lot of players that I had known from my earlier days of watching local football in the Corinthians team, many of whom I had not seen for some years. At the buffet after the game, it was therefore only natural to renew old acquaintances and arrange for a set of fixtures from Gordon, in order that I could attend some of the Corinthians future games. Those buffets were to be an important and most enjoyable feature of the match day for both the Corinthians and Nomads, along with the drink in the bar afterwards- so much so, that opponents who did not cater were often removed from the following season's fixtures.

The switch to watching more of the Corinthians than the Nomads games came as a result of Carl Ward's controversial sacking as captain of the cricket club's first team. After running our football team at the Vagrants for the 1995/96 season in which the football, I must admit, was rather ordinary (I think that we only won one out of the fourteen friendly games which I had managed to arrange with various Sunday League clubs) and served more, I think, as an excuse for socialising and lengthy Sunday drinking sessions than anything else. However, it was during these Sunday games that two major cricketing appointments were first muted and then accepted at the club's Annual General Meeting. The first was Carl's appointment as captain to go with his role as secretary and the second was my own appointment as match secretary of the cricket club.

With typical enthusiasm, I fulfilled the role during the summer of 1996 and the club, for the first time ever, with Carl's support, introduced an idea which I had previously seen work well in football, when a Junior Club was started.

All junior members were enrolled and they formed the club's teams at various age group levels, as well as receiving coaching. Trips were organised to Old Trafford to watch games of cricket at a first class level. Two junior members were invited down to each first team home game, along with their parents, to act as match day mascots, receiving free refreshments for the day and their names on a matchday programme, which had been introduced for the very first time. The interest which this brought about saw the junior membership in the club very nearly double overnight and, coupled with the appointment of Indian professional, K.V.P.Rao, who stayed at my home for that summer and performed so admirably in the Premier Division, enabled the club to finish in a very respectable mid table position, a position which it has not been able to achieve very often since. The future for the club looked promising and it had been brought about by an invigorating youth policy.

With hindsight, however, I believe that the formation of the football team, which lasted just the one season, had a downside to it. Players who had not been involved began to feel as though they were being isolated and a split started to occur in the cricket club between the players who were involved in the football and those that were not, which was to quickly see Carl removed as captain. In my opinion, this was rather harsh because at the original Annual General Meeting he had been re-elected but in a special Annual General Meeting, called by his opponents within the club, he was forced to relinquish the position. He instantly resigned and accepted an offer to play for local rivals, Nantwich Cricket Club.

I resigned in sympathy against his dismissal but, for one season, continued to administer both the under eleven and under thirteen teams, where we had made such good progress, having contacted local schools, such as St Mary's, where their headmaster, Alan Rogan, had invited us to help with bringing cricket into the school for the first time and our coaching had been so successful that they had managed to get into the last four of the local schools competition and had provided us with several members of our under eleven team that had won several games in a season, a feat never before achieved.

So, with Carl moving not just away from Crewe Cricket Club but also in his own personal life to Telford and to a new teaching appointment, the association that he had with the Nomads began to weaken and therefore only naturally, as I knew more of the Corinthian team, I started to follow their progress closer but have always kept in touch with the Nomads and watch them whenever possible.

The area, over the years, had often seen a Crewe Corinthians team taking part in its football competitions but somehow, by the time that the mid fifties had arrived, no team under that name existed.

Therefore, in 1957, the present Crewe Corinthians Football Club was formed by Gordon Anderson with help from three other gentlemen, W.T.Butler, A.Preece and M.G.Wakelin and their first game was played on 21st August 1957, at Stoke Heath against the Royal Air Force Tern Hill, which resulted in a rather embarrassing eight goals to one defeat, despite having only been losing two goals to one at half time.

The Corinthians have always had a full and varied fixture list, brought about as a result of Gordon's great knowledge of people and teams on the "friendly circuit", with games against opponents from Merseyside, North Wales, Staffordshire and throughout Cheshire, all played on Saturday afternoons on a purely ` friendly' basis.

The only exception to this being the annual Northern Cup competition, which was started by the clubs on the circuit in 1982. It was the brainchild of Gordon, who sat as its chairman from its inauguration until his death in 2004, and also incorporated a similar competition for League teams in the area, with their finals usually played on a top non League ground at the start of May. It was aimed at maintaining interest in the closing months of the season, when it had been found that friendlies had often been called off due to a lack of interest from players who had had their ration of football for the season.

In its first season, the competition comprised of just eight teams and commenced in March. Very quickly, however, the number was increased to thirty two, with the competition commencing in January, before reverting back to allow for sixteen teams but retaining a January starting date.

It was, ofcourse, a just reward for the Corinthians, when they became the first winners of a competition, open by invitation to teams within a fifty miles radius of Northwich.

The competition has not always been trouble free though. It has caused rifts at clubs, who have looked to strengthen their teams by bringing in players in preference to regular members of the team, which has often resulted in them losing a dependable member and it has also been responsible for disputes between clubs, as too much significance may have been placed towards the competition at the expense of good club relations.

A major example of this occurred in 1993, when our rivals, Crewe Nomads, succeeded in reaching the final, where they were due to play the Corinthians. Unfortunately, on the date fixed for the final, a number of the Nomads players were unavailable, having to play cricket that day in the senior local League. Asking for a re-arranged date, preferably in mid week, which they considered could be done as both sides were local and as such had no travel difficulties in meeting an evening kick off, they were angry when the committee of the competition, under the chairmanship of Gordon, refused their request and ordered that the game should be played on the original date. This refusal to switch the date of the game annoyed the Nomads so much that they withdrew from the competition and Marple, whom they had beaten in the semi-final, were reinstated in order to play the Corinthians in the final. The end product was that the Corinthians won the trophy that day for the second time and that the Nomads have never re-entered the competition, despite several attempts by people, including myself and Gordon, to bring them back into the fold, where they would be more than welcome, having played for well over fifty years on the circuit.

The next time that the Corinthians appeared in the final was in 1996, when they were beaten by an impressive Chester College of Law team on the ground of Nantwich Town, where they were to return three years later to beat British Steel Vets in the final by two goals to nil, courtesy of goals from Kevin Edwards and John Stevenson.

In April 2005, an outstanding win was achieved in the quarter final against highly fancied Liverpool Ramblers who, incidentally, are Liverpool's oldest known club, coming into existence before both the Everton and Liverpool Football Clubs. Ramblers had always given the Corinthians their highest respect by playing their first team, who normally just play public schools, rather than their second eleven, who play the other teams on the circuit. However, for the Northern Cup they normally revert to fielding their first team and usually with a great deal of success.

Unfortunately, our win that day did not bring the reward that the team had wanted so much to honour Gordon with, after his death in the summer of 2004. A semi final defeat against Port Sunlight, decided by penalties after extra time, was a cruel way to go out of a competition that had meant so much to everyone that season.

However, the following season, in May 2006, the team were to rectify matters in style by convincingly beating Liverpool Liobians in the final at Radbrook Hall by 6-0 , to at last lift that coveted trophy, which had meant so much to many of the older members of the squad after Gordon's death.

Since 2003, the club has been playing on their latest ground behind the Lamb at Willaston, the home of Willaston White Star, after moving from the Barony Park in Nantwich after the pavilion had been destroyed by vandals and inadequate changing facilities were temporarily having to be used.

On moving to play behind the Lamb, the Corinthians have entered Willaston White Star's annual Commander Bayley competition. This is an end of season knockout competition for teams comprising of a number of non league players and with the Corinthians having a team playing regular non league friendlies, was an ideal competition to enter. The team were supplemented by the permitted number of league players, such as Ian Lee and Robbie Hancock, who already play with the Corinthians but also play on a Sunday for Willaston Villa/Peacock and Wickstead respectively in the Sunday League.

The first season saw the club acquit itself excellently by reaching the final, before losing out in a pulsating game to Morrisons by the odd goal in seven, described by many of the veterans who had supported the competition over many years as, 'one of the best finals played'. The game had seen the Corinthians two goals down inside the first twenty minutes, drawing level with two early goals in the second half, before conceding a further two but pulling one back with ten minutes to go and in a frantic finish just missing out.

The following year, 2004, saw the team reach the semi final, where they were drawn against a strong Post Office team, featuring a former Crewe Alexandra midfield player, Mark Gardiner. The team lost by the single goal and to make matters worse had their young goalkeeper, Danny Reade, who was incidentally the following year to sign for Nantwich Town to become their regular custodian in their North West Counties team, sent off by referee David Bloor, for foul and abusive language, after contesting a harmless goalkick or corner situation. However, some forty eight hours later, they had been re-instated, as it appeared that the Post Office had played a player whilst under suspension and some of our lads had got wind of this fact and made an appeal, which was successful.

Not the best way of progressing, I know that Gordon was disappointed to have had to progress that way. It was certainly something that I had no knowledge of, being most surprised on the Saturday before that final on the Sunday, when I found out that the Corinthians had been reinstated into the competition.

On a very warm day, the team ran out very easy winners by six goals to one over Sydney Arms, having had a dream start of four goals in the first twenty five minutes.

The result was even more incredible bearing in mind that the nucleus of the team had themselves been on the receiving end of a trouncing just eight days before. With the progress of the team in the Commander Bayley, the management team of Kevin Edwards, Roger Woodward and Gordon, had felt it necessary to play a game on the preceding Saturday to their semi final in order to keep the players on their toes.

We therefore arranged a game on Legends, the home ground of Bentley Motors, between the older Corinthians and the young Corinthians Sunday League side, a team that Gordon had helped me set up at the start of that season. The youngsters recorded a very emphatic nine goals to one win that day over their more experienced opponents, with Craig

Mayman stealing the show with four goals, which earned him a place in the squad to contest the final.

With the addition of the four permitted league players for the final, Danny Reade, whose father, Clive, was ofcourse our regular Saturday afternoon keeper, Ian Lee, Gary Wood and Donny Brown, the player-manager of Willaston White Star, who, although in the veteran stages of his career, had vaste experience at senior Non League level, the team were to perform admirably to ensure that the Corinthians picked up the trophy for the first time since their foundation in 1957, although a Crewe Corinthians team had been winners of the competition some seventy years previously.

The final was the last time that Gordon was to watch his beloved Corinthians side and it was only fitting that it was he who, the players had demanded, should go up to receive the trophy at the end of the game.

The following day, I called to see him at Margaret's bungalow and we had a good chat about the way that he would like to see the Corinthians heading and he expressed great pleasure at the good progress our young Regional League team had made in their first year.

We all knew that Gordon was very ill, suffering from prostrate cancer, a condition that he had had for the last two years or so, but it still came as a deep shock when, just ten days after that final, I received a telephone call from Margaret to tell me that Gordon had passed away.

Unfortunately, the following year the team failed to retain the trophy, going out to a young Willaston team by three goals to nil but they did go out with the knowledge that they were knocked out by the eventual worthy winners of the competition.

Gordon had always been very traditional in his outlook on football, with more than a hint of the values that had been instilled into him during his public school upbringing, which made him so unique in the present day game.

The Corinthians' shirt was always black and white, with black shorts and black and white socks and with the badge of the club embroidered on the shirts, which were never numbered. The shirt could take different formats of black and white, striped, quartered or just white with black edgings. It therefore came as a surprise when, in 2002, the lads running the team for him managed to purchase a set of red and white striped shirts, which Gordon reluctantly accepted. However, on the formation of our Regional Sunday League team in 2004, Gordon was more than happy to offload and revert to his more traditional black and white striped shirts. Imagine what his feelings would have been on the day, in April 2005, when the lads had managed to purchase a set of replica West German shirts and turned out in them for their Northern Cup tie against Liverpool Ramblers. Even Gordon's dog, Paddington, who accompanied him to so many games over the years, had to be black and white!

My first season of watching the Corinthians on a regular basis was the 1997-8 season and over the following seven seasons whilst Gordon was alive, I reckon that I watched over two hundred games and clocked over six thousand miles travelling with him in his car, starting off religiously, until the last two years, from the Earl public house, which in those early days was known as the Earl of Crewe, a meeting point for close on forty five years, before being changed to the Peacock in Willaston.

The Corinthians have played their home fixtures at the Barony in Nantwich, the Cotton Arms in Wrenbury, Nantwich Town's London Road ground and the King George Playing Fields, before the latest move to Willaston White Star's ground, behind the Lamb Hotel, who, courtesy of the landlady, Lorraine, provide the Corinthians with such good refreshments after the end of each game- a feature of the Saturday game that was always held high in Gordon's priorities.

Very nearly every game in which I have watched the Corinthians play has always been competitive but played in the right spirit. Players who have misbehaved have nearly always been substituted by their own team, allowing referees to enjoy the game. The only exception to this was in a game refereed by young Dave Bloor, who had reason to send off two opponents from a Merseyside team that we were beating rather handsomely at the time, for persistent bad language and dissent. In true Corinthian spirit, Gordon brought two of his own players off the pitch, in order to at least level the sides numerically and not rub salt into the wounds of his opponents any more than need be. I am not saying that this should happen but it made sense on the day to do so, after all, we were not playing for the town hall clock!

It was the same for teams turning up short of substitutes. In the event of an injury and a team being short of a substitute, it was expected that their opponents would loan one of their own players in order to ensure that the game was played on an equal footing wherever possible.

This would result in the social side going amicably, creating many long term friendships and associations over the years, which have made this type of football so enjoyable to the thousands that have played it.

Even Gordon's not just the customary handshake at the end of the game but the old public school outcry of "three cheers" for his opponents would herald a feeling of total sportsmanship.

A brutal or late challenge, of which there were some, saw the customary heartfelt apologetic hand being sincerely offered to the victim, who would accept, without question, that apology.

One of the funniest episodes to happen to Gordon and myself occurred in our Northern Cup semi final at Wirral Vets when, with the game won convincingly near the end, Gordon started to watch a game on the adjoining pitch. As both games finished at the same time, Gordon found himself in conversation in the dressing room with an official from the other game and on closing, the official invited Gordon to their after match buffet and asked Gordon to follow him in his car, which we duly did. Gordon had, somehow, become under the misconception that this chap was an official of the Wirral Vets, who we had played that day. We followed the gentleman concerned and Gordon began to talk to all and sundry for a good half hour, during which time, I was concerned that none of our own players had arrived for the buffet. On drawing Gordon's attention to this fact, he eventually summoned up the courage to ask for the name of the team who were offering us their hospitality, only to find out that it was the team who had played on the adjoining pitch. To make matters worse, nobody in the room knew of where our opponents had arranged for our buffet to be held. Rather sheepishly, we left the room, thanking them for their hospitality and tried to find out where our own players had gone but without success. On arriving back home, both Gordon and myself received phonecalls from anxious players wondering where we had got to. Needless to say, we had some rather embarrassing explaining to do.

Tradition always went hand in hand with Gordon's Corinthians. Gordon rewarded any of his players who had accumulated one hundred games with a special commemorative plaque with the club crest on, these being presented annually at the club's annual dinner, at which, another of the club's traditions - the toast which Gordon made, was always the same- the Queen, the ladies and finally, the Corinthians themselves. At Presentation Evenings, only one award was ever made to the players, other than those centenary plaques, and that was the Player of the Year award which, under true Corinthian spirit, was never allowed to be won consecutively by any player.

Gordon's knowledge of the circuit was of the highest order, gained over nearly fifty years of playing on the left hand side of the pitch, from left back to left winger, followed by holding the joint role of secretary and chairman after he had finished playing.

In the later years, he came to rely heavily on Kevin Edwards, who phenomenally has averaged a goal a game in over five hundred appearances and Roger Woodward, a defender, with over three hundred appearances spread over the last twenty plus years to get him his players. Both probably knew Gordon as well as anybody and it is only fair to say that without the help from Roger and Kevin, the club would not have continued for so long. Indeed, when the Corinthians celebrate their fifty years, no higher praise could possibly be bestowed on anybody more than these two true Corinthians, who both took Gordon to their heart and ensured the continuation of the club. Since Gordon's death, help for Kevin and Roger has been found with the appointment of Andy Jones as manager and Dave Lewis as treasurer.

The majority of the team have been with the club throughout my association with it. Goalkeeper, Clive Reade, now in his fifties, had, in his prime, played for Crewe Alexandra reserves. Gareth Wlliams, one of two brothers, Aidan being the other, both utility players, had, like Robbie Hancock, a striker and Chris Lee, a midfield player, all played in a high standard of football, Mid Cheshire League or higher, on a Saturday. Chris had also played on a Sunday for Rolls Royce during our successful period of the eighties. Donny Brown, a central defender or midfield player, had experience with Winsford United in the Cheshire League and Paul Mayman, had experienced an illustrious non League career with Nantwich Town, Northwich Victoria and Telford United, after a spell in the Football League with Crewe Alexandra, which resulted in him winning two non League international caps for England in the early eighties and three F.A.Trophy final appearances with Telford United. Then there are lads who have played local football, like Simon Wall, with Wellcome Foundation and who for many years had also played rugby union for the local Crewe and Nantwich Club, Richard Fitzgerald, Phil Bowen, Ian Lee and Gary Heathcock and more recently, Richard and Danny Dodd, whose father, Richard, previously played for the Corinthians, and are somewhat the youngsters of the team by at least twenty years!

Hopefully, all of these players will see in the fiftieth year of the Crewe Corinthians Football Club, along with our younger Sunday Regional League team, in order to honour a man who epitomised the Corinthians spirit so much and who, at the Annual General Meetings, always allowed his players a say but somehow, in the end, to quote a famous song title, always did it my way.

Gordon Anderson was simply ` Crewe Corinthians'.

CHAPTER TWELVE: AND SO TO TODAY'S CORINTHIANS TEAM IN THE REGIONAL LEAGUE.

Towards the end of the 2002/2003 season, Gordon had privately spoken to me on our return from away games about his concern that the present Corinthians team, at that time averaging forty years of age, may not survive until 2007, to see in the fiftieth year. This had always been Gordon's wish, having seen his local rivals, Crewe Nomads, celebrate their fifty years a few years previously. We had talked about bringing in some young players into the team. The most obvious way of doing that was through Paul Mayman's son, Craig, who at seventeen, was now considered old enough and bringing with him some of his football mates.

Craig had played with a host of Lads and Dads Junior teams, such as Willaston White Star, Willaston Wasps, Shavington Shooters and Wolverton until, due to poor running of the League, which often resulted in managers not finding out until sometimes as late as Friday that the League had arranged a game for them for the Sunday, which in turn caused so much frustration for both managers and their players, who then had to re-organise their weekends in order to fulfil fixtures that could have been better arranged. This situation had resulted in many clubs resigning and the League for that age group failing to provide an adequate number of fixtures for the season. For many lads aged fifteen, school games, totalling no more than ten in a season, were therefore the only organised eleven a side football in the area.

It was at this point that I was brought into the equation. To fill the void, I decided to approach Dave Long to see about the possibility of starting a seven-a-side competition for under seventeen year olds at the Vagrants. At the time, only small side games for adults existed at the local sports centres. Three of the lads keen to start up a team were the first ballboys that Dave Long had taken on at the Vagrants, namely Craig and his two schoolmates, James Butler and Ritchie Sutton. Dave agreed that there was a scope for a small side football competition for under seventeen year olds, provided that I was willing to organise it, which I duly agreed to do. Invitations were sent out to all schools, asking if they could give the newly formed League space on their noticeboard and asking for applications from interested teams. I also managed to obtain a list of all the teams in that age group that existed in the Lads and Dads local Football League and wrote to them all asking for any interested parties to contact me. The League was allocated the whole area of the astroturf, which easily accommodated two pitches, on one midweek evening for ninety minutes, allowing twelve teams to enter.

Craig had decided to enter a team and, with myself having to try to remain neutral, his mother, Diane, was appointed adult in charge. The team, a year younger than most in the League, comprised of lads from St.Thomas More and Shavington School, with Richard Douglas, Ritchie Sutton, Joel Thompson, Jordan Mayes, Peter Murphy, Matthew Hole and James Butler joining Craig from St Thomas More and Wayne Beggs, Jamie Roberts and Dave Griffin from Shavington and just Danny Mair from Malbank, calling the name of their team, 'Madhatters'.

We managed to get together ten clubs for that first season and in September 2000, became the first League to play small sided football under floodlights for juniors in the Crewe area.

We had our own select band of referees, Ken Saunders, Danny Craig and Willie Beech, who did such sterling work, although on one occasion, Danny took matters a bit too far, when he sent of Joel Thompson for time wasting five minutes from the end of the game with Joel's team winning by eleven clear goals. The punishment for that offence was a thirty five day suspension and the payment of seven pounds administration fee.

The League was a huge success in its first year, filling a void in junior football for lads of that age.

Despite being a year younger than several of the teams, which at junior level is a big handicap, they convincingly won both the Winter and Summer League, with Craig scoring a phenomenal ninety goals, seventy one in a winter programme of twenty seven games and nineteen in fourteen in the summer.

The competition has continued to flourish, thanks to the far sightedness of the Vagrants, who hopefully will reap the benefits as these lads go older and hopefully remain loyal. My only real disappointment was the fact that Dave Long had organised, for the first time in six years of competitions at the Vagrants, a presentation evening and yet, as Champions of the Junior Section, not one player attended to receive their awards.

The lads had won the competition so easily that they decided not to reapply for the Junior Section but to enter a team in the Adult Section, even though the majority of the team were still only fifteen. This was to give them a nice introduction into playing against adults, without the physical vigour that existed in the eleven a side game. To their credit, they finished a respectable mid table. Unfortunately, because the whole team was from the same year at school, they were unable to commit the time to competing in the Summer League because of taking their GCSE exams and that signalled the end of the Madhatters seven a side team.

For the whole of the following season, the lads therefore played little or no competitive football. Half way through that season, in January 2003, I was approached by Craig and Richard Douglas to see if there was a possibility of forming a team. I knew that Gordon quietly had reservations about the ability of the Corinthians to still be playing four years on, in August 2007, when the club would reach that magical fifty years of existence. The idea of the formation of a younger Corinthians side sounded an excellent idea to both Gordon and myself and so we informed the two lads to start getting a team together.

The first two or three months were spent watching games in the Crewe Regional Sunday Football League, as this was the League which we had decided to apply for, afterall, it was pointless applying, if the lads were not confident that they could compete at that standard.

In April, confident in their ability to be able to compete, I approached the secretary of the League, Jeff Minshull, to formally make our application. Jeff had been the long serving secretary of the League who, over the years, had spent numerous Saturday's refereeing the Corinthians, which made him very supportive of our application and support was also to be found amongst other members of the Executive Committee. Treasurer, John Hulse, who had had spells with both the Nomads and the Corinthians as a goalkeeper many years previously and chairman, John Cotton, whom I had known for many years from both football and cricket, were both supportive of our application.

Together with Crewe Hall, a team from the rival Cheshire and Border Counties League, who were managed by Tony Beeston, the clubs accepted our application for membership to the League, by increasing the Second Division from twelve to fourteen teams to accommodate us both.

Sadly, League secretary, Jeff Minshull, was to pass away before our season started but the League came across an excellent replacement in Mike Hargrove, who had, many years previously, been secretary of Hays Chemicals, when Craig's father, Paul, had played for them. Mike's ability as secretary makes for a very well administered League which we have been proud to have been a member of and which hopefully, as I promised on the night when we were elected, that we would become a club that the League could be proud of, by being disciplined on the field and organised off it.

The real driving force behind the formation of the team was Richard Douglas. It was his idea to start up a team and he was therefore responsible for getting most of the players in that first year, along with being instrumental in getting Jed Hulme, the manager of his old Wolverton team, to be our first manager. My role was to ensure that they had the necessary criteria to meet League requirements and to get them into the League, which had been achieved quite comfortably.

Richard Lee Douglas was born in Crewe on 15th September 1985, one of four children to Colin and Christine, his elder sister being Leanne and with two younger brothers, Robert and John. Until 2004, Colin and Christine had quite admirably been foster parents for fifteen years to over thirty children. `Dougie' has therefore never been allowed to be spoiled and I am sure that it is this aspect of his character, of having to live with so many different types of personalities, coupled with his one hundred per cent commitment, both on and off the field, that I, as secretary, have found invaluable and make him a good club captain..

It came as no surprise to me when he informed me that his first experience as a captain occurred at the age of just ten when, as captain of his Gainsborough Junior School, under the management of Mr Shackleton and headmaster, Alan Jennison, they won the Crewe and District Junior Football League. On mentioning Gainsborough Junior School, memories came flooding back to me as to how, during my days at Everton Football Club, the school had suffered from the cruel hands of arsonists and Alan, who I had known through Crewe Cricket Club, had asked for prizes for a raffle that they were doing in order to raise funds to rebuild the school and I had donated a football, which I had got the Everton team to sign.

Richard went on to play for the town representative junior school team, along with four other members of today's Corinthians, Craig Mayman, Wayne Beggs, Matthew Hole and Adam Longley, going on to become beaten finalists in the Alderman More Trophy, a competition open to town teams in the North West.

To commence his secondary school education, Richard moved to St Thomas More where, along with Shavington School, they dominated the first two years of school football, winning the title in the second year by winning every game. The rivalry that existed between the Shavington and St Thomas More lads was friendly but competitive and featured some excellent games over their years at school. Coincidentally, so many of those lads that have appeared in the Corinthians team over the first few years, such as Andy Lofkin, Steve Fidler, Stuart Evans, Wayne Beggs, Jamie Roberts, Dave Griffin, Kevin Sharp, Graham Smalley and Adam Longley came from Shavington, with Richard, Craig Mayman, Matthew Hole, Mike Field, Declan Small and Will Ryder from St Thomas More.

After leaving school, Richard studied Sport at South Cheshire College for two years, before starting employment as a trainee manager with the Lyceum Theatre, following a spell working part time for the Council as a lifeguard at the local swimming baths.

The next connection came about as a result of Richard playing for the successful Wolverton team from the age of eleven. Managed by Jed Hulme, Richard was instrumental in persuading Jed to become manager of the new Corinthian team, bringing along with him Jed's own son, Jez Tagg, Ricky Barlow, whose father Colin had played for me some twenty years previously at the Youth Centre and Neil Forbes.

Being realistic, because of the player's inexperience individually and the fact that so many had not even played any eleven a side football for a full season, I felt that we would really struggle initially and gave a wry smile when a challenge to get twenty five points in the League in order to earn a free night at a presentation evening was made to them by our manager, Jed Hulme.

Training started in earnest, twice a week on a Wednesday evening and a Sunday morning, some six weeks before our opening League game, scheduled for the beginning of September 2003.

The basis of the squad comprised of Richard Douglas, who could play in defence or midfield, Craig Mayman, a midfield player or striker, Ricky Barlow, a left sided player, equally at home in defence or midfield, Jez Tagg, a striker and Neil Forbes, a goalkeeper, who had been with Jed at Wolverton in that last year, to which we added Neil's brother, Danny, a full back. Two lads from St Thomas More, Mike Field, a defender and Will Ryder, a utility player were enrolled, as were Jamie Roberts, a left back and Danny Mair, a striker, who had played with the Madhatters seven a side team Danny Forbes enlisted a lad a year younger than the majority of our team, who were at the time seventeen, in Steve Jones, a striker or midfield player. The squad was strengthened with the addition of three lads, just a year older than the majority. Michael Ollier, a full back, Michael Craggs, a striker, who had been paperlads for me during my spell as a newsagent and winger, Leslie Chetwood, who was employed by Jed in his off licence. Finally, the squad was given its one experienced player, when Jed signed Andy Simpson, a defender or midfield player, who, in his thirties, had played for Elephant in the League. After a few training sessions, Andy, quite optimistically, forecasted that he felt we could get ten points that season- still relegation material but more optimistic than myself, not as optimistic as Jed, though, who gave the team a target of twenty five points that first season.

So, those players formed the squad which we went into our first League game with, taking just three months to put together. Our only disappointment in the pre-season build up was our failure to convince a young midfield player called Ben Roscrow, whose father Shaun had played with such distinction in the League for many years, to play for the team, after he had impressed in training, which, at the time, set a damper on whether we were capable of attracting the quality of player to us which we knew that we required in that first season.

On applying to join the League at the Annual General Meeting, I had assured voting clubs that, both on and off the field, our conduct would be a credit to the League but stated that it would be three or four years before our true potential would come through on the pitch.

All grass roots teams depend upon their players paying for their football and the new young Crewe Corinthians team were no different. With one exception, Andy Simpson, the majority of our squad were seventeen or eighteen years old and money at that age is even harder to come by. Gordon had generously given us two sets of second hand kit, the red and white striped shirts, which he was more than relieved to dispose of in order that his Saturday team could revert back to their traditional black and white, along with a set of very old black and white striped shirts. In addition, he had also paid our County Football Association affiliation fee. However, this still left some two hundred pounds required in order to pay competition fees of one hundred pounds and a further fifty pounds for both insurance and footballs. To meet this expenditure, we decided to levy each player ten pounds membership for the season, which we felt that by paying this membership fee it would go a long way to proving their commitment to the club for the season. This still left the actual match expenditure for the hire of the pitch, for which I had managed to obtain for us the pitch at Brine Leas School, along with the referees fees for our home games, which would run out at approximately sixty pounds per home game and that was without the cost of paying for the kit to be washed after every game, this being done free of charge by our manager and his wife. We therefore decided to charge a three pounds match fee in order that this expenditure could be met. Like all other clubs, however, there are always unforeseen items of expenditure on the horizon. To meet these costs, clubs, such as ourselves, each year have to run some kind of raffle, which for us featured goods from Jed's off licence being raffled off at Christmas.

On Sunday 31st August 2003, our season finally got underway with a League fixture against Belle Vue at the local Legends Sports Ground. It was a real honour that Gordon, by now suffering from ill health, managed to make it down to see our first game. Unfortunately, despite our opponents playing the second half with ten men after having a player sent off, we could make little impression as an attacking force in the game, although our effort could not be faulted, as we went down to a two goals to nil defeat. The consolation was that the team which finished the game that day were all under the age of eighteen and were probably the youngest team ever to play in a Crewe Sunday Regional League game.

The next three games were to bring home the struggle on the pitch that I expected us to have in our first season, although the performances gave me renewed hope that, given time, we would be able to compete in the League.

The second game that we played actually saw us score our first goal in the League. After rarely looking like scoring on the previous Sunday, five days later in an evening game, done to avoid fixture congestion at the end of the season, on Friday 5th September 2003, against fellow newcomers, Crewe Hall, Danny Mair scored a goal well inside the first minute, in what I am sure will be one of our fastest ever goals. However, we still went down by four goals to two and further defeats were inflicted by Peacock/Willaston Villa by five goals to nil, then at the Express, by three goals to one, in a game in which we encountered a problem that, unless drastic action is taken, will be like a cancer in the grass roots game. Both teams turned up to play but unfortunately no referee was present. On this occasion, both teams agreed that our manager, Jed Hulme, who had a few years previously refereed games in the Lads and Dads League, could fulfil the role. To anybody caring about the continuation of the grass roots game, the referee must be treated with respect and players and club officials must show appreciation for his efforts and realise that he will not get all of his decisions correct.

Four consecutive defeats but the players knew and appreciated the task ahead of them in the League and knew that it would take time to succeed. Not just were they young, with an average age of just seventeen in an adult League, they were also relatively inexperienced, having spent twelve months not playing eleven a side since leaving Lads and Dads football. Their reward was to come however in the last of three evening games, courtesy of goals from Craig Mayman and Steve Jones, which were enough to see the team earn their first point in a drawn game against Hop Pole at Brine Leas School on Friday 12th September 2003. That first point was a major highlight in the history of our club. It gave me a feeling of pride equivalent to anything that I had witnessed in the game, including even the fantastic days when Everton had picked up the Championship, F.A.Cup or European Cup Winners Cups in those glory days of the mid eighties.

Better was to follow however as, just two days later on the same venue, we picked up our first ever victory against a nine man Railway team by the odd goal in three, courtesy of goals by Craig Mayman and Ricky Barlow.

Following on this win and boosted by the signing of Andy Lofkin, the first quality addition to the original squad, a real character who can play anywhere in the back four and who never fails to give maximum effort, Andy was instrumental in the team getting their first win against an eleven man opposition, when fellow strugglers, Salvador, who we knew that if we were to avoid having to apply for re-election, we would have to obtain good results against, were beaten by three goals to one. The goals in that game coming courtesy of Craig Mayman, Danny Mair and a rare goal by the skipper, Richard Douglas, whose enthusiasm took him past two defenders in a run which started midway in his own half before, just at the last moment, losing control of the ball as it ran towards the opposing keeper. Chasing a hopeless cause, he was rewarded when the unfortunate keeper's clearance rebounded off him, to record for the skipper, his first and only goal of that season.

Only two more draws were achieved before Christmas, one against Fox Elworth and the other against Vine who, along with Salvador, would offer us our best opportunity of avoiding the re-election bottom two placing, as we also went out of all four Cup competitions in the first round. During this period of time, we strengthened our squad by signing Steve Fidler, a promising young goalkeeper who, hitherto, had only played in goal in seven a side competitions but whose agility and willingness to work at his game had impressed me and Stuart Evans, a winger, also aged seventeen, who had been recommended to me by Paul Stonehewer, the manager of the Crewe and District F.A.youth team and whose uncle, Dave Cooke, was assistant manager of Shrewsbury Town and whose grandfather, Gordon Cooke, had played for Crewe Alexandra in the early fifties. In addition, Andy Simpson, the elder statesman of our team, had brought to us an experienced Richard Gillett, who played as a striker.

Immediately after Christmas, important wins against the Vine, in what was, as far as the re-election places were concerned, a six pointer and Willaston Villa/Peacock, whom we had lost five goals to nil against in our third match, saw us reach the fifteen points mark and a lofty fourth from the bottom spot and had shown just how quickly the team were progressing. Results, as one would expect from a relatively inexperienced team, were inconsistent- but to me that was the best that I could ever have imagined them to be in our first year. The only real beating which we had to endure was a ten goals to nil defeat by the Champions elect, Elephant, as Dave Hanson, the top goalscorer by a long way in our League that season, gave a very accomplished display. This defeat however saw the debut of a young full back, Ross Bettison, who came on as a substitute and who must have been so shell shocked that we never saw him again. Fortunately, that low ebb was soon to be improved upon, as wins over Salvador and Railway, gave us "doubles" over those teams and took us up to the twenty one point mark and virtually assured us that we would not have to apply for re-election.

In our penultimate game of that first season, a win by the odd goal in nine against Belle Vue, who we had lost to so easily in the first game, had shown just how much the team had improved throughout the season. It had taken them to the twenty four points mark, just one point required to achieve the target set by manager, Jed Hulme, for a free end of season evening but with just one game left - against Beeston Hotel whom, earlier in the season, we had lost nine goals to three against and who were now riding high, having got to the final of our Divisional Cup. Unfortunately, we lost that game but Jed decided that the players had so thoroughly deserved their evening that, at a cost of several hundred pounds to his wife, Emma and himself, the function was arranged.

On that night, however, we were unaware of an award that we were to receive a few weeks later at the League's Annual General Meeting when, along with Salvador, we were awarded the Good Conduct Cup, after only having received one booking for the whole of the season. The culprit for that booking, our skipper, Richard Douglas, who picked up the award on behalf of the club, to add to the award that we had already bestowed on him as our Player of the Year, as voted for by his fellow players and the management- a fitting reward for the lad who had been so instrumental in starting the team.

By the end of our first season the team had really come of age, which they proved by beating the Corinthians Saturday side by nine goals to one in an end of season challenge match. Gordon had been so impressed by the team's improvement throughout our first season and no doubt, would have been proud of their achievement in winning the Good Conduct Cup, just as I had been on us being presented with it on the evening, having given the undertaking at our first League meeting that our behaviour on the field and organisation off it would make us worthy members of the League.

For the record that season, two players, Jez Tagg and Ricky Barlow were ever presents with Craig Mayman and Jez Tagg being the highest goalscorers with thirteen and twelve respectively.

Of the squad that played that first season, Andy Simpson, Mike Field, Danny Forbes and Steve Jones had intimated that, for one reason or another, they would not be playing football on a Sunday for the following season. Other players such as Michael Ollier, Michael Craggs, Leslie Chetwood, Danny Mair and Will Ryder had failed to establish themselves in the team. Jed therefore decided that the squad had to be strengthened. Fortunately for us, Nantwich Town youth had become too old for the Staffs County Youth League and as many of the lads in our team knew a number of the Nantwich lads, we were able to recruit three excellent young players in Wayne Beggs, in my opinion, one of the best young midfield players in the area, who had decided to delay going to university for a year, David Griffin, a cultured defender, who we knew could also do an excellent job in midfield and who, only a few months previously, had had an England under eighteen schoolboy trial and finally, but not least, Graham Smalley, a midfield player, who had arrived in the area a few years previously from the south. In addition to these three, Stuart Wilkinson, an eighteen year old defender, nicknamed "Studs", was signed from Coppenhall, where he had won a Cheshire and Border Counties Sunday League Championship medal the previous year. Will Ellis, Richard Kearns and Luke Forrester, a defender, midfield player and striker respectively, were all signed after impressing in training, along with Jason Heath, a speedy winger, who is known better by his nickname of "Liggy" but the newcomer who was to make a real impact in that first half of the season was a young striker, Kevin Sharp, who had been invited to come down to training but who, on that first night, was so nervous that he had to be persuaded to take part. By the time Christmas had arrived, his twenty goals at more than one per game, including all four goals in his first full appearance against Express, had taken us to the top of the League,

Off the field, we were also to make important signings that were to play such an integral part in the success which was to follow. Russell Tagg, uncle to Jed's son, Jez Tagg, and a relation to Ernie Tagg, who, in the sixties, had been manager of Crewe Alexandra, had watched a few of our games in our first season and had been sufficiently impressed to be persuaded into coming along as coach. Russell had had a vaste amount of experience as a defender with local clubs, the main one probably being Faddiley. Russ quickly made an impression with our players at the pre-season training sessions which had started some six weeks before the start of the season on a Wednesday evening and Sunday morning.

The combination of Jed and Russ very much resembled one which occurred at Manchester City in the months just before I joined them in 1972 between the extrovert coach, Malcolm Allison, to whom I would associate Russ and the father like figure of Joe Mercer, who fits to a tee, Jed.

The hard work put in by Jed, Russ and the players in the pre-season was to be so instrumental in the excellent start to the League campaign that we had, which saw us gain outstanding victories against AC Wickstead by four goals to two, in which Craig Mayman became our second player to score a hat-trick, after Jez Tagg had achieved the feat against Willaston Villa/Peacock the previous season. This was then followed by an excellent three goals to nil win against Nantwich Town, who were favourites for the title, having just missed out the previous season. A further victory in a pulsating game against Sydney Arms, where our opponents reduced our four goal half time advantage to just one, which we held on to only as a result of one of the best saves that I have ever seen in local League football in the last minutes by our goalkeeper, Steve Fidler, saw us top of the League at the end of the first month of the season.

The downside to having a young team, and with us every player in the team was aged eighteen, is the fact that their future careers are still in the melting pot and as a result of this, we lost our regular left back, Jamie Roberts, who left to go to university. Fortunately, an excellent replacement was found in another of the Nantwich Town youth team from the previous season. Matthew Hole who, just like Wayne Beggs, Dave Griffin and Graham Smalley, had featured in a Nantwich Town youth team that had become too old for the Staffs County Youth League but, just like David and Graham, had continued to play at London Road in the reserve team, was signed. Matthew had also played in the Madhatters seven a side team and had attended St Thomas More School alongside Richard Douglas and Craig Mayman, who had been so instrumental in bringing so many of the lads to the club and so, it was only natural that when Jamie left to go to university, Matthew was approached to sign.

In the League, the rich vein of form continued and saw us top of the League at Christmas but the gloss was removed when we heard that our goalkeeper, Neil Forbes, would be entering hospital early in the New Year for an operation to a long standing knee problem and would be unavailable for much of the remainder of the season. This had left Steve Fidler as our only recognised goalkeeper, which led to us signing Chris Murray, who had impressed when playing for Hop Pole against us and who, on hearing about our goalkeeping predicament, approached us with a view to signing.

The trouble for us lay in the fact that several other Hop Pole players had also became dissatisfied with playing for their club and they became the third team that season, out of twenty eight that had started in the League, not to finish the season. The effect was that we had six points expunged from our record whilst third place, Beeston Hotel, who at the time were still considerably behind both ourselves and Nantwich, had been beaten heavily at the start of the season by the Hope Pole and had that defeat expunged from their record and with it, also improved their goal difference, compared to our own, by fifteen.

Teams dropping out of Leagues in mid or late season can make a mockery of a season's football . This very real problem is something which all football bodies need to look at and have very strong legislation in hand, even to the extent, I believe, which suspends the re-registration of all players of any club which has to resign for the remainder of the season, in order that they, the playing members, make every effort to ensure that their club fulfils its obligations to the other clubs in the League.

As we approached the final six weeks of a season in which, during its eight months, we had at some time in each of those months been at the top of the League, both ourselves and Nantwich Town Regional, who had games in hand but were still a few points adrift, suddenly, because of Hop Pole's resignation, found ourselves pressured from Beeston Hotel who, along with AC Wickstead and Audlem DK., were starting to put together a winning run.

A fourth broken bone in two years, two hand and two feet, forced our captain, Richard Douglas, to miss three weeks of the run in. In the seventeen games that he had played, we had won sixteen and drawn one but in the six which he had missed, we had won only one, stressing his importance to the team at that time. A replacement, with a similar commitment, had to be found for the run in. Here, we dropped in lucky. Chris Hollins, although still in his early twenties, was Richard's boss at the local swimming baths and although not having played eleven a side for a few years, soon showed the drive and ability which he had shown in his earlier days as a junior with Stoke City.

A further misfortunate hit the club when David Griffin, suffering from a blood disorder, became the second of our players to have to be admitted to hospital. Although missing "Griff" and Neil Forbes, the club spirit, in which the players club together for a get well card and gift, was to see them through to the successful conclusion of the season but not before a disastrous, yet memorable game at Audlem on Easter Sunday, which saw us throw away a two goal lead.

In that eventful game at Audlem, we had our first ever player, Will Ellis, one of our least offensive players, sent off, after which, we lost a two goal lead. We were, however, to score what I would select as our best ever goal and indeed one of the best goals that I have witnessed in local football which, incidentally, was also our one hundredth goal of the season. From a Craig Mayman corner, a volley from David Griffin from twenty plus yards flew into the net. However, unfortunately for David and ourselves, still in the title race, this was to be his last game for a month, as illness was to force him to miss three games, before returning for the final two. The defeat at Audlem, our third of the season, gave Nantwich Town Regional the advantage for the Championship, and it looked as though we were going to pay dearly for the defeats earlier in the season against Willaston Villa/Peacock and Salvador, both lower half of the table teams, from whom we had only acquired four out of the twelve points at stake.

This indeed proved to be so, as Nantwich Town Regional picked up the necessary points required from their games in hand to ensure that the last game of the season between the two of us was an academic affair, with pride being kept by both sides, as honours were shared with a 2-2 draw.

Our runners up position was secured on Sunday 1st May 2005, in what to Jed and myself was a red letter day in the team's short two year history and one which will always feature in the history of the Crewe Corinthians Football Club. It marked the day when, at Bunbury, playing Beeston Hotel, we clinched promotion to the Premier Division of the Crewe Regional Sunday League, courtesy of a 5-3 victory, the goals coming courtesy of a Kevin Sharp hat-trick, Jez Tagg and a goal from Wayne Beggs, who scored the all important equaliser, which eased the nerves after Beeston had taken a surprise lead.

The chase between Kev and Jez for top goalscorer in effect being decided that day, Kevin's two extra goals ensured a quite phenomenal total of thirty seven for the season in all League and Cup ties compared to a superb thirty five goals by Jez. Seventy two goals out of a final figure of one hundred and eighteen had been scored by the two and when one added the double figure contribution from two midfield players, Wayne Beggs and Craig Mayman, a total of ninety eight out of one hundred and eighteen goals had phenomenally been scored by just four players. Despite this tremendous achievement however and the fact that, as far as I can make out, we actually scored more goals than any other local team that season, Kevin did not finish top scorer in our Division, that honour going to Ben Spruce, of Nantwich Town, who profited from the fact that our two strikers, Kevin and Jez, had shared so many goals between them. In relation to this, the League's top scorer for its Premier Division was less than half of what these three lads had achieved, showing that scoring in the Premier is somewhat harder.

Scoring goals had been an important facet to our play during the season but it had also been a tremendous team effort. When we had started in the Regional League as a bunch of untried seventeen year olds, I had always believed that it would take a minimum of four years to be promoted. We had aimed at just trying to avoid having to apply for re-election in the first year, followed by relative safety the second, a mid table to top half position in the third year, with a real chance of promotion in the fourth season as our lads would then be in their very early twenties and have a few years experience behind them. Their progress had surprised me but not so much our coach, Russell Tagg, his assistant, Stuart 'Goggsy' Roberts and our manager, Jed Hulme, who remained confident from the start of our second season as to our potential.

Sunday 1st May 2005, also heralded a piece of fund raising which both Jed and myself were to be very proud of. We had decided to do a sponsored walk that Sunday morning to Bunbury for our game, being the longest journey that we would undertake in the season, some fourteen miles in all. We decided that we should seek out sponsors, with half of the proceeds going to charity and every player was given a form to obtain sponsors.

At the time when we were planning our sponsored walk, an article had appeared in the local press concerning the young baby son of Crewe Alexandra forward, Steve Jones, who had suffered from serious complications following his birth which had necessitated the Special Baby Care Unit at the local hospital. This had reminded Jed's wife, Emma, about the birth of their own son, Josh, and how he had required the attention of the Unit at his premature birth and also, with their younger son, Jack, a few years later, when he too was in need of the facility. Therefore, it was only fitting that the charity which we would be walking for, with a fifty per cent donation of all funds raised, was the local hospital's Special Baby Care Unit.

In a marvellous achievement, six hundred and forty pounds was raised inside three weeks by just twenty people, which resulted in a cheque being donated to the Special Baby Care Unit at Leighton Hospital for three hundred and twenty pounds.

The walk, luckily for us, took place in dry conditions, an overnight thunderstorm fortunately passing away just an hour before our scheduled seven o'clock start that Sunday morning. A walk, which took us three and a half hours, was completed just half an hour before kick off time and the feeling of pride as we, and I am sure that I speak for Jed as well, arrived at the ground, to be met by the applause from all our players, who had worked so hard to raise money for the cause, was just reward.

On the field, the team also did their job perfectly to win promotion. This was the best feeling that I had experienced in over forty years of being involved in football, either professionally or at grass roots level. It had been brought about not so much by us achieving promotion so soon after starting the team, after all, I had experienced major trophy triumphs in the eighties at Everton which were equally exhilarating but it was the feeling that we, as a club, through the efforts of Jed, myself and the players, had also put something back into society by our efforts with the sponsored walk.

The day that Jed, Emma and myself went to the local hospital to hand over the cheque to the staff of the Baby Care Unit and the reading of the letters from the grateful parents of the young babies that had need of the expertise which the Ward offered, made us all realise what a deserving cause we had worked for and how proud I was of the efforts made by the young members of our team to raise the sort of money that they had done, in order to benefit the hospital on the successful completion of the walk by Jed and myself.

The success of the walk had gone a long way to prove to me how grass roots clubs, such as ourselves, could help both local deserving charities and at the same time help themselves financially. It had been a day that I hope many of our lads came to appreciate more the real values behind life.

Our pride was further increased when, a few weeks later, we received a letter from the hospital stating that the money had been put towards a pump for the unit, on which they had placed a plaque with the words, `With Love from Crewe Corinthians' inscribed.

The team's share of the sponsorship money was spent on their Presentation Evening held at the Earl, three weeks after the finish of the season.

The League had allocated us fourteen individual plaques but we had decided to reward every player who had played and this necessitated additional plaques having to be purchased in addition to the trophies for the major awards of Player of the Year, as voted for by the players, which went to Jez Tagg, Manager's Player of the Year going to Richard Douglas and a bottle of champagne going to Wayne Beggs, who finished runner up in both awards, Kevin Sharp, who won the Top Goalscorer award and finally, a very deserving award in my opinion for the Clubman of the Year, which went to Jason Heath, who, although not a regular in the team, never missed a game or training session all season and without players such as him, clubs, such as ours, would struggle to continue.

All our awards were presented by two of the town's very special football celebrities, Frank Blunstone and Johnny King.

Both had started their illustrious football careers in the early fifties at Crewe Alexandra as a left wing partnership, John playing inside with Frank on the left wing, before moving their different ways, Frank to Chelsea and John to Stoke City, although many of the experts in those days felt that they should have been sold as a left wing partnership, such was their influence on the Crewe team in those days.

Frank had gone on to play for the full England team on a number of occasions and rather aptly, in Chelsea`s championship year of 2005, had been a member of the only previous Chelsea championship winning team exactly fifty years ago, which rather intrigued the Londoner in our team, Graham Smalley, who is a keen Chelsea fan and who, on the night, had the honour of meeting one of the Chelsea legends.

Talking of legends and there is no bigger local legend than "Kingy". John, having left Crewe for Stoke City, then featured in their team for a good number of years and acquired honours for England at "B" level, before spending a season at First Division, Cardiff City, returning to Crewe in the twilight of his career, for what was then a club record transfer fee of six thousand pounds, repaying it in his first season by plotting the club to promotion for the first time in its long history.

No better two footballing ambassadors could we have had than these two local legends to celebrate our first local success but even though John and Frank presented all the awards to the lads, the biggest cheer of the night came about as a result of our young mascot, Jack Hulme, received his award from his favourite player, Andy Lofkin, who lifted the little lad skywards, much to the amusement of Frank and John, whose faces I was watching at the time.

I was so proud that evening- a special team on a very memorable evening with two very special guests and hosted so well by the staff of the Earl, especially Kate and Lydia, who had supplied us with such excellent hospitality at the end of each game, when twenty or so thirsty footballers would return there to have their thirst quenched and talk over the game, a feature which is so priceless in today's grass roots game and without which, the game, as we know it, would be so much poorer. Plus, ofcourse, it also gave me the opportunity to collect those important match fees!

Finance is, and always will be, an integral part of the grass roots game. Match fees and a small annual subscription account for most items of expenditure, such as pitch hire, referees fees, League fees, insurance and footballs but that still leaves a fair size hole when it comes to kit.

Just like the professional game, grass roots clubs have endeavoured to try to attract sponsors, who are normally friends or family to one of the team members, who are willing to pay out a few hundred pounds to help our worthy cause, by supplying them with the necessary revenue to purchase a match kit in return for having their company name on the shirt. It is these people who do more for grass roots teams than do our own governing authority. Our own sponsor, Len Evans of D.L.Evans Ltd, a roofing contractor, came as a result of one of our players, Stuart Wilkinson's girlfriend, Danielle, being the daughter of the sponsor and his generosity, as indeed the thousands like him around the country, puts to shame the governing bodies in the game, by doing far more to help clubs continue and not overprice the grass roots game to the players, many of whom are just mere teenagers starting out in life and not as yet good wage earners.

During a season, most grass roots players will fork out about one hundred pounds a year to play for their team, provided that they do not fall foul of the County Football Association's big money earner - the disciplinary code of payments, which can see a player further the coffers of the wealthy County F.A. to the tune of eight pounds per caution and four times that amount for a sending off. It has always baffled me as to how the authorities can justify that amount of money. I can appreciate a nominal charge made to the club to notify them of a player's sending off, or the date of any suspension that he receives for acquiring several bookings in a season, but I can not see why the County have to notify us of a caution, at the cost of eight pounds, when no appeal can be made anyway. Surely, the referee can notify the two clubs at the end of a game of any cautions which he has had to administer and that would save a lot of time and money. The financing of the recording of bookings at County Headquarters should come from these nominal charges and our affiliation fees. This makes me feel that the high administration fee charged by our football authorities is just a money making racket to pay for their posh offices and staff wages and give them a bank balance which we never hear about, as they convey an attitude that certainly does not give the clubs a feeling that they are there to serve us.

Another problem which the football authorities will have to face up to in the very near future is the decline in the numbers playing the eleven a side game at the grass roots level. County Football Associations throughout the country should look to redress this problem, as I am sure that the same situation of dwindling numbers of teams for the eleven a side game that exists in our area is prominent throughout the country, as the growth of the small side game continues, mainly because players realise that they can get their ration of football far cheaper and with far less aggravation than that inflicted on it by the authorities on our eleven a side game and ofcourse, with the changing social climate, getting up early on a Sunday morning, having spent Saturday evening in the pubs and clubs, which now have far longer opening hours following the relaxation of the law, does not seem so appealing to today's youngsters.

Incidentally, on discipline and the role played by our County Football Association, I would point out that in our first season, we, along with Salvador, acquired just one booking in a full season, to win our Sporting Cup. What did we receive from our County Football Association to congratulate us on that achievement, which could only be bettered by not having a booking at all, the answer-sweet f.a.! and do not tell me that it would have been too much trouble for the County to write and congratulate teams, such as ourselves, as we regularly receive correspondence, which includes advertising material from companies, who no doubt pay the County F.A for this service- but there again, why should they thank us, after all, we did not contribute much to their wage bill!

The next disturbing contact that I had with the County Football Association came as a result of our team training at the Brittles in Wistaston on a hard court forty square metre floodlit training area. After the training session, I spoke at great lengths with our manager, Jed Hulme, about the lack of use the area received because of its surface. Jed realised the potential of the area and we approached Eric Swan of the local Wistaston Parish Council regarding the possibility of astroturfing the area. Jed was willing to fund over sixty per cent of the required costs as his part of a partnership with the local authority to install the astroturf to the already floodlit area which would benefit the population of Wistaston. We were convinced that there was a need for an astroturf five a side court and so the Wistaston Parish Council put forward its proposals for a grant to the County Football Association. We received notification to go down to the County Football Association Headquarters to meet with the County officials.

Feeling optimistic, with approximately seventy five per cent of the funds available and looking for a grant of somewhere in the region of fifteen thousand pounds, I went with John Moore, the chairman of the local district Council, to attend a meeting, with a business plan which had taken many hours to draw up, only to be told straight away that, because of the size of the playing area, it was a non starter. Apparently, to apply for a grant, a minimum playing area of sixty by forty metres was required, ours being twenty metres short in length. Our County must have known that fact before we spent a wasted day at our own expense meeting them. So, several years on, the Brittles still have a floodlit area hardly used for football which should have been in full use throughout the week but ofcourse the County, or some other organisation, still have that money in their bank account earning interest.

The build up to the 2005/2006 season was to see the team clinch its first trophy when we landed the annual Wrenbury Tournament, beating the Plough of the Mid Cheshire Sunday League in the final by four goals to one, courtesy of a brace from Craig Mayman and Jez Tagg and winning all four of our group games.

In the pre-season leading up to our introduction into the Premier League, we strengthened our squad still further with three more talented youngsters, although two of these were really to act just as replacements to two of our key players, whose future careers were very shortly that season to take them away from the Crewe area - a problem that we seemed to have faced before.

Kevin Sharp, our leading goalscorer the previous season, had been successful in joining the Marines and Wayne Beggs, a key midfield player, had been selected to go to university. In their places came Shaun Gilraine, a midfield player, who was to be re-united with the three ex Nantwich Youth team players that we already had in our squad, along with Adam Longley, who had been the goalkeeper of that Nantwich Town team and whose father, Nick, had played a number of games in goal for Crewe Alexandra in the Football League in the eighties. The squad was also strengthened with the signing of Adam Peberdy, another nineteen year old - just like virtually every member of our squad, who was a striker, joining us from Wrenbury, where he had already appeared in the Premier League.

We had set ourselves up nicely for that first crack in the Sunday

Premier Division and an opening fixture against one of the areas oldest clubs, Willaston White Star, and to compete against the likes of Bentley Motors, managed by Les Wain, a local lad who had represented England at schoolboy level, before going on to play for Crewe Alexandra and featured in the Northwich Victoria team that had reached the fourth round of the F.A.Cup.

The opening game against Willaston White Star saw us have mixed fortunes. An excellent 3-2 win was overshadowed by a serious knee injury to Andy Lofkin, which was to see the big hearted defender out for the remainder of the season.

Our form continued to fluctuate in the League, but was good enough to consolidate our position in the Premier Division, finishing above the relegation zone, as Bentley Motors made a clean sweep of three of the four local trophies open to them- who stopped them from winning all four? Crewe Corinthians.

Although our form in the League had been inconsistent, in the Cups it had been a different matter. A cup run that had seen us convincingly defeat The Bank Regional, our old rivals from the Second Division days, who previously went under the name Nantwich Town Regional and who, only the year before, had pipped us for the Championship and Nantwich Young Farmers, set up a Final against Bentley Motors on the ground of Nantwich Town Football Club.

Bentley Motors had already beaten us 8-0 and 6-1 in the League but only two weeks before, we had managed to give them a scare in a semi-final before going down by the odd goal in three. This certainly gave the team heart and they thoroughly deserved their extra time win by two goals to one, courtesy of goals from Adam Peberdy and substitute, Jason Heath, who chose just the right time to get his first and only goal of the season.

Bentley Motors went on to win the League, being undefeated for the second consecutive League campaign, and also ended up winning our League's other Knockout Trophy by beating Willaston White Star, and the coveted Crewe F.A. Sunday Cup by beating Crewe Athletic 7-0, to complete another remarkable season, in which they proved to me to the best team that the area had seen in over forty years of Sunday football. Our pride was that we were the only team to beat them in a full season.

Good teams build on success, as I had experienced at Everton. The question remained, would these lads?

Only time will tell how we continue to venture, but one thing is for sure, my journey in football from the Football Association to Crewe Corinthians calling at Manchester City, Traffic, AFC Bwanas Knockers, Cholmondeley County, Crewe Alexandra, Everton, Crewe Youth Centre, Rolls Royce and Leeds United has seen me come across so many different characters but all with one common feature, a love of the beautiful game and I have enjoyed every minute of it.